CHRISTINA LAMB was named Foreign Correspondent of the Year in 2002 for her reporting on Afghanistan in both the British Press Awards and the What the Papers Say Awards, and awarded Foreign Affairs Writer of the year by the Foreign Press Association. Her original despatches from Afghanistan during the Soviet occupation won her Young Journalist of the Year. She is also the author of the best-selling *The Africa House* and *Waiting for Allah*. She is married with a young son and is a roving foreign correspondent for the *Sunday Times*.

From the reviews:

'Award-winning foreign correspondent Christina Lamb has written an inspiring and moving account of Afghanistan's plight . . . Lamb shows that, despite attempts to destroy the country and its culture, its soul remains uncrushed.'

MARIANNE BRACE, *Independent on Sunday*

'Deeply penetrating, informative and always engaging . . . Through the dispiriting events under which Afghanistan continues to be submerged, Lamb continually finds delightful people who have latched on to the fact that Faith is an ecclesiastical word for credulity, and offer some hope for the country's future.'

CAL McCRYSTAL, *Financial Times*

'Lamb has a curiosity that demands she listen to anyone – warlord, reluctant torturer, Pakistani intelligence officer, family of the last man hanged . . . And beyond the door of the "Golden Needle Ladies' Sewing Classes" in Herat, Lamb is awed by that cultured city's resistance . . . which, as [she] understands, matters more than pages of guns and rubble.'

VERONICA HOWELL, *Guardian*

'A remarkable blend of outrage, compassion and hope, Christina Lamb's book is an alternately horrifying and uplifting insight into the Taliban regime.' JUSTIN MAROZZI, *Evening Standard*

'This book is in the best tradition of classics by British adventurers such as Robert Byron, Peter Levi and Eric Newby. In fact, Lamb's empathy for the people she meets is such that her writing outdoes that of her stuffier male forebears. For Lamb, the country is more than just magnificent landscape and proud history. She has a long perspective from which to observe what she sees, having made a trip into Soviet-occupied Afghanistan at the end of the 1980s with a young Hamid Karzai, now the country's dapper president ... Her book boasts genuine journalistic exposés as well: she tracks down a Taliban torturer and discovers the Herat literary classes which, masquerading as sewing circles, concealed their activities from the religious police. After receiving a series of heartfelt letters about life in Kabul under the Taliban, she hunts for the young woman who wrote them.'

MARCUS WARREN, *Daily Telegraph*

The Sewing Circles of Herat

MY AFGHAN YEARS

CHRISTINA LAMB

Flamingo
An Imprint of HarperCollinsPublishers

Flamingo
An Imprint of HarperCollins*Publishers*
77–85 Fulham Palace Road,
Hammersmith, London W6 8JB

Flamingo is a registered trade mark of
HarperCollins*Publishers* Limited

www.harpercollins.co.uk

Published by Flamingo 2003
9 8 7 6 5 4 3 2 1

First published in Great Britain by
HarperCollins*Publishers* 2002

Author photograph by Caroline Forbes

ISBN 0 00 714252 8

Set in PostScript Linotype Minion with
Castellar and Janson display

Printed and bound in Great Britain by
Clay Ltd, St Ives plc

This book is dedicated to Lourenço
who thinks Mummy lives on a plane
and the fond memory of Abdul Haq who told me
'You're a girl. You can't go to war in Afghanistan.'

CONTENTS

ACKNOWLEDGEMENTS

It was a gold-inscribed invitation landing on my mat on a dark rainy November morning in Birmingham that first took me to Pakistan and thence to Central Asia and I will always be grateful to Benazir Bhutto for inviting me to her wedding and opening up an entrancing new world to me.

This book would not have been possible were it not for the tremendous generosity of Afghans throughout Afghanistan and the countless mujaheddin who back in the late 1980s put up with having a young English girl travelling with them.

In particular I would like to thank my friends Hamid Karzai, Hamid Gilani, Ahmed Wali Karzai and Jamil Karzai, all of whom did their best to make me feel like part of their families as well as the late Abdul Haq, who teased me mercilessly, but was one of the most courageous people I have ever met. He firmly believed that Afghans needed to sort out their own problems rather than outsiders and was to pay for his convictions with the tragic deaths of his wife and son, murdered in Peshawar, then the loss of his own life, captured in Jalalabad and hanged while trying to raise a force against the Taliban in October 2001. In July 2002, his elder brother Haji Qadir was gunned down in Kabul, less than a week after becoming Vice President.

In Kabul, I am grateful to Mr Shah Mirzad of Shah Books for managing to keep so many wonderful books on Afghan history hidden from the Taliban and for permission to reproduce one of his postcards, and to Dr Eric Laroche of UNICEF for sharing his thoughts on a society he knows and loves.

In Pakistan, Dr Umar Farooq has always been a loyal friend as have Nusrat Javed, Bashir Riaz and Husain Haqqani. I would like to thank Ijaz-ul Haq for spending so much time explaining his father General Zia's vision for Afghanistan and Iftikhar Gilani for giving me some insight into the Pashtuns. There are many other people who cannot be named because of the risks they have taken in speaking to me.

I would also like to thank Dominic Lawson, editor of *The Sunday Telegraph*, and Con Coughlin, executive editor, for their encouragement and for allowing me time off to write. Some of the material in the book has already appeared in the paper. I would like to thank too Robin Pauley, former Asia editor of the *Financial Times* and Jurek Martin, former foreign editor, for their encouragement when I was first starting out.

As my travel companion on much of the more recent part of this journey and fellow detainee during two tense days and nights being held by Pakistan's military intelligence ISI, photographer Justin Sutcliffe deserves a special mention. Were it not for his ingenuity in smuggling his spare phone into captivity, we would not have been able to alert our newspaper to our plight. Many of his wonderful photographs appear in the book.

Paul Marsden, MP for Shrewsbury, helped rescue us from the ISI, being manhandled by Baluchistan police in the process, and kindly rearranged his whole schedule to stay in Pakistan until we were safely out.

Princess Homaira Wali, eldest grandchild of the king of Afghanistan, could not have been more generous with her time and friendship in showing me round Rome and I will always think of her when I hear the song *Mack the Knife*.

I would like to thank my good friends Professor Akbar Ahmed and John Witherow for taking time from their extremely busy lives to read the manuscript and make invaluable comments.

As always, my wonderful agent David Godwin who perhaps alone knows what this book means to me, and my fantastic editor Arabella Pike for her late night e-mails of encouragement and for commissioning a book on the Amazon and ending up with a memoir of Afghanistan.

Last, but very definitely not least, I would like to thank my Mum and Dad for looking after their grandson whenever his mother had a chapter to finish, my husband Paulo for making the most inspiring cappuccinos every morning, and my son Lourenço for keeping me aware that it is not always necessary to fly to the other side of the world and dodge bullets to have an adventure.

London, July 2002

LIST OF ILLUSTRATIONS

Illustrations in the text:

Plate section:

Great Mosque at Herat, 2001 © *Justin Sutcliffe.*

Sultan Hamidy's blue glass, 2001 © *Justin Sutcliffe.*

Doves at Mazar-i-Sharif © Abbas/*Magnum Photos.*

Timur besieging Herat, 15th century © *British Museum/Bridgeman Art Library.*

The Remnants of an Army by Lady Elizabeth Butler (1846–1933) © *The Bridgeman Art Library/Tate London,* 2002.

Afghan forces rise against the British Garrison in Kabul in 1841, illustration by R. Caton Woodville © *Mary Evans Picture Library.*

Kandahar Lady of Rank, Engaged in Smoking, plate 29 from 'Scenery, Inhabitants and Costumes of Afghanistan' by Robert Carrick (1839–1904) © *Stapleton Collection/The Bridgeman Art Library.*

Umeer Dost Mohammed Khan colour lithograph by Louis Hague from 'Characters and Costumes of Afghanistan', written by Captain Lockyer Willis Hart, published 1843 © *Private Collection/ The Bridgeman Art Library.*

King Abdur Rahman (1880–1901) from *Under the Absolute Amir of Afghanistan* by Frank A. Martin (*Bhavan Books and Prints, New Delhi 2000*).

King Amanullah and Queen Soraya in Europe, 1929 © *Topham Picturepoint.*

Princess Bilquis, her husband and daughters in Kabul, 1970 © *Julian Simmonds.*

King Zahir Shah in exile, 2002 © *Julian Simmonds.*

The Red Army entering Afghanistan, 1979 © *PA News.*

More than one million Afghans were killed during the Soviet occupation © *PA News.*

Mujaheddin on a Russian tank in Kandahar, 1988.

Mujaheddin graveyard.

The old Afghan practice of severing the heads of captives © *Steve McCurry, Magnum Photos.*

Buzkashi © *Reuters/Popperfoto.*

A young boy flies a kite in Kabul, 2001 © *Reuters/Popperfoto.*

Izatullah the kitemaker © *Justin Sutcliffe.*

The author crossing into Afghanistan, 2001 © *Justin Sutcliffe.*

Shoe-shopping in Herat, 2001 © *Justin Sutcliffe.*

The fourth-century, 170-feet high Buddha of Bamiyan © *Jenny Matthews/Network.*

The Buddha of Bamiyan destroyed, 2001 © *Reuters/Popperfoto.*

Refugee children in Maslakh camp, 2001 © *Justin Sutcliffe.*

All pictures without credits are from the author's personal collection.

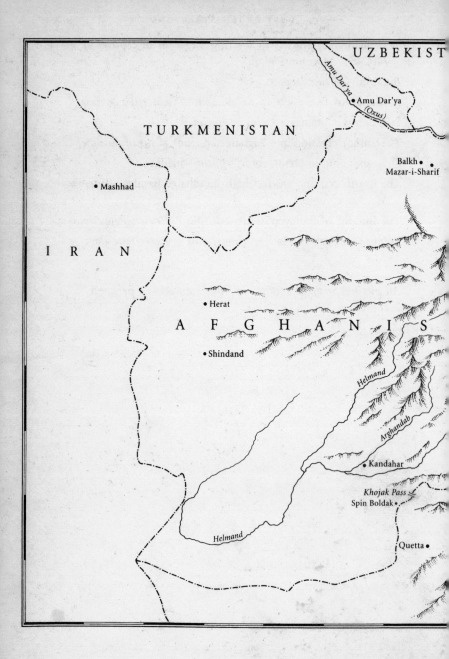

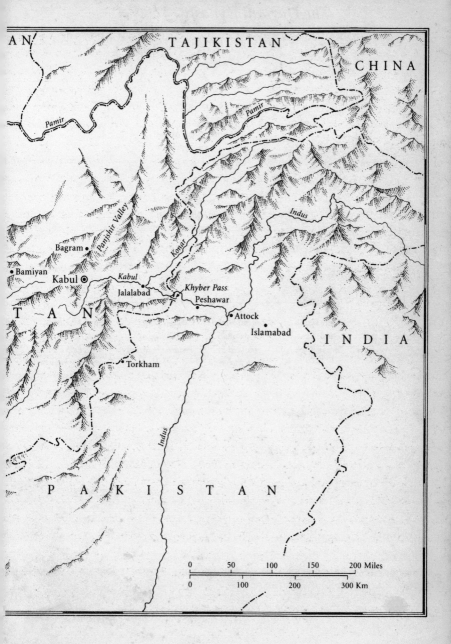

AN
TAJIKISTAN
CHINA

Pamir

Pamir

Indus

Bagram •
Panjshir Valley

Konar

• Bamiyan

Kabul ◉   *Kabul*

Jalalabad •   *Khyber Pass*
• Peshawar

T   A   N

• Attock

Islamabad •

I   N   D   I   A

• Torkham

Indus

P   A   K   I   S   T   A   N

0	50	100	150	200 Miles
0	100	200	300 Km	

The Durrani Dynasty

SADDOZAI

Ahmad Shah Abdali
1747–72

Timur Shah *
made Kabul capital
1772–93

────── 26 sons ──────

Humayun
blinded by
Zaman Shah

Zaman Shah (e)
1793–1800
blinded by
Shah Mehmud

Shah Shuja
1803–9 (e)
restored to throne
by British
1839–42 *

Shah Mehmud
ousted Zaman Shah
with help from
Fateh Khan Barakzai
1800–3
1809–18 †

(b) blinded
(e) exiled
* murdered
† 1818–26 civil war

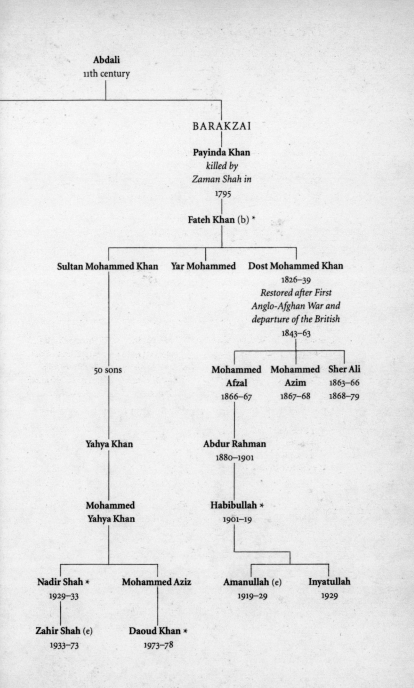

Abdali
11th century

BARAKZAI

Payinda Khan
killed by
Zaman Shah in
1795

Fateh Khan (b) *

Sultan Mohammed Khan   **Yar Mohammed**   **Dost Mohammed Khan**
1826–39
Restored after First
Anglo-Afghan War and
departure of the British
1843–63

50 sons

Mohammed   **Mohammed**   **Sher Ali**
Afzal   **Azim**   1863–66
1866–67   1867–68   1868–79

Yahya Khan   **Abdur Rahman**
1880–1901

Mohammed   **Habibullah** *
Yahya Khan   1901–19

Nadir Shah *   **Mohammed Aziz**   **Amanullah** (e)   **Inyatullah**
1929–33   1919–29   1929

Zahir Shah (e)   **Daoud Khan** *
1933–73   1973–78

If you should ask me where I've been all this time
I have to say 'Things happen'.

PABLO NERUDA, *No Hay Olvido*, There's No Forgetting

Peace is not sold anywhere in the world,
Otherwise I would have bought it for my country.

GIRL IN AFGHANISTAN, 'Lost Chances' UNICEF Report,
2001

Beginnings

M Y STORY like that of Afghanistan has no beginning and no end. The Pashtuns say that when Allah created the world he had a pile of rocks left over from which he made Afghanistan, and just as the historians seem unable to agree on when or how that far-off land of hills and mountains got its name, settling on the exact moment when it became part of my life seems an arbitrary process.

There is a dreamcatcher over my desk, a small cylinder made with loops of tiny seeds out of the bottom of which dangle four small bunches of turquoise, scarlet and yellow macaw feathers. Crafted by Indians who still live by the old ways in a remote river inlet of the Amazon, it is meant as its name suggests to catch dreams, filtering out the nightmares and only allowing through the good ones. As I begin to write in the pale light of dawn, I suddenly notice it moving, the feathers fluttering wildly even though there is no wind in my small study. I check the window and it is firmly closed yet the coloured feathers refuse to still.

On my desk is a handful of letters from a woman of about my own age in Kabul. She risked her life to get them to me and this is also her story. But if I must choose a moment to start my tale it would be when I was twenty-one years old, a graduate of philosophy at university and of adolescence in British suburbia, stumbling out of a battered mini-bus in the Old City of the frontier town of Peshawar, dizzy with Kipling and diesel fumes. Clenched in my hand was a suitcase I could barely lift, containing everything I imagined I would need for reporting a war, from packets of wine gums and a tape of Mahler's Fifth to a much-loved stuffed pink rabbit, missing one ear.

If I close my eyes, I can conjure up the image of standing there, momentarily unsure in the dust-laden sunset, a gawky English girl, surrounded by motor rickshaws painted with F-16 fighter jets, beggars with missing arms or legs or faces eaten away by leprosy, and men in large turbans or rolled woollen caps selling everything from hair-grips to Shanghai White Elephant torches and wearing rifles as casu-ally as Londoners carry umbrellas. The streets were ancient and narrow with two-storey wooden-framed buildings and across one hung a giant movie placard of a sultry raven-haired beauty drawing a crimson sari across cartoonish eyes. Everywhere such faces, carved with proud features as if from another time, some wise and white-bearded in sheepskin cloaks, others villainous with kohl-rimmed eyes. These were the Pashtuns of whom Sir Olaf Caroe, the last British Governor of the Frontier, had written 'for the stranger who had eyes to see and ears to hear . . . here was a people who looked him in the face and made him feel he had come home'.

A rickshaw took me to Greens, a hotel mostly frequented by arms dealers, where I was given a room with no curtains. I lay on the thin mattress, looking northwest to a sky dark with a serrated mountain range. Beyond those dragon-scale peaks lay Soviet-occupied Afghani-stan, the remotest place I had ever imagined suddenly only forty miles away.

If ever there was a country whose fate was determined by geogra-phy, it was the land of the Afghans. Never a colony, Afghanistan has always been a natural crossroads – the meeting place of the Middle East, Central Asia, the Indian Subcontinent and the Far East – and thus frequently the battlefield and graveyard of great powers. Afghans spoke of Marco Polo, Genghis Khan, Alexander the Great, and Tamerlane as well as various Moghul, Sikh and Persian rulers as if they had just passed through.

The Red Army were the latest in a long line of invaders going back to the fourth century BC when Alexander the Great spent three years crossing the country with 30,000 men and elephants, taking the beautiful Roxanne as his wife en route. During the nineteenth century, the country's vast deserts and towering mountains provided the stage for what became known as 'The Great Game', the shadowy struggle between the British Empire and Tsarist Russia for dominance in the region, in which many of the players were individual officers or spies, often as young as I was when I first stepped out of that Flying Coach.

Peshawar had once been part of Afghanistan, used by its kings as their summer capital, and that first night in Greens was the start of two years which turned everything I had known or valued upside down. Coming home again would never be the same.

Smuggled back and forth across the Khyber Pass in an assortment of guises and on a variety of transport with the mujaheddin, I found them brave men with noble faces who exuded masculinity yet loved to walk hand-in-hand with each other and pick flowers, or who would sit for hours in front of hand mirrors clipping their nostril hairs with nail scissors. They exaggerated terribly, never claiming to have shot down just one Soviet helicopter but always seven. Yet they were poetic souls such as Ayubi, one of Commander Ismael Khan's key lieutenants in western Afghanistan and a huge bear of a man in a Russian fur hat who would silence a room by walking in, but who on bidding farewell, penned me a note in the exquisite loops and swirls of Persian script saying 'if you don't think of me in 1000 years I will think of you 1000 times in an hour'.

Crouching in trenches watching the nightly show of red and green tracer-fire light up the sky, breakfasting on salted pomegranate pips as rockets whistled overhead, I was supremely happy and alive. With the confidence of youth, I thought I was indestructible.

Part of the charm was the romance of being with people fighting for a cause after a childhood on the not exactly lawless borders of Surrey and south London where the local idea of rebellion was to go shoplifting in Marks & Sparks, and the biggest challenge finding a way home after missing the last train back from a concert at the Rainbow Theatre. Even at university, the only issues we could find to protest about were rent increases and the investments of Barclays Bank in South Africa's apartheid regime. I had read Hemingway, got drunk and melancholic on daiquiris, and longed for a Spanish Civil War of my own.

But for me Afghanistan was more than that. It was about being among a people who had nothing but gave everything. It was a land where people learnt to smell the first snows or the mountain bear on the wind and for whom an hour spent staring at a beautiful flower was an hour gained rather than wasted. A land where elders rather than libraries were the true source of knowledge, and the family and the tribe meant far more than the sum of individuals.

When I returned to Thatcherite London where the streets were full of people rushing, their faces seeming to glitter with greed, Afghanistan felt like a guilty secret, my Afghan affair.

At a dinner party in north London, I listened to friends bragging about buying Porsches with their bonuses and sending out from their offices for pizzas and clean shirts because they were clinching a deal and could not leave their desks. I wanted to tell them of a place where every family had lost a son or a husband or had a leg blown off, almost every child seen someone die in a rocket attack and where a small boy had told me his dream was to have a brightly coloured ball. But, when I began to talk about Afghanistan, I watched eyes glaze and felt as if I was trying to have a conversation about a movie no one else had seen.

Over the next few years, I moved to South America then North, to South Africa then southern Europe, and found new stories, friends and places. Yet like an unfinished love affair, Afghanistan was always there. Every so often I got a call from people from those days and, to my shame, would see the message and not reply. Occasionally I saw a deep enamel blue that reminded me of the tiled mosque in Mazar-i-Sharif, ate an exquisite grape that reminded me of Kandahar where locals boasted they grew the sweetest in the world, or smelled a pine tree that brought back the horse-drawn tongas jingling along the avenues of Herat. My travels took me to remote parts of Africa and, lying under a star-sprinkled sky in northern Zambia, I suddenly remembered years before sleeping in the Safed Koh, the White Mountains near Jalalabad, silenced by the immensity of the heavens and a commander telling me that every star is a dead mujahid.

I returned to Pakistan whenever there was a change in government or military coup, which was often. The refugee camps into which a quarter of Afghanistan's population had poured were bigger than ever and people talked of a sinister new group called the Taliban led by a mysterious one-eyed man.

My Afghan friends were still there, life passing them by. The dashing young guerrillas had turned into balding middle-aged men with potbellies and glasses, left adrift by the West's abandonment of their cause. Increasingly contemptuous of Pakistan where they had to live but which they blamed for all Afghanistan's woes, one old friend called Hamid Gilani told me with glee that an Italian restaurant called *Luna Caprese* had opened in Islamabad and suggested we dine there. When I arrived, there was an open can of Coca-Cola at my place. 'It's special Coke to drink a toast to the old days,' he laughed. Lifting it to drink, I realised he had filled it with illicit red wine.

Behind Hamid's glasses I could see crescents of tears rimming his eyes. 'Seeing you cleans my heart', he said. 'You have a husband, a baby, a job and a home and I salute you. I am a man who has given his youth to the struggle for a place that no longer exists.'

Suddenly on September 11th all that changed as half a world away two planes smashed into the World Trade Center and another into the Pentagon. Danger had come out of a clear blue sky and nothing would be the same again. Watching the horribly compelling scene over and over on my television, holding my two-year-old son Lourenço who kept shouting 'Mummy, plane *crashing*', I listened to the pundits pontificate on who might be responsible. That the planes had been hijacked by suicide bombers immediately pointed to the Middle East. Saddam Hussein, Washington's arch-enemy, was top of the list of suspects. But there was another name. That of Saudi-born terrorist Osama bin Laden. Not only had he repeatedly vowed war on the West, but, said one expert, he had even sent a message from his lair in Afghanistan to an Arab newspaper a few weeks earlier saying that he was planning a spectacular attack.

Afghanistan. It was as if a ghost had walked across my grave. As the map came up on the screen to show viewers the whereabouts of this forgotten country squashed between Iran, Pakistan, the –stans of central Asia and one thin arm just touching China, I instinctively clutched at my neck for the silver charm I used to wear on a chain. The charm was a map of a far-away country with the words *Allah-o-Akbar*, God is Great, etched across it in lapis lazuli, and it had been given to me years before by a tubby commander with a short beard and twinkling eyes called Abdul Haq with whom I once used to eat pink ice-cream.

Twelve years had passed since I had last breathed the air of Afghanistan. In that time large parts of its capital had been turned to rubble in fighting, tens of thousands more people killed, the regime of the one-eyed mullah had locked away its women, hanged people from lampposts, smashed televisions with tanks and silenced its music, and for the last few years even the rains had stopped. Would I still find the cobalt blue of the mosque in Mazar-i-Sharif where the white doves flew, the smell of pines on the hot Wind of One Hundred and Twenty Days in Herat, the same burst of sweetness on the tongue from the grapes of Kandahar?

On my desk next to my computer, the holiday faces of my husband

and son smiled out trustingly from a snapshot in a yellow frame and in my drawer were thick files of invoices for mortgage and utility bills, nursery fees and guarantees for all manner of electrical appliances. Did I really want to return to that unforgiving land of rocks and mountains stained by the blood of so much killing, or a place inside me when I was young and fearless with all my life and dreams ahead of me? And if I did rediscover that person would I destroy everything I had? The dreamcatcher seemed to know.

1

The Taliban Torturer

'The evil that men do lives after them,
the good is oft interred with their bones.'
SHAKESPEARE, *Julius Caesar*

THE INSTRUCTIONS FROM the commanding officer were clear. 'You must become so notorious for bad things that when you come into an area people will tremble in their sandals. Anyone can do beatings and starve people of food and water. I want your unit to find new ways of torture so terrible that the screams will frighten even crows from their nests, and if the person survives he will never again have a night's sleep.'

I listened in horror. We were sitting at a table in the orchard of the Serena Hotel in Quetta in early October and the evenings were just starting to turn cold. There was a homely scent of apples from the trees all around and the sound of water trickling through narrow pebble-filled canals crisscrossing the orchard. Up above, the Milky Way cut a dusty path through a sky sprinkled with stars. I remembered long ago, on a chilly mountaintop in Paktia, a mujahid telling me that this was the trail left by the Prophet's winged horse Buraq as he galloped towards the heavens.

Sitting at the table with me were Jamil Karzai, the young nephew of an old friend Hamid Karzai, who handed me a letter that I did not open till later, and three people Jamil had brought to talk to me. All three had been members of the Taliban but it was one in particular who was holding my attention.

His name was Mullah Khalil Ahmed Hassani and he was a small thin man who seemed anxious to be liked, with the pinched face and restless hands of one whose darkness hours are constantly haunted. His eyebrows were unusually highly arched under a gold-embroidered Kandahari skullcap that perched rather than fitted on his head, and as he spoke shadows played in the dark recesses of his face. He looked like a torture victim. Instead, as a member of the Taliban's feared secret police, for the previous three and a half years he had been one of the perpetrators charged with carrying out the commanding officer's instructions.

Aged thirty and married with a wife and a one-year-old baby daughter, he was a graduate in business studies and had been working as an accountant until he joined the Taliban. Like many in the movement, Khalil had been largely educated in Pakistan where he had grown up as a refugee, and two of his elder brothers had died fighting among the forces of Gulbuddin Hekmatyar, the most fundamentalist of the seven mujaheddin leaders, in the jihad, or holy war, against the Russians. But his family was well off, owning lands and several houses in Kandahar to which they returned after the war, while he remained doing a degree at Peshawar University. Although he had introduced himself as Mullah Hassani, he explained with a nervous laugh, 'I became a mullah just by joining the Taliban. I'm not a religious scholar.'

'Like many people, I did not become a Talib by choice,' he continued. 'In early 1998 I was working here in Quetta as accountant for a company trading dried fruit, almonds and pistachio nuts when I got a message that my grandfather, who was eighty-five, had been arrested by the Taliban in Kandahar and was being badly beaten and would probably die. They would only release him if we provided a male member of his family as a conscript, so I had to go.'

Many of Khalil's friends had already joined the Taliban. Some

because their families had been told their lands would be confiscated if they did not, though a few got round this by paying a bribe of $20 a month not to be conscripted, a huge amount in a country where the average salary is less than $200 a year. Others had been lured into its ranks with offers of money and Datsun two-door pick-ups with bumper bars – the vehicle of choice of the Taliban – which were provided to the leadership by smugglers and drug-barons in return for being able to ply their lucrative trade as Afghanistan became the world's largest producer of opium[1]. The deliberate destruction of the irrigation channels by the Russians during their ten-year occupation meant that poppies were all that would grow in much of the country, and were the main crop in the south-western provinces of Helmand, Zabul and, to a lesser extent, Kandahar. Although the Taliban had banned the consumption of narcotics as un-Islamic, and in July 2000

[1] According to the US State Department, Afghanistan's opium crop in 2000 was 3,656 tonnes, 72 percent of the world's total, compared to 31 percent in 1985. Production fell in 2001 after the Taliban banned the growing of opium poppies, but in 2002, following the fall of the Taliban, Afghanistan became the world's biggest opium producer again.

had banned cultivation of opium poppies, the trade continued and the country remained one of the world's major trafficking routes, known as the Golden Crescent.

Assigned to the secret police, Khalil patrolled the streets at night looking for thieves and signs of subversion. Initially he thought the Taliban were doing an effective job. 'It had been a crazy situation after the Russians left,' he explained. 'In Kandahar warlords were selling everything, even stripping the telephone wires, kidnapping young girls and boys, robbing people and blocking the roads, and the Taliban seemed like good people who brought law and order.'

This was something I had heard over and over again. Afghanistan is roughly speaking, split into north and south by the Hindu Kush. To the north are mostly Persian and Turkic peoples, and to the south the Pashtuns, while Tajiks and Hazaras live in the mountains. By the time the Taliban emerged in 1994, ethnic and tribal divisions in a land awash with weaponry[2] had turned the country into a shifting patchwork of fiefdoms run by warlords who switched sides with bewildering frequency.

The predominantly Tajik government of President Burhanuddin Rabbani controlled Kabul and the northeast, backed by commander Ahmad Shah Massoud, the famous Lion of the Panjshir, but was under siege from the forces of the fundamentalist Gulbuddin Hekmatyar based to the south, a man who had once stopped an interview with me because he could see my ankle. Herat and the three westernmost provinces were ruled by Ismael Khan, an egocentric mujaheddin commander whose men wore black and white checked scarves, called him 'Excellency' and carried pictures of him with flowing black beard on a white horse. Mazar-i-Sharif and the six northern provinces were governed by the vodka-swilling Uzbek warlord General Rashid

[2] The combination of US and Soviet aid probably made Afghanistan the world's largest recipient of personal weapons during the 1980s, according to figures from the 1991 SIPRI Yearbook on World Armaments, with total weapon imports greater than those of Iraq. For more details *see* Barnett Rubin.

Dostum, who had been on the Soviet payroll during the jihad. Dostum's 20,000-strong Jawzjani militia was so terrifying that they were known as *galamjam* or carpet-thieves, the ultimate Afghan insult. After the collapse of the Communists, he had subsequently allied with and betrayed just about every faction and at the time of the emergence of the Taliban had just switched his support from Rabbani to Hekmatyar. In the mountains of central Afghanistan, Hazaras ran the province of Bamiyan. A *shura* of bickering commanders in Jalalabad governed the three eastern provinces bordering Pakistan.

The worst situation was to the south of the Hindu Kush among Pashtuns, Afghanistan's largest ethnic group, particularly around Kandahar. Gul Agha, the Governor, son of the late Haji Latif, a notorious bandit-leader turned mujaheddin commander, was said to have controlled no more than his office and the stretch of road outside. Small-time warlords and petty commanders had stripped the city of anything that could be sold for scrap and set up their own checkpoints.

Everyone talked of the chains across the roads, five on the main street of Kandahar, fifty just on the two-hour sixty-five-mile stretch between Spin Boldak and Kandahar, each manned by different warlords demanding money. Businessmen and truckers were paying far more in bribes to transport things than the value of the goods themselves. Wali Jan, *sardar* of the Noorzai tribe, and owner of a petrol station and one of the principal bazaars in Kandahar, whom I met at his marble-floored house in Quetta, told me he had happily given money to Mullah Omar. 'It had been a terrible situation,' he explained. 'The roads were full of dacoits and we had to pay a fortune to transport our stuff and our market was full of thieves.'

Then there were the rapes. No one slept safely in their homes as young girls and boys were kidnapped and violated, causing many parents to stop sending them to school. According to Taliban legend, the whole movement was sparked off in the spring of 1994 when a commander paraded on his tank around town a young boy that he had taken as his bride after a dispute with another commander who had also wanted to sodomise the boy. Another version was that a commander had abducted two young sisters from the village of Sanghisar where Mullah Omar preached at the small local mosque, taken them to his military camp and repeatedly gang-raped them. Mullah Omar was said to have gathered thirty men and attacked, hanging the commander from the barrel of his own tank.

Later interviews with some of the founding members of the Taliban, as well as villagers from Sanghisar and officers from Pakistan's Inter-Services Intelligence (ISI), which gave military and financial support to the movement, cast doubt on both these versions and made it clear that it had been planned for some time with active recruitment going on among *madrassa* students in Baluchistan. However war-weary the population and eager for change, it seems inconceivable that a bunch of illiterate small-town mullahs and religious students could have masterminded the often sophisticated military offensives that saw them capture ninety percent of the country within four years, not to mention economic measures such as flooding the currency markets of Mazar-i-Sharif with counterfeit Afghani notes to destroy confidence in the local administration. All of this pointed to the involvement of the ISI, which for years had been trying to install a sympathetic government in Kabul. General Nasirullah Babar, Interior Minister in the government of Benazir Bhutto who was ruling Pakistan at the time the movement emerged, publicly referred to the Taliban as 'our boys'. Whatever the truth there is no doubt that initially Mullah Omar and his men were seen as noble figures simply intent on restoring law and order to the country, then to hand over control to someone else.

'Mullah Omar told me we don't want chairs, you tribal leaders can have those, we just want food for our men,' said Wali Jan. 'For the four days it took them to capture Kandahar our *nan* shops gave all the bread they produced to them. We also gave them watermelons. Then they said they wanted to take Herat which was good for us as we import through Iran and wanted that road cleared so we gave them money and they captured Herat and again Mullah Omar told me don't worry, we don't want chairs. They also said we don't want taxes, just *zakat*, the Islamic tax, just 2.5%. But they cheated us for they took the chairs and then they started taxes, demanding more and more money.'

Patrolling the streets of Kandahar in his black Taliban turban, Mullah Khalil Hassani also felt cheated. Throughout 1998 the leadership began issuing more and more radical edicts and his duties changed. Instead of searching for criminals or subversives, the night patrols were tasked with finding people watching videos, listening to music, playing cards or chess, or keeping birds, something that had always been popular in Kandahar where people would train so-called Judas pigeons to lure birds from other people's flocks and capture them. Men sporting beards that did not meet the regulation length of being long enough to squeeze a fist around it and still have some beard protruding at the bottom, were to be arrested and beaten, as were any women who dared venture outside the house in squeaky shoes, white shoes, or shoes that clicked. Even owning a kite became a criminal offence.

One of Wali Jan's market stalls was burnt down for selling Malaysian soap because printed on the green and yellow packets was a silhouette of a woman; another for stocking washing powder with a photograph of a housewife and children. 'It was a nightmare – the police were always confiscating food because they had pictures of people on them,' he recalled. 'We had to close down the photo booths and video shops, and could no longer sell music, only the Taliban Top Ten.' According to him, the Taliban's favourite singer was a man called Siraji, who intoned monotonous war chants inciting people into battle with lyrics such as:

> *This is our house, the home of lions and tigers*
> *We will beat everyone who attacks us*
> *We are the defenders of our great country.*

'They banned everything,' he continued. 'The only entertainment was public executions. The only safe activity was sleeping. Once I asked Mullah Omar what people were supposed to do for enjoyment and he said, "walk in gardens and look at flowers". But the funny thing is after he took over there were five years of drought and everything died so there weren't even flowers.'

'Was there a list of forbidden things?' I asked Khalil. 'Not exactly a list,' he replied. 'Most of the things we knew and notices would come round with new ones as well as orders, such as to keep our turbans straight.' He thought for a while then asked for a sheet of paper from my notebook and wrote down the following, adding to them throughout our conversation as he remembered more. I later had it translated.

1. All men to attend prayers in mosques five times daily.

2. No woman allowed outside the home unless accompanied by a *mahram* (close male relative such as a father, brother or husband).

3. Women not allowed to buy from male shopkeepers.

4. Women must be covered by burqa.

5. Any woman showing her ankles must be whipped.

6. Women must not talk or shake hands with men.

7. Ban on laughing in public. No stranger should hear a woman's voice.

8. Ban on wearing shoes with heels or that make any noise as no stranger should hear a woman's footsteps.

9. Ban on cosmetics. Any woman with painted nails should have her fingers cut off.

10. No woman allowed to play sports or enter a sports club.

11. Ban on clothes in 'sexually attracting colours', (basically anything other than light blue or mustard).

12. Ban on flared trousers, even under a burqa.

13. Ban on women washing clothes in rivers or any public place.

14. Ban on women appearing on the balconies of their houses. All windows were supposed to be painted so women could not be seen from outside their homes.

15. No one allowed to listen to music.

16. No television or video allowed.

17. No playing of cards.

18. No playing of chess.

19. No flying of kites.

20. No keeping of birds – any bird-keepers to be imprisoned and the birds killed.

21. Men must not shave or trim their beards which should grow long enough to protrude from a fist clasped at the point of the chin.

22. All men to wear Islamic clothes and cap. Shirts with collars banned.

23. Anyone carrying un-Islamic books to be executed.

24. Ban on all pictures in books or houses.

25. All people to have Islamic names.

26. Any street or place bearing a woman's name or any female reference to be changed.

27. All boy students to wear turbans.

28. Any non-Muslim must wear a yellow cloth stitched onto their clothes to differentiate them.

29. All sportsmen to have legs and arms fully covered.

30. All audiences at sporting events to refrain from cheering or clapping but only to chant Allah-o-Akbar.

'Basically any form of pleasure was outlawed,' said Khalil, 'and if we found people doing any of these things we would beat them with logs soaked in water like a knife cutting through meat until the room ran with their blood or their spines snapped. We did different things, we would put some of them standing on their heads to sleep, hang others upside down with their legs tied together, and stretch the arms out of others and nail them to posts. Sometimes when their spines were broken we would throw bread to them so they would try to crawl. Then I would write the report to our commanding officer so he could see how innovative we had been.

'Once in Kandahar Jail, I watched the prison superintendent Mullah Burki beat people so harshly that it was impossible to tell afterwards whether or not they had been wearing clothes and when they drifted into unconsciousness we put salt on the wounds to make them scream.'

The state of terror spread by the Taliban was so pervasive that it began to seem as if the whole country was spying on each other. 'As we drove around at night with our guns, local people would come to us and say there's someone watching a video in this house or some men playing cards in that house,' he said. 'I was shocked. We are a land of feuds and I suppose some people were using us to settle old scores.'

After Kandahar, Khalil was put in charge of secret police cells in the provincial capitals of Ghazni and then Herat, a once beautiful Persian city in western Afghanistan that had suffered terribly under the Soviet occupation and had fallen to the Taliban in September 1995. It was renowned as a highly-cultured place where women would dance at weddings and many girls had been in school until the Taliban closed them all down. Mullah Omar was infuriated when 150 women dared appear on the streets of Herat to protest against the closure of the female public bath-houses. Khalil and his men were told to be particularly cruel to the Heratis who were Persian-speaking and had a large Shia minority, unlike the Pashto-speaking Taliban who were all Sunni Muslims. Speaking in Persian was forbidden and a strict curfew imposed from 8 p.m. to 7 a.m. Anyone out on the streets in those hours, even for emergencies such as illness or giving birth, was arrested. 'Some Taliban had been killed by the ordinary people in Herat,' he explained, 'so we were told to beat them much more harshly.'

Another group that came in for particularly harsh treatment were the Hazaras who make up about 19 percent[3] of the population and live mostly in the infertile central Afghanistan highlands of Hazarajat as well as large communities in Kabul and Mazar-i-Sharif. Persian-speaking Shias with flat Asiatic features, the word 'hazar' in Persian means thousands and they were said to be descended from Genghis Khan and his hordes of Mongol warriors who had swept through the region in 1221–2. Genghis Khan detested cities because they deprived his warriors' horses of grazing and he razed them wherever possible, wiping out the ancient cities of Balkh, Herat, Bamiyan and Ghazni, leaving only a single watchtower at Bamiyan, and slaughtering so many of the inhabitants of Balkh that a visitor reported arriving and finding only dogs.

The Hazaras had grown to expect a rough time from Pashtun rulers. In 1838 Alexander 'Bokhara' Burnes, a young Scot whose book *Travels into Bokhara* had been a bestseller, was sent as British emissary to the court of Dost Mohammed supposedly on a trade mission but in fact part of a network of British agents in Central Asia gathering intelligence about Russian plans to secure warmwater ports to the south which they had coveted since the time of Peter the Great. In his subsequent account *Cabool*, he wrote of the Hazaras as 'oppressed

---

[3] Population figures in Afghanistan can only be estimates and are all hotly disputed by the various ethnic groupings. The CIA World Fact Book 2001 puts the population at 26.8 million of which 38 percent are Pashtun, 25 percent Tajik, 19 percent Hazara, 6 percent Uzbek and 12 percent other.

by all the neighbouring nations whom they serve as hewers of wood and drawers of water', adding that 'many are sold into slavery and there is little doubt that they barter their children for cloth'. Worse was to come in the 1890s when the British-backed king Abdur Rahman massacred thousands and took thousands more to Kabul as slaves. When the Tajiks took power in Kabul, a minority themselves, they too did not spare the Hazaras. In 1993 Ahmad Shah Massoud's men swept through the capital's Hazara suburbs, killing an estimated 1000 civilians, beheading old men, women and children and stuffing the bodies down wells, cutting off hands and throwing them to dogs, and raping the women.

But the Taliban took this discrimination to new extremes. Not only did they see them as heretics – at almost five million people the Hazara make up Afghanistan's largest Shia community – but they also resented the active role of women in Hazara society and the way they dressed, provocatively as the Taliban saw it, wearing bright full skirts and boots as well as lots of silver bangles and earrings and not covering their faces.

In August 1997, having captured Kabul but failed to take Mazar-i-Sharif, Taliban forces blockaded Hazarajat, cutting off all four access roads in an attempt to starve the one million Hazaras living just below the peaks of the Hindu Kush. No notice was taken of outraged protests from foreign aid organizations such as Oxfam that these people in the provinces of Bamiyan, Ghor, Wardak and Ghazni would die because their crops had failed in the continuing drought and they had already slaughtered all their animals and eaten all the grass.

Then, after finally capturing Mazar-i-Sharif in August 1998 when General Dostum fled to Uzbekistan and several of his commanders switched sides, the Taliban launched what witnesses described as 'a killing frenzy' in retaliation for the heavy casualties suffered when they had tried to take the city the previous year. Driving through the streets with white Taliban flags flying from their Datsun jeeps and machine guns mounted on the roofs, they peppered the streets with bullets. One witness described seeing them mow down a group of women on their way to a wedding, a small boy pushing a cart of bread and an old man grinding wheat. After one day of indiscriminate killing, they focused on the Hazaras, carrying out a house-to-house search for anyone of fighting age in the Hazara areas and shooting them on the spot, usually in the face or testicles.[4]

The new Governor of Mazar-i-Sharif, Mullah Manon Niazi, who had distinguished himself as Governor of Kabul by stepping up the number of public executions, announced: 'Hazaras are not Muslim, they are Shia. They are *kofr* (infidel)'. This was taken as official licence both to rape and kill. Shia patients were dragged from hospitals and shot and Mullah Niazi forbade their relatives from removing the bodies from the street for five days until wild dogs had eaten them, as Dostum's men had done the same to the Taliban the previous year. Thousands more were imprisoned in metal shipping containers twenty to forty feet long that had been used to bring in Cold War arms supplies, and then were either left to asphyxiate or shifted to prisons in the south.

Some of these containers arrived in Herat where they came under the guard of Khalil Hassani and his men. Describing what happened as 'among the worst of so many bad things', he recalled: 'One day when I was in Herat several old Russian trucks were brought from Mazar-i-Sharif on the way to Kandahar. They were carrying metal shipping containers inside which were Hazara prisoners. There were about 450 of them and they were all women and children – I suppose the men had been killed. It was still summer and the trucks were left in the square for two days in the baking heat and the children were crying for food and water but our instructions were to give them nothing and we refused to let them out of the containers for toilet or anything. I can still hear the noise, the desperate banging on the

---

[4] For more details see the Human Rights Watch report of November 1998 – 'Afghanistan: The Massacre in Mazar-i-Sharif'.

metal and the muffled cries that gradually grew softer. It was more than 40°C outside and must have been like a furnace inside. The old and the babies must have been dead.'

Coincidentally, that afternoon before meeting Khalil, I had wandered around the suburb of Kirani on the outskirts of Quetta, a labyrinth of mud-walled houses and tiny stores, which is mostly home to Hazara refugees. In a small dirt-floored mosque with no roof I came across a huddle of about thirty hungry and frightened Hazara women and children in vividly coloured but very dirty clothes, and a few old men. They told me they had travelled twenty days to come to Pakistan by truck then foot, from a village near Bamiyan, the town famous for the giant Buddhas carved into its mountains, which the Taliban had blown up earlier in the year in defiance of worldwide protest. Having got all the way to Pakistan, they had discovered they could not enter the refugee camps as the borders were officially closed so they could get no aid and would have to keep moving around or risk being picked up by police and dumped back at the border.

'We left because we had nothing to eat,' explained Asma Rosaman, a woman in a bright cerise dress with a red-rose patterned shawl, her three sons and three daughters clutching at her wide skirts. Usually refugees at least manage to bring out a quilt to sleep under and a kettle and pot. These had absolutely nothing with them beyond the clothes on their backs and stories of being forced to watch their men-folk burnt alive as the Taliban rampaged through their villages, demolishing their houses, raping women and killing the men.

'My husband was killed when we escaped,' said Asma in a voice too tired of tragedy to be emotional. 'The Taliban followed us on horses. He was carrying our household goods so he was behind and they shot him. He was a wheat farmer but we had not had wheat for a long time because there was no rain. One lady in the village was pregnant and they locked her in her house and set fire to it with her children screaming. They killed children with steel rods and plucked out eyes. I saw them dynamite a cave where 200 people had taken shelter. I closed my childrens' mouths so that no one would hear them. They killed 3000 people in one month.'

This was probably not an exaggeration. The details took a long while to come out in the world, only when the first refugees started to arrive in Pakistan, but testimony collected by human rights organizations suggests that between four thousand and six thousand people were massacred in Bamiyan after its surrender that August of 1998.

Another woman called Peri Gul with eyes like black olive pits tugged at my arm. 'There were 300 killed in my village,' she said. 'They locked my husband in our house and set fire to it and beat me when I tried to run inside. Afterwards I had to beg bread for my three sons and daughters. Every house was burnt and they sprayed the fields with chemicals and set fire to them so no one had food. Mostly we just scraped moss from rocks. I even thought about selling one of my children but who would buy? Nobody had anything.' I guessed she was in her mid-20s, ten years younger than me, but she looked old enough to be my mother. Clutching my hand with her calloused dirt-encrusted fingers, she sobbed, 'We were innocent people just trying to survive. First they starved us then they murdered us. Why didn't anyone do anything?'

Such stories were so inhuman sometimes I would just want to snap shut my notebook and run away. There were more than three million Afghan refugees in Pakistan and it wasn't as if it was just the occasional individual with a sad story, it was everyone. I felt like a parasite, sucking up all these tales of tragedy to regurgitate in newsprint for people thousands of miles away, and with no tangible advantage for those I interviewed. I had no answer to why the world had done nothing.

Back in the 1980s when I had lived in Pakistan before, I had interviewed lots of refugees, sometimes spending the night in the camps. But then the Afghans had only suffered eleven years of war, their men were defeating the Russians, and there was still hope in their eyes. Now they had been through twenty-three years of war; their men were killing each other and their eyes were blank. As I watched these Hazara mothers unable to feed their babies, I thought of my own well-fed son back home, dressed in a different outfit every day, a wooden train set taking over the living room, parties with cake and balloons, holidays in the sun. I couldn't imagine looking into those trusting blue eyes knowing I had no food for him and no place for him to sleep. At a store nearby, I bought them a sack of rice, some bread and apples and some blankets, and their gratitude only increased my guilt. It was not enough, it never would be.

In the orchard that evening, we took a break to go and help ourselves to the barbecue, steaming slices of *saji*, leg of lamb rotating on an enormous skewer, and for a while we talked of other things. I showed them the photograph I carry of my husband who has the dark eyes and olive skin of the Moors who once ruled Portugal. 'He looks like an Afghan,' said Khalil approvingly.

By the time the inevitable pot of green tea arrived, there was a bitter chill and the orchard had emptied of diners. But Khalil had more to tell. Between postings for the secret police, he had spent some months as a bodyguard for Mullah Omar, the spiritual leader of the Taliban. He came from the same branch of the Ghilzai tribe and so was trusted.

Holding my teacup in both hands to keep them warm, I asked him to describe Mullah Omar. One of the most enigmatic things about the Taliban was the reclusiveness of their one-eyed leader. Not only had he never travelled outside Afghanistan, Mullah Omar had barely visited his own country. He had only twice gone to Kabul, preferring to rule from his adopted home of Kandahar though he was actually born in Tarin Kot in Uruzgan, the mountainous province north of the city. He had never given interviews to western journalists, and he had refused to meet with western diplomats.

No pictures of him hung in government offices. Newspaper articles about him were always illustrated by the same blurred photograph taken from television footage of him in Kandahar holding up the Sacred Cloak of Prophet Mohammed at a special gathering of Taliban in 1996. At this ceremony, he had himself declared as Amir ul Momineen, Commander of all Islam; it was also the first time the cloak had been taken out for more than sixty years.

All that was known about Mullah Omar was that until 1994 he had been a simple village mullah in Sanghisar, a small community of mud-walled houses an hour's drive north of Kandahar. He was about forty, bearded, wore a black turban and had only one eye, having lost the other in a Soviet rocket attack during the jihad in the 1980s, supposedly clawing it out of the socket when he realised that he had been blinded. Even the one eye was sometimes disputed. A few days earlier a friend of a friend had come to my hotel, whispering because of all the ISI officers in the lobby, that he had a picture of the real Mullah Omar. I opened the envelope to see a small black and white passport photograph of a man with a turban and two eyes.

Khalil was not very enlightening on his appearance. 'He looks normal, medium height, a bit fat and has an artificial eye which is green.' He had more to say on his personality. According to Khalil, Mullah Omar modelled himself on Caliph Umar, a seventh-century leader of Islam who had been declared Amir ul Momineen of the peoples of Arabia and was the second Caliph after the death of the Prophet Mohammed. A simple man who owned just one shirt and one mantle, and who ordered his own son killed for immorality, Caliph Umar used to disguise himself in ragged clothes to mingle incognito amongst the common people. In the same way, Mullah Omar would go out of his compound at night on his battered old motorcycle to find out what his people were saying about him in the bazaars and *chai-khanas* or tea-houses.

Khalil said that Mullah Omar presented himself as a man of simple tastes but though he berated his cook every day for serving meat when his soldiers in the field had none, he ate it anyway, and he liked listening to war-chants and riding his Arabian horse around his compound. In fact Khalil had quickly come to the conclusion that the great enigmatic mastermind behind the Taliban was just simple-minded. 'Mullah Omar knows only how to write Omar and to sign his name,' he said. 'He's completely illiterate.'

I had been told the same thing a few days earlier by General Ishaq, administrator of the hospital in Kandahar that used to treat Mullah Omar, and a former general in the Afghan army. 'His doctor told me he thought that the rocket had left bits of shrapnel in his brain. He said Omar likes sitting at the wheel of one of his cars making engine noises and that he had days of terrible headaches and mood-swings when he would not see anyone and dreams when he thought he was having visions.'

For Khalil, coming into such close contact with the Taliban leader-ship was what made him lose faith in the whole movement. 'It is the first time in Afghanistan's history that the lower classes of the country are governing and by force. There are no educated people in this administration – like Mullah Omar they are all totally backward and illiterate. They have no idea of the history of the country and they call themselves mullahs but have no idea of Islam. Nowhere does it say men must have beards or women cannot be educated, in fact on the contrary the Koran says people must seek education.'

For all the Taliban leader's avowed simplicity and proclaimed intention of returning Afghanistan to the time of the Prophet, 1400 years earlier, Khalil said Mullah Omar loved the trappings of power. Not poor himself, he had however been shocked by the lavishness of Mullah Omar's house, set in a vast walled compound with a mosque, guesthouse, its own farm, stables and houses for the uncle who acted as a father-figure and all his relatives. Built in 1997, all paid for by Osama bin Laden, it had specially reinforced walls and roofs, six feet thick and cushioned with car tyres, to withstand even a cruise missile. He had even had a road moved because it went too close to the compound.

The main house where Mullah Omar lived with his three wives and five children was in an inner walled area. In front of the wrought-iron entrance gate was a fountain flowing over a fibreglass sculpture of a fallen log dotted with small Miami Beach-style plastic palm trees. The house itself was a two-storey building, set either side of a central courtyard which contained a water purification system and was painted with murals of the scenic attractions of Afghanistan including the fort at Kalat, the minaret at Jam, the mosque of Herat and oddly one of the swimming pool at the Intercontinental Hotel in Kabul, but not of course of the Bamiyan Buddhas. Whichever wife was in favour would sleep on the same side of the house as Mullah Omar while the other two would sleep in the other section with the children.

Just outside the inner compound was the guesthouse, a bungalow with a large patio with columns painted like tree trunks and walls decorated with gaudy flower murals. Mullah Omar spent the mornings there, sitting on a bed with a tin of money and a walkie-talkie by his side, receiving his commanders, handing out cash and issuing instructions, usually sent out on paper chits.

Khalil said he sometimes saw Osama bin Laden at Mullah Omar's house, arriving in a black Land Cruiser with tinted windows, usually in a convoy of seven or eight cars at a time. 'His bodyguards were all very tall people, Sudanese I think, with curly hair and all with wireless sets and earpieces like those American bodyguards. Sometimes I went to Mullah Omar's house in Uruzgan when they went hunting for birds or deer together or fishing with dynamite.'

The more he saw of them together the more he became convinced that the Taliban were not really in control. 'We laughed when we heard the Americans asking Mullah Omar to hand over Osama bin Laden,' he said. 'The Americans are crazy. Afghanistan is not a state sponsoring terrorism but a terrorist-sponsored state. It is only Osama bin Laden that can hand over Mullah Omar not vice versa.'

During his time in the Taliban, Khalil had attended two Arab-run training camps, one in Jari Dasht, the Yellow Desert, four hours from

Helmand, an area with its own airstrip where Arab sheikhs used to go hunting, and one near Herat. 'We were taught by Pakistani military trainers how to shoot exact targets and how to move along the ground in the front-line,' he said. They were also told that if they died while fighting under the white flag of the Taliban, they along with seventy-two members of their families would go to paradise. They were also given blank marriage certificates signed by a mullah and encouraged to 'take wives' during battle, basically a licence to rape.

Being ordered to the front-line was to provide Khalil's chance for escape: 'We were sixty-two friends sent to Bagram, north of Kabul, and our line was attacked by the Northern Alliance and they almost defeated us. Many of my friends were killed and we didn't know who was fighting whom, there was killing from behind and in front. Our commanders fled in cars leaving us behind so we also escaped, walking all night.

'I was very afraid of being caught. I got away but then I was stopped by a line of Arabs who demanded to know why we were escaping. For two days we were under their arrest then taken back to the front-line.'

One night he was put on watch and saw a truck of sheep and goats coming through the lines from Northern Alliance territory so he jumped in and got to Kabul and from there back to Kandahar. There he was arrested and put in jail for eight days and interrogated but managed to get out to Quetta through the intervention of some relatives who were high-ranking Taliban members.

Since leaving the Taliban, Khalil had been living back in Quetta with his wife and baby daughter, and was looking for work. Although he insisted that the Taliban had become an organization 'in name only', he feared for his life and I wondered why he had taken the enormous risk of speaking to me. 'I want people to understand,' he said, shaking his head. 'I have done terrible things and the only way I can make up for it is to tell the world the truth about these people.'

Kabul, September 24 2001

Respected Mr Jamil Karzai

Salam alay kum
I hope you and the rest of your family will be alright. I
received your letter and I informed other female members of
ours, Farishta, Najeba, Sadaf and Maryam about your
request to write to a lady journalist who writes for the
Sunday Telegraph of Britain.

Respected Karzai, we here really appreciate what you do
for the new generation of Afghanistan and we are really
worried about your life too. Please be careful.

Here is the letter for Miss Christina Lamb.

Dear Christina

Jamil Karzai has written about you that you are a nice kind
beautiful and helpful lady and has asked us, specially me to
write a letter about our life under the Taliban regime and I
hope this will help you outside understand the feelings of an
educated Afghan female who must now live under a burqa.

My name is Fatema, this is my real name but please I ask
you to use this name of mine Marri, as what we are doing is
dangerous. I'm thirty years old and live in a three-roomed
flat with my family on a big estate, it's called Microrayon. I
was born here in Kabul and I graduated from the twelfth
class of Hishai Durrani High School, our biggest girls' school.

*I speak Dari, Pashto and English. I think you are surprised I
know English but my father was a diplomat and my mother
an English teacher. My mother went to university in India.
So don't worry.*

*I know from our friend that you have a kind husband
and a beautiful son and you travel the world reporting and
meeting people. I dream of a life like that. It's funny we live
under the same small sky yet it seems we live 500 years
apart.*

*You see us now in our burqas like strange insects in the
dust, our heads down, but it wasn't always this way. I do
not remember much before the Russian invasion as I was
only eight when they came and I felt bad then when I saw
the soldiers with their white faces and hair because my
parents said they had made slaves of us but even at that
time we still went to school. Women worked as professors
and doctors and in government. We went for picnics and
parties, wore jeans and short skirts and I thought I would go
to university like my mother and work for my living.*

*I know in the villages many schools had been destroyed in
the war but here in Kabul we were lucky. Only when the
Taliban came were all the girls' schools and university closed.
When the mujaheddin came to Kabul my school was closed
for a year because of all the fighting which was very bad
particularly here in Microrayon and we were the first line of
battle, but then I finished school and became a teacher. I
particularly liked science and wanted to go to university to
study science but there was no money because my father had
lost his job.*

*When the Taliban came to Kabul, it was September 1996,
they told us all to stay at home. They announced it on the
radio just like they announced we all had to wear burqas. I
had never worn one before, they were something from the*

village, and it was like not being able to breathe or see, just seeing in front through that small square like a cage, and in the summer it is so hot and the sun blinds you. I fell over twice the first day.

In our house behind all the burqas and shalwar kamiz is a red silk party dress, my mother's from the time when the king was in power and my father in the foreign ministry. Sometimes I hold it up against me and imagine dancing but it is a lost world. Now we must wear clothes that make us invisible and cannot even wear heels. One of my friends was beaten with cable for wearing white shoes because the Taliban said, 'how dare you wear the colour of our flag', and another because they said they could hear her shoes click on the pavement.

You might think we women are doing nothing but my friends and I struggle for the rights of Afghan women working secretly here for the Afghan Women's League, trying to educate our women and young girls. Some of our members make nan bread and distribute it to widows, there are so many widows from this long war, you see them in all streets in the city begging in their torn clothes but the Taliban beat them and say they are not allowed out without mahram, that's what we call men relatives like a husband or father.

My sister and I hold secret English and science classes in our house. It is hard as all the time we fear someone might report us and we cannot get books. Our students pay a little and we use it for firewood to keep warm. We do not even have a blackboard. We tell them do not bring bags and sometimes we stop for weeks because we have heard the Taliban are onto us. We thought about contacting an NGO but we are worried the Taliban would find out. Some other schools have been found and the teachers beaten.

We have small rebellions. Maybe you do not know we are

forbidden to wear make-up under the burqa but I have a red lipstick. One of my friends runs a secret beauty salon in her bedroom.

In my family I am the eldest and apart from my sister Latifa, I have two brothers. One is a tailor, the other still a student but in school now all he learns is the Koran and the Hadith, not science or foreign languages. Science was my favourite subject. I wanted to be a science teacher.

Life here is very miserable. We have no rights at all and we have asked many times other countries of the world for help but they have been silent. Now we heard about this attack on the towers in America with many people dead and my father says the Americans will come and remove the Taliban but we do not dare hope. I wonder, maybe the world will think all Afghans are terrorists and we are not. It is the Arabs, who drive around in their Datsuns with black windows and live in big houses behind high walls in Wazir Akbar Khan and buy their foods in tins in the import shops in Chicken Street. If you saw how we lived, you would know we cannot be terrorists, we are the forgotten people.

We do not have schools, the doors of education are closed on all, especially us. I don't know if we will ever go to school again. We cannot paint or listen to music. The Taliban ran their tanks over all the televisions.

We asked the world, are we not human beings? Do we not deserve to live in peace? Can we not have rights as women in other countries?

I do not know what you want me to write to you. If I start writing I will fill all the paper and my eyes will fill with tears because in these seven years of Taliban no one has asked us to write about our lives. In my mind I make a picture of you and your family. I wonder if you drive a car, if you go out with friends to the cinema and restaurants and

dance at parties. Do you play loud music and swim in lakes?
One day I would like to see and I would also like to show
you a beautiful place in my country with mountains and
streams but not now while we must be hidden. Maybe our
worlds will always be too far apart.

Marri

2

Mullahs on Motorbikes

*Unlike other wars, Afghan wars become serious
only when they are over*
SIR OLAF CAROE

TRAVELLING IN AFGHANISTAN was like wandering through
the shadows of shattered things. Khalil Hassani's story had
meant more to me than he realised for Afghanistan had left its own
dark place in my mind. When he spoke of Kandahar, I pictured a
land the colour of dust, its old caravan trails littered with burnt-out
tanks and dotted with bombed terracotta villages which from a distance resembled the ruins of some forgotten civilisation and probably
looked little different to when Alexander the Great founded the city
in 330 BC giving it his name, Iskandar in Arabic. But I saw something
else too.

The first time I went to Kandahar I was on the back of a mullah's
motorbike and thought it the most desolate place on earth. Nothing
but tufts of coarse grass grew on the stony plains and the distant
mountains were barren and flesh-coloured. The turban wound round
my head offered scant protection from the ancient grit driven into
my eyes and mouth on a scorching desert wind that was said by
Kandaharis to be so hot as to grill a fish held on an upturned palm.

It was 1988 and the giggling mullahs on motorbikes who taught me to tie a turban and shared their rations of fried okra and stale *nan* bread with me under Soviet tank-fire, would later become the Taliban. No one had heard of the Taliban then, it was just a word in Pashto that meant 'seekers of knowledge' or religious students. And not many journalists went to Kandahar in those days. The journey to Afghanistan's second biggest city was complicated and dangerous, starting off from the remote desert town of Quetta where the earth seemed in a constant state of tremor and to which flights were sporadic.

Most reporters covered the war from Peshawar where there was a five-star hotel and the seven mujaheddin parties fighting the Russians had their headquarters, making it easy to arrange trips 'inside', as we called getting into Afghanistan. There was an American Club where one could drink Budweisers, eat Oreo Cookie ice-cream and listen to middle-aged male correspondents in US Army jackets with bloodstains and charred bullet holes on the back hold court with stories of conflict and 'skirt' from Vietnam to El Salvador. Their eyes had seen so much that they saw nothing, they knew the name and sound of every weapon ever invented, their faces were on the leathery side of rugged and even at breakfast there was Jim Beam on their breath. One of them wore hearing aids which he informed me loudly was because of 'bang bang'; most had children in various places but never carried their photographs, and all of them went to the Philippines for R and R.

It was different for me. I was a young girl in a place where women were regarded as property along with gold and land – the three zs of the Pashtuns, *zan*, *zar* and *zamin* - and kept hidden away behind curtained doorways. The closest I had ever come to war was doing a report for Central Television News in Birmingham on a cannon used in the Battle of Waterloo that 'Local Man' had rescued from the sea. I found the weapon names confusing with all the acronyms and numbers and for a long time couldn't even tell the difference

The Kandahar desert had been turned into a battlefield.

between incoming and outgoing fire. I was young enough to believe I could change the world by writing about the injustices that I saw and foolish enough to think that I could be a witness without bearing any responsibility. What I knew of the Afghans was a romanticised vision distilled from Rudyard Kipling's *Kim* and various nineteenth-century British accounts such as the first by Mountstuart Elphinstone who went out to parley with the king on behalf of the East India Company in 1809 and wrote, 'their vices are revenge, envy, avarice, rapacity and obstinacy; on the other hand, they are fond of liberty, faithful to their friends, kind to their dependents, hospitable, brave, hardy, laborious and prudent.'

After having taken various 'resistance tours' inside from Peshawar, I decided to go to Kandahar largely because I liked the name. Alexander the Great had conquered many peoples and founded a number of cities on his long march from Macedonia towards India, most of which bore some variation of his name. But there was something magical about the name *Kan*-dahar, which pronounced with the stress on the first syllable and a long breath at the end, seemed to convey a sense of longing for the place.

Kandahar was where everything had started. Under the shimmering turquoise dome that dominates the sand-blown city lies the body of Ahmad Shah Abdali, the young Kandahari warrior who in 1747 became Afghanistan's first king. The mausoleum is covered in deep blue and white tiles behind a small grove of trees, one of which is said to cure toothache, and is a place of pilgrimage. In front of it is a small mosque with a marble vault containing one of the holiest relics in the Islamic World, a *kherqa*, the Sacred Cloak of Prophet Mohammed that was given to Ahmad Shah by Murad Beg, the Emir of Bokhara. The Sacred Cloak is kept locked away, taken out only at times of great crisis[1] but the mausoleum is open and there is a constant line of men leaving their sandals at the door and shuffling through to marvel at the surprisingly long marble tomb and touch the glass case containing Ahmad Shah's brass helmet. Before leaving they bend to kiss a length of pink velvet said to be from his robe. It bears the unmistakable scent of jasmine.

In a land of war, the tomb of Ahmad Shah is a peaceful place. Only the men with stumps for legs and burqa-clad war widows begging at its steps hint at the violence and treachery which has stalked Afghanistan since its birth as a nation-state, founded on treasure stolen from a murdered emperor. Part of that treasure was the famous Koh-i-Noor diamond, then said to be worth enough to maintain the whole world for a day and now among the Crown Jewels under twenty-four-hour guard in the Tower of London, stunningly beautiful but blighted by an ancient Hindu curse that the wearer will rule the world but if male will suffer a terrible misfortune.

A member of the war-like Pashtun tribe of Abdalis, Ahmad Shah

---

[1] Until Mullah Omar took it out in November 1996 and displayed it to a crowd of *ulema* or religious scholars to have himself declared Amir-ul Momineen, Prince of all Islam, the last time had been when the city was struck by a cholera epidemic in the 1930s.

was commander of the bodyguard of Nadir Shah, the great Persian conqueror who in 1738 had captured Kandahar from the Ghilzai, another Pashtun tribe and traditional rivals of the Abdalis. Nadir Shah moved east to take Jalalabad, Peshawar, Lahore and finally Delhi, where angered by locals throwing stones at him, he ordered a bloodbath in which 20,000 died. He left laden with treasures of the Moghuls including the fabled Peacock Throne of Emperor Shah Jahan, creator of the Taj Mahal, which was solid gold with a canopy held up by twelve emerald pillars, on top of which were two peacocks studded with diamonds, rubies and emeralds. Among the precious jewels he packed on his camels was the Koh-i-Noor, named after his exclamation on first seeing the 186-carat stone, describing it as 'koh-i-noor!' or 'mountain of light'.

After India, Nadir Shah travelled west, conquering as he went, but with the Koh-i-Noor in his turban, he became more and more ruthless, convinced that everyone was trying to kill him, even his favourite son Raza Quli whom he had blinded. One night in 1747, travelling on yet another military campaign, someone stole into Nadir Shah's tent and stabbed him to death. Ahmad Shah fled the camp with his 4000-strong cavalry and headed to Kandahar, taking much of the emperor's treasury, including the cursed Koh-i-Noor.

Freed from Persian domination, the Abdalis held a *jirga*, a tribal assembly of elders and religious leaders to decide on a ruler. After nine days of discussion they settled upon the twenty-five-year-old Ahmad Shah, partly for his charisma, partly because he was a Saddozai, from the tribe's most distinguished line, partly because a holy man stood up and said he should be, and largely because he had a large army and lots of treasure. A sheaf of wheat was placed on his head as a crown.

Ahmad Shah's affectation of wearing a pearl earring from the looted Moghul treasures led his subjects to call him Durr-i-Durran, Pearl of Pearls, and the royal family became known as the Durrani clan. He set up a *shura* or tribal council to govern the country, and, quickly realising that the best way to control Pashtun tribes was to indulge their taste for warfare and plunder, he used Nadir Shah's booty and a succession of military adventures to keep them in check. Helped by the fact that to the west Persia was in disarray after Nadir Shah's death, and to the east the Moghul Empire was crumbling, Ahmad Shah ended up carving out the second greatest Muslim empire after the Ottoman Empire, taking Kabul, Peshawar, Attock, Lahore, and eventually Delhi.

Never the most modest of men, he had coins minted with the inscription, 'the Commandment came down from the peerless Almighty to Ahmad the King: Strike coins of silver and gold from the back of fish to the moon'.

After his successes in India, Ahmad Shah moved west to capture Herat which was still under Persian rule, then north of the Hindu Kush to bring under his control the Hazara of Bamiyan, the Turkmen of Asterabad, the Uzbek of Balkh and Kunduz, and the Tajik of Khanabad and Badakshan to create Afghanistan as it is today. But he had to keep returning to India where his territories were threatened by the Hindu Maratha armies from the south. Invading India for a fourth time, he acquired Kashmir and Sindh.

Yet he always missed his homeland. A deeply religious man and warrior-poet, he wrote of Kandahar:

> Whatever countries I conquer in the world
> I can never forget your beautiful gardens
> When I remember the summits of your beautiful mountains
> I forget the splendour of the Delhi throne.

Each time he left Kandahar there were plots to overthrow him, often by his own relatives and whenever he returned home from extending his empire, Ahmad Shah would spend the first few days executing dissidents. A later king, Abdur Rahman Khan, would refer to his country as Yaghistan or Land of the Unruly, and as the great Afghan scholar, the late Louis Dupree remarked, 'no Pashtun likes to be ruled by another, particularly someone from another tribe, sub-tribe or section'.

In an attempt to deter the pretenders, the king started executing not only the plotters but also ten randomly chosen members of each sub-tribe involved, yet the intrigues continued. A sword wound on his nose turned ulcerous and cancer began eating away at his face, leaving him in terrible pain and according to accounts of the time, forced to wear a silver nose, with maggots from the wound dropping into his mouth whenever he ate or drank. The Sikhs raised an army and rebelled in the Punjab, forcing him to return to India a fifth, sixth, seventh and eighth time, twice destroying the Sikh city of Amritsar in his anger but never really succeeding in defeating them. Other parts of his empire broke away, some declaring independence, while Murad Beg, the Emir of Bokhara, took others.

Despairing of the land he had created, in 1772 he died alone and in agony in the Suleyman Mountains east of Kandahar, aged only fifty. He left thirty-six children including twenty-three sons most of whom thought they should be his successor. From then on the Durranis lost Punjab, Sindh, Kashmir and much of Baluchistan as two Durrani branches, the Barakzai and Saddozai – and family members within – tussled for control. With no outsiders to unite against until the first British invasion in 1839, soon everyone was fighting and blinding everyone else for power in each region, fathers against sons, brother against brother, uncle against nephew and one wearer of the Koh-i-Noor after another met a violent death.[2] They even had a name for it – *badshahgardi*, which means ruler-turning.

But in his heyday Ahmad Shah had ruled an empire stretching

[2] The Koh-i-noor left Afghanistan when it was given by Shah Shuja to Ranjit Singh, the wily one-eyed ruler of Punjab, as payment for helping restore him to the Kabul throne in 1839, then was appropriated by the British after the defeat of the Sikhs and annexation of the Punjab in 1849. It was the prize exhibit in the Great Exhibition of 1851 and was then recut to the present 109 carats and worn in the crowns of Queen Victoria, Queen Mary and Queen Elizabeth, but no kings for it is still considered unlucky for males.

from the Amu Darya or Oxus River in the north to the Arabian Sea, from Mashad in the west to Delhi in the east, as well as Kashmir, Sindh and most of what is now Baluchistan. One way or another the Durrani dynasty he founded was to rule Afghanistan till the Communist takeover in 1978 and most Afghans regard him as the father of the nation, referring to him as Ahmad Shah Baba.

There was another reason for wanting to go to Kandahar. In Peshawar I had met a direct descendant of Ahmad Shah Abdali, a Kandahari called Hamid Karzai. Educated at a private school in the Indian hill-station of Simla, followed by a master's in political science at Delhi University, he was about thirty and spoke the old-fashioned English of newspapers in the subcontinent, addressing women as 'ma'am' and using expressions such as 'turning turtle' and 'miscreants'.

Hamid was unlike anyone I had ever met. He wore a leather jacket and jeans, yet walked with the bearing of a king. In a city where men did not consider themselves dressed without rocket-propelled grenades or Kalashnikovs across their shoulders, he was polite and gentle and liked reading English classics such as George Eliot's *The Mill on the Floss*. He had a beaked nose and a bald round head that cocked from side to side like a bird as he fixed deep brown eyes upon his listeners. With me he would talk about English music and literature, the feeling that he had lost his youth, and his hatred for Pakistan and his life there. But the greatest passion in his voice came when he spoke of Kandahar with its orchards and running streams, grapes which he said came in forty varieties, not just green and black as I had known in England, and deep-red pomegranates so sweet and luscious that Persian princesses dined on them and lovers wrote poetry about them. He told me too of great tribes and heroic clashes and had a sense of history and being part of it unlike anyone I had ever come across. His eyes would bulge with anger as he talked of centuries-old feuds between his tribe and another.

His tribe were the Popolzai, a Durrani clan that could trace their origins back to the fifteenth century and had given the king the land to build Kandahar as his capital. Once I asked him to tell me their story. 'It's too long,' he laughed, telling me only the part about an Abdali khan who was so old and weak he could no longer mount his horse and beseeched his four sons to help him. The first three all laughed and refused. But the youngest, whose name was Popol, put him on his back and carried him, so when the old man was dying, it was Popol he named as his heir.

Though Hamid was not the eldest of the seven sons of Abdul Ahad Karzai, leader of the Popolzai, he was the only one not to have gone into exile and thus regarded as the probable successor. His brothers all lived in America where they ran a chain of Afghan restaurants called Helmand in Chicago, San Francisco, Boston and Maryland.

He too had been planning to move abroad but after the Soviets took over and imprisoned his father, he abandoned his studies in India to travel to Pakistan and visited a refugee camp near Quetta where he found himself surrounded by hundreds of Popolzai. 'They thought I could help them just because of who I was,' he said. 'But I was who I was only because of them. They were such brave people, it made me feel humble and guilty about my privileged life and I became determined to be the man they thought I was.'

His house in Peshawar bustled with tribal elders, large men with complicated turbans, sitting cross-legged on floor cushions in various rooms, drinking green tea from a pot constantly replenished by a small boy, and unwrapping small silver-foil Hershey Kisses sent by Hamid's brothers. Some of his visitors looked wild and unwashed and seemed from another century entirely to Hamid, but he listened to them with great respect and gave them food and shelter, while he himself lived very simply, using any money he acquired to help his tribesmen.

'I've always had this drive. It's something in me, this great love for the tribe,' he said. Yet growing up he had hated what he called the 'tribal thing' and had been eager to escape Kandahar and go abroad. Had the Russians not invaded, his dream had been to become a diplomat, perhaps even Foreign Minister one day, but the war had changed everything. His skill was with words rather than guns so he became spokesman for the National Liberation Front of Professor Sibghatullah Mojadiddi, a royalist from a prominent Sufi family and one of the most moderate – and thus worst funded – of the seven leaders.

This was the job he was doing when I first met him in 1988 but by then he was disillusioned with the mujaheddin leadership. It should have been a time of jubilation – the defeated Russians had agreed to leave and their troops would soon be heading back across the Oxus River in a humiliation that would help trigger the collapse of the Soviet Union. But the cost had been enormous – 1.5 million Afghans had lost their lives and more than 4 million become refugees – and the mujaheddin had failed to agree on any credible government to replace the Soviet-backed regime. As far as Hamid was concerned the seven leaders were not interested in the future of their country and had all become corrupt and power-grabbing, people who would have been nothing in the traditional tribal set-up but now lived in palatial houses in Peshawar with fleets of Pajero jeeps and dollar accounts overseas.

Mostly he blamed ISI, in particular General Hamid Gul, the agency's manipulative director who initiated the policy of bringing Arabs to fight in Afghanistan and made no secret of his desire to see his protégé Hekmatyar installed in Kabul running a 'truly Islamic state'. Because US support for the mujaheddin to fight the Russians was a covert CIA operation, ISI had been in charge of distributing all the arms and money as well as providing the Americans with intelligence. The agency was in effect controlling Afghan policy. It was ISI that had created the seven mutually hostile parties back in 1980, following the well-tried British divide-and-rule policy, and it was made clear to refugees that a membership card for Hekmatyar's Hezb-i-Islami was a fast track for obtaining flour and cooking oil while joining the royalists meant a long wait. ISI was mistrustful of anyone from Kandahar, remembering how the Durranis had once controlled a large part of what was now Pakistan, and refused to recognise Pashtun nationalist organisations. Instead, they diverted the lion's share of aid and weapons to fundamentalists such as Hekmatyar who received half of the US$6bn provided by the US and Saudi Arabia, telling the Americans quite erroneously that his men were more effective on the battleground.

'The Russians may have destroyed our territory but the Pakistanis have destroyed our liberal culture,' Hamid complained. 'I can never get married in this country because I don't want to subject my wife to this kind of life.' Saddened that the jihad was ending in disarray and he had sacrificed his youth and studies for 'nothing', he often talked about giving it all up and moving to Europe. Instead, increasingly he began to believe that the future of Afghanistan lay with some of the leading commanders and the tribes, the same view I was hearing from Abdul Haq, the young Kabul commander who lived a couple of streets away from me in Peshawar's University Town and where I would often drop in to persuade him to send me with his fighters to Kabul.

'You're just a girl,' Abdul Haq would always say, laughing at my irritation, and then moving on to politics. 'We commanders did our job fighting and expected the leaders to do theirs. Now it seems we might have to do that too,' he grumbled, painfully shifting the artificial foot which he had to wear since stepping on a mine in 1987. 'We have been loyal and are still loyal but if the leaders cannot come together we cannot just sit by and let the country be destroyed.'

One day Hamid told me of an independent group known as the Mullahs Front fighting around Kandahar. He was going to visit and offered to take me with him. 'You must go to Kandahar. That's the real Afghanistan,' he said in his emphatic way, a tic vibrating in his cheek.

*   *   *

Hamid Karzai in Kandahar, 1988.

Our journey began in Quetta, a small lawless town centred round a bazaar of small shacks from which moneychangers somehow sent money all round the world, merchants displayed sacks of cumin and saffron, and reams of bright silks, and where men wore shirts embroidered with tiny mirrors and jewelled sandals with high heels. It seemed on the very edge of the earth, surrounded by the rifts and caramel-coloured escarpments of the Baluchistan desert, and at the time the only hotel was the New Lourdes. A colonial place in the cantonment with a lush lawn that looked as if it should have peacocks, its rooms did not appear to have seen a duster since Pakistan's creation in 1947 and were heated by complicated Heath Robinson-style boilers of brass pipes and tin funnels that emitted periodic roaring noises sending the whole contraption rattling. Flushing the toilet flooded the room and the only light came from a lamp with no plug, just bare wires twisted straight into sockets.

My fair hair, green eyes and pale skin made it very hard for me to disguise myself as an Afghan guerrilla and on previous trips across the border, I had travelled as a woman refugee, my face and body hidden by a burqa, and sometimes provided with a small child to hold my hand for authenticity. But the Mullahs Front would apparently be a laughing stock in Kandahar if a woman was seen amongst them so this time I went dressed the same as the fighters I was travelling with, in shalwar kamiz, loose pyjama trousers made of many yards of cotton which hang in folds from the hips tied with pyjama cord and a long shirt, and heavily turbaned, with a grey embroidered Kandahari shawl thrown carelessly over the shoulder.

As always with Afghanistan, the journey, which had been delayed for days, finally started in a great hurry in the dawn hours then involved endless waiting, changing vehicles five times. I began to sympathise with Frank Martin, an Englishman who worked from 1895–1903 as Engineer-in-Chief to king Abdur Rahman then his son Habibullah, and whose account of his travels into the country in the party of an Afghan prince I had been reading. 'It is not in the habit of the people to rush things,' he wrote. 'Their custom is instead to put off all they can until tomorrow, or the day after that for preference.' Unlike the exasperated Mr Martin, we did not have to wait for a man with a drum to go out in front of us, nor another carrying a huge gold embroidered umbrella as sunshade to protect princely skin. Even so the sun was setting by the time we ended up in a Pajero jeep heading out of town, the desert-mountains rising smudged and Sphinx-like in perfect Turner colours either side of us. Apart from Hamid, my travel companions were Abdul Razzak, one of Kandahar's leading commanders known as the Airport Killer for his daring raids on the airport, and Ratmullah, a chubby sub-commander with an impressively twisted turban, a loud belly laugh, twinkling black eyes and bushy black beard.

Deep into the night, we climbed the Khojak pass, passing trucks gaudily painted with mountain scenes or Pathan beauties and inlaid with intricate metalwork which hid secret compartments. We were in tribal territory and the only industry in these barren lands was smuggling – and abduction. For most of the way the road intertwined with the British-built railway as it twisted in and out of the mountains. According to local legend, the chief engineer committed suicide because he had made a bet with his colleague leading the drilling team from the other side that they would meet in the middle on a certain date. When they did not he thought he had miscalculated and their two tunnels had failed to join up. The day after his death the tunnels met and the 3.2-mile-long Khojak tunnel, the longest in South Asia, now graces Pakistan's five-rupee note.

It was almost midnight by the time we crossed the border to be greeted by the red flares of the heavy guns from nearby Spin Boldak, which the mujaheddin were trying to capture. The blurred face of Yunus Khalis beamed down from a calendar on the wall of the compound where we stopped for the night. One of the fundamentalist leaders, Khalis was a ferocious henna-bearded seventy-year-old with a sixteen-year-old wife, and virulently anti-royalist. Yet Hamid was welcomed with great enthusiasm, everyone coming to pay respects. As we squatted on the floor for dinner with a group of large men after the usual long guttural exchange of Pashto greetings, Abdul Razzak, who was himself a member of Khalis, explained, 'parties mean nothing here. We just go with whoever gives us arms. None of the Peshawar leaders would dare come here.'

The men laid their Kalashnikovs down by their sides as boys too young to fight brought a pitcher of water and grubby hand-towel for us to wash, going round the room in order of seniority, serving me last. The only sound was the smack of lips and tongues as we scooped greasy goat stew out of an aluminium bowl with stretchy Afghan bread, washing it down with curd in iced water. On the dried-earth walls our silhouettes flickered in the light of the oil lamp.

It didn't seem very long after we had gone to sleep, huddled on flea-ridden cushions under quilted coverlets in shiny pink and red material, when we were woken by wailing. It was prayer time. Outside, where the daystar had not yet faded from the sky, the men were laying down their shawls on the ground and prostrating themselves, shawls flapping in the wind and rockets thundering in the dust not far away as they held their palms in front of their faces and mouthed the words '*Bismillah ar-Rahman ar-Rahim*', in the name of Allah, the Beneficent, the Merciful.

The boys brought breakfast – a pot of green tea thick with sugar, which they poured into small glasses, boiled sweets from Iran, and a tray of hard bread left from dinner, as well as dry lentils, which the commanders cracked noisily between their teeth. I went outside to brush my teeth in water left from the previous night's hand-washing. Abdul Razzak and some of his mujaheddin were crouched in the early sun, brushing their teeth with twigs or clipping facial hair, using their small round silver snuffboxes as mirrors.

We set off through the desert, not the majestic sands of T.E. Lawrence or Wilfred Thesiger, but endless grey plains which absorbed and amplified the beating sun and abandoned villages that had been turned into battlefields scattered with spent ammunition. In one village we got out and wandered around, identifying the bombed-out remains of the clinic, the prison and the school, one wall covered with children's charcoal drawings of Soviet helicopters shooting down stick people. The mujaheddin leapt onto the burnt-out hull of a tank for me to photograph them, striking poses with their Kalashnikovs and rocket-launchers. Two ragged children suddenly emerged from one of the ruins, hand-in-hand, their faces and eyelashes grey with dust, the only survivors, begging for food. I could not imagine what

they were living on and they fell upon my packet of emergency digestive biscuits, stuffing them into their mouths.

We were supposed to follow in each other's footprints because of land-mines but the dust kept blowing them away. There was dust everywhere, coating my clothes, in my hair, my ears, my fingernails and mouth, the wind lifting it up in columns so that sometimes it was difficult to see, and giving everything a gritty feel. It was at least 40°C, and my thirst made my head ache, but instead of water Ratmullah appeared clutching marigolds which he shyly presented me for my hair and laughed when I tucked them behind my ears. Like many mujaheddin, I often saw him walking around casually clutching a flower, sometimes hand-in-hand with a friend. Later, when I got to know him better, I asked him why they loved flowers so much and he replied; 'because they are peace and beauty and everything we have lost'.

*   *   *

The author on a destroyed Soviet tank, near Kandahar, 1988.

Our destination was Abdul Razzak's secret training camp cum *madrassa* or religious school in an area called Khunderab, inside a narrow gorge hidden by overhanging mountains, the entrance blasted out of the rock with dynamite. A guard sat at a table, an old black telephone in front of him. Abdul Razzak explained it was part of a wireless phone system captured from the Russians, and enabled camp-guards to call a military post on top of the mountains where they had men stationed with anti-aircraft guns if an enemy approached.

The camp, which acted as a training and rest camp for fighters for the Mullahs Front, had existed for about a year, moving there after the previous site was bombed by Soviet Mig 17s for seventy-four hours continuously, destroying all their weapons and killing fifty men. 'There were forty planes dropping 3000 bombs,' said one man

with what I presumed was the usual Afghan exaggeration of multiply-ing everything by ten, 'it was the only day we couldn't pray.'

Prayer was an important feature of camp-life. The camp was home to eighty men and forty-two students aged from eight to eighteen and Abdul Razzak took me to see the school where children studied the Koran and Arabic. We watched a recitation lesson, boys rocking back and forth as they intoned the words of the Koran, and Abdul Razzak gave some religious books he had brought from Quetta to the white-bearded teacher. Hamid told me that for boys educated in *madrassas*, the rocking becomes such a habit that later in life they cannot read without it. Had we but known it, we were seeing the incipient Taliban. In my diary I wrote: 'Mohammed Jan is eight. After Koranic lessons he learns how to load a BM12'.

Next we saw the boys' dormitory – camouflaged from above with a roof of tree branches and hay that allowed air to circulate, keeping it cool inside. A small boy sat in the doorway cleaning a pile of Kalashnikovs. There seemed to be weaponry everywhere. 'We have thirty-five RPG7, forty-two RR82mm recoil rifles, seven anti-aircraft guns,' said Razzak. They also had two Stinger missiles left of an initial six which they received in November 1987, kept under twenty-four-hour guard, though they happily took them out to pose for photographs. Nine hundred of these heat-seeking missiles had been provided by the Americans to the resistance in 1986–7 along with British Blowpipes and were thought to have turned the tide of the war by countering the threat of Soviet air superiority though many were instead sold on to Iran, forcing the CIA to launch a buyback programme which did not stop them later turning up everywhere from Angola to Algeria.

The camp was run by Abdul Razzak's friend Khadi Mohammed Gul who said he was twenty-eight but looked at least ten years older. He told me he had wanted to be a mullah, a village priest, but had joined the resistance and in 1983 been captured by the Soviets and sent to Pul-i-Charki, the notorious prison on the outskirts of Kabul. Run by KHAD, the East-German trained Afghan secret police, it held around 10,000 political dissidents. He was there for four years until he was released in a prisoner swap when Razzak captured a top commander from the Afghan regime.

Survivors of Pul-i-Charki were rare and I asked him about life there. 'We knew whenever the Soviets had suffered heavy casualties because they would take a whole lot of prisoners, remove their blood for transfusions then shoot them,' he said. He also told of awful tortures. 'Sometimes it would be electric shocks to the nose, ears, teeth and genitals, so many that now I am impotent. Other times they tied us to trees with our feet on broken glass and left us for several days until the wounds went rotten and there were maggots inside. Another punishment was to give us food with laxative or something bad in to cause diarrhoea then leave us in a room one meter square so we would have to live in our own excreta for days. Sometimes at night they would call someone's name and we would know he was being shot but we would say "bye!" as if he was going for a trip but we knew he'd never come back.'

The words hung heavily in the air and we sat there for a while in silence. Then I asked to see the rest of the camp. There was a clinic with a few lint bandages and a box of aspirins where a doctor was cleaning a horrible suppurating wound on the thigh of a fighter who sat silently despite the agonising treatment, and a bakery where young boys were slapping flat wide oblongs of dough onto the wall of a large clay pot buried in the ground with hot coals in the bottom to make *nan*, the traditional unleavened bread. Some other boys were scrubbing clothes in the small river and it was hard not to notice the red staining the water. A few goats and sheep were grazing and there was a small plantation of okra or ladyfingers as well as several apple trees so the camp was more or less self-sufficient.

The camp had strict rules, one of which was 'men must be taught religious teachings as much as possible'. Everyone was checked at the gate and there were heavy penalties for sneaking out weapons or ammunition.[3] 'You see we are not like those other groups which steal

---

[3] 'Salah furush', or weapons seller, had become a term of abuse in Afghanistan as many commanders enriched themselves by selling off arms or signing false receipts to the ISI for more arms than they actually received, getting a kickback in return.

the money and sell the arms to the Iranians,' said Gul. 'This is what jihad is meant to be.' He pointed out that many villagers used the clinic, which was the only medical facility for perhaps fifty miles, and all wanted their boys to be accepted to study at the school as free board was provided.

It was the first time I had seen a mujaheddin group making an effort to provide facilities to civilians. At the main gate as we were leaving, an exhausted ten-year-old boy named Safa Mohammed had just arrived 'to join the resistance' after a fourteen-hour walk through the mountains. 'My father was killed by the Russians and I ran away from my mother,' he said. 'First I want to study but when I grow up I will carry a gun and kill Soviets.'

It was evening as we drove away, bumping across rutted mountain tracks, headlights off to avoid being spotted by a Russian plane. The area was heavily mined so two brave men walked in front of the wheels of the jeeps, testing the ground as we followed slowly behind. Of all the many ways to die or be injured in Afghanistan, mines were the scariest. The Soviets had scattered them everywhere, including what the mujaheddin called jumping mines, designed to bounce up and explode in the genitals, and even some disguised as pens and dolls to entice children. Most were butterfly mines dropped from the air, which maimed rather than killed and thus took out more resistance firepower as men would be needed to carry the victim. No one knew how many mines there were – the latest figure from the US State Department was more than ten million – nor their where-abouts, for contrary to all rules of warfare the Soviets had not kept maps.

I had seen far too many victims in the hospitals of Peshawar with legs or arms blown off, eyes missing or guts hanging out, as well as all the people in the bazaars and refugee camps with stumps for limbs and had taken to identifying interviewees in my notebooks as 'man with beard and *two* eyes'. My head throbbed from concentrating as I scoured the land in front for mines and scanned the skies, for somewhere among the many stars there might be a Soviet Mig.

It was 2.30 a.m. when we arrived at our destination of Argandab, a valley of orchards about ten miles west of Kandahar which Alexander the Great had used as a camp for his army of 30,000 men and elephants and was now an important base of the resistance. Mujaheddin love gadgets and someone turned on flashing fairy lights to herald our arrival after all our efforts to be invisible. The rumble of guns was not far off but I fell asleep to the soothing sound of running water from a river.

As we breakfasted the next morning on salted pomegranate pips, I saw that the whole area was pitted with holes from bombs, in between which were clusters of mujaheddin graves made from little piles of stones with small tattered green flags stuck on top. The shelling was relentless, sometimes so near that dust sprayed over us, but none of the mujaheddin sitting around seemed to pay any attention to it. Hamid told me that when he was growing up this had been a favourite picnic spot with its orchards of apricots, pomegranates, peaches, figs and mulberry trees but that was hard to imagine. The crop had all been destroyed in the fighting or rotted because there was no labour for picking and the Russians had destroyed the *karez*, or irrigation channels to stop the mujaheddin using them for cover. As we talked a delegation of Popolzai arrived, led by Mullah Mohammed Rabbani, overall commander of the Mullahs Front, all of whom seemed overjoyed to see Hamid, embracing him to the right, to the left and right again in the traditional way, then shaking his hand.

I began to realise the importance of his visit and the risk he was taking. He had told me the previous day that he was high up on the Soviet hit list and I wondered whether the fact that we were bombed everywhere we stopped was really a coincidence. I wished he wouldn't keep radioing everyone to say we had arrived. That morning as we sat under a tent of camouflage material, he told me, 'The first casualties in Kandahar were forty from my family. The four most important were taken to the Governor's house, laid on a big rug and huge rocks thrown on them from above to smash their skulls. Afterwards the carpets had to be taken to Bawalpur to be washed.'

There was a roar of engines and several turbaned men on motor-bikes shot into the orchard. It was incongruous seeing these medieval bearded figures on their Yamaha motors and I started to laugh, but Hamid got up to greet the heaviest one. I recognised Ratmullah, who had left us the previous day and was now back with some of his fellow-fighters.

'The bikes are the best way to get around quickly and not to be seen,' he explained as he dismounted. 'Anything bigger gets picked out and shot.' When there was a lull in the shelling, we set off on the motorbikes, bumping across plains which looked like the set of a war movie crisscrossed with muddy trenches, something I had never seen before in Afghanistan. I held on to the back of Ratmullah's bike, shouting 'you're Allah's Angels!' which he didn't understand but we both laughed, my turban unravelling all round my face as we hurtled along.

Passing a tall concrete silo for storing wheat, we were suddenly riding along a paved highway, the Herat–Kandahar road. The stretch we were on was controlled by mujaheddin and just in front of a blue-domed tomb which had somehow survived intact and that housed a mujaheddin camp, they had built a wall along the road consisting of tanks and armoured personnel vehicles turned on their sides, moving each one into place after it had been destroyed. I counted eighty-two. It felt very exposed particularly as we came to a bend in the road beyond which we could not see. 'Is this safe?' I shouted to Hamid but his words were lost in the wind and I only caught what sounded like helicopter. Later he told me he had said we were fine as long as no helicopters came in which case we were dead.

It was a relief when we turned off the road and rode through some

Motorbikes were less likely to be spotted by Soviet planes.

orchards of rotting pomegranates. In the distance we could see plumes of thick black smoke. Finally we came to Malajat, an area that had seen so much fighting that all its inhabitants had fled, leaving just the resistance. The mujaheddin post where we were to stay was the homeliest I had seen, the usual earthen-walled house but with a garden decorated with pots of pink and red geraniums and a small shed which turned out to be an improvised shower-room where one stood under an upside-down water bucket full of holes.

The commander of the post was Bor Jan, a squat man with a shaved head who looked like a friar in his black robes and served us green tea and boiled sweets using a Russian parachute as a tablecloth. He had been an officer in the Afghan army but at the time of the Communist takeover went into a *madrassa* where he joined forces with fellow religious students Abdul Razzak and Mullah Mohammed Rabbani. 'Of the original ninety persons there are only eight of us left,' he said. 'I cannot describe the suffering.

'We went to join Harakat of Maulvi Mohammed Nabbi Mohammedi because at the beginning that was the most powerful group militarily. To start with we just had a few guns from the gun-shops at Darra [a Pakistani tribal town famous for copying guns] but we captured more and slowly spread. We were the first mujaheddin to do conventional fighting – trench warfare – because the terrain here is not suitable for guerrilla methods. In 1982 we left Harakat and joined Khalis to get better arms.

'The Front was started by Abdul Razzak and he sent sub-commanders to various districts whom he had recruited directly and pays all their expenses. Now we have two thousand people in three areas – Argandab, Malajat and Zabul.'

I asked about the command structure and Bor Jan explained; 'We communicate by letter because we don't have radios and even if we did maybe they wouldn't be safe. Usually we carry out joint operations where each sub-commander brings five or ten men and then the spoils are divided. Disputes are resolved through local systems of elders or religious scholars but if that fails they go to a special Islamic court where a man called Maulvi Pasani decides.'

All of them were very bitter about Pakistan and the Peshawar leaders. 'For every one rupee aid given to the resistance, we get one *paisa*. We only have two clinics for our wounded in Quetta which is two days away while there are hundreds in Peshawar.'

Although Bor Jan claimed to be helped by the civilians inside the town, he said his men often went hungry. 'Once during heavy Soviet bombing we had no food for twenty-five days and we lived on grapes. Now we keep leftover bread in bags and store it for hard times.' He pulled out a sack to show us and I felt a piece of the bread. It was rock hard. 'Last winter we lived on this for one hundred and eighty-two days,' he said.

We stayed at Bor Jan's post for about a week. I was not allowed to venture outside the post as it was made clear that it would look extremely bad for the Mullahs Front if it got out to anyone, particularly other mujaheddin, that they were harbouring a Western woman.

They seemed far more worried about this than about being attacked by the Russians. I grew to hate my turban, which was hot and heavy in the boiling desert sun, my hair damp and sweaty underneath, but I was never allowed to remove it. 'Remember, you are a Kandahari boy,' they said to me, something I discovered had hazards of its own in a region where men are known for their liking of young male flesh.

One afternoon another motorbike roared up and we were joined by Ehsanullah Ehsan Khan, another Popolzai, whom everyone called Khan Aga or Uncle Khan. Frowning at me, he said he was the son of Saleh Mohammed Khan who initiated the 1954 insurgency against the liberation of women and burnt the movie hall and girls' school. 'The Communists took him to the Governor's house and dropped a stone on his head,' he added.

There was not much to do. Once we went on a crazy night-time raid on a government defence post in the centre of the city which involved us leaving the motorbikes in a flour-mill, tiptoeing past a Communist post so close that we could hear the radio inside, then hiding in the woodcutters' bazaar until a signal was given at which everyone fired their weapons then fled back through the empty streets and along the ridges between irrigation canals.

Mostly we did nothing. I became accustomed to sitting in Bor Jan's garden writing my diary with bullets whizzing one side and rockets the other, and chatting to his men. When they were not cleaning their guns, clipping their nose-hairs or tending their beloved flowers, those that were literate would read the Koran. There was none of the hashish smoking I had encountered on previous trips though plenty of chewing – and spitting – of tobacco. I was provided with a Kalashnikov-wielding bodyguard, a solemn-faced nineteen-year-old called Abdul Wasei to stand in front of the door while I washed off my coating of dust in the bucket-shower, which after a week without washing, felt like a five-star bath. They even made me a bed, which was wonderful until I realised that I was sleeping on boxes of ammunition.

Abdul Wasei, a nineteen-year-old former raisin cleaner who was my bodyguard.

Ratmullah had found a little sparrow, which he tied by string to a multi-barrel rocket-launcher and it would jump around squawking. Some of the fighters amused themselves by firing their Kalashnikovs near it and betting how high it would jump.

One day Bor Jan told us we were going to attack the airport. The plan was to depart at dawn but we left in the late morning, about twenty of us, all on motorbikes. I sat behind Ratmullah, trying to

Ratmullah.

balance without touching his body so as not to offend him and
consequently almost falling off. It felt good finally to be outside the
post until in a field of green corn we passed an abandoned tractor,
the driver's body hanging awkwardly over the side. His brains had
been blown out.

We hid the bikes in a branch-covered hole in a mulberry wood
and, passing under a Koran held up by Ratmullah, we ran through
the trees and down into one of the trenches that the mujaheddin had
dug around the city. In the distance were some hills, beyond which

was the airport. Some of the men took up position behind the trench in a tower used to dry grapes and began firing rockets at the airport, hoping to blow up a plane or an oil-tanker, though it seemed to me much too far away.

A shout went up and I just caught the fleeting panic on Ratmullah's usually serene face before he pulled me to the ground under his huge weight. Two Russian tanks had appeared on the crest of the hill and were rolling down towards us. There was a dull thud as one of them fired and the grape tower behind us went up in smoke. As hot dust and rubble rained down on us Abdul Wasei dragged me into a shelter dug into the side of the trench. We could hear the cries and whimpers of the wounded but there was nothing we could do. If we emerged from the trench, we would be shot.

For two days we stayed there trapped while the tanks resolutely refused to go away. The cries behind us stopped and the silence was almost worse. We had nothing to eat or drink and my tongue felt thick in my mouth. There was a pool of muddy water in the trench and the others scooped it up with their hands and drank. Dead mosquitoes were floating on top but in the end I gulped down the dusty-tasting water, wryly remembering the British diplomat in Islamabad who had advised me 'whatever you do, take your own cup to Afghanistan to avoid catching anything'. Ratmullah suddenly jabbered excitedly in Pashto, holding something up in his chubby hands. It was a mud-crab. I watched in horror as he bit into it, making noises of delight. Soon everyone was looking for mud-crabs and chewing them happily.

Finally on the second day the tanks retreated back up the hill, presumably deciding we must all be dead. We ran crouching along the trench then out and back into the mulberry woods where our bikes were still where we had left them. When we got back to the post and were sitting drinking green tea, I put on my radio. After the usual crackle and static, I found BBC World Service and the

Eating mud crabs in the trenches.

unmistakable gravelly voice of Louis Armstrong singing *What a Wonderful World*. It was one of those moments you know you will never forget. Exhilarated at still being alive, I asked Abdul Wasei if he was ever scared. He shook his head. 'That would bring dishonour on my family. A coward running away will not be buried in Muslim rites. Instead he becomes a ghost so will never reach Paradise.'

That night as it was our last dinner before leaving, we had rice with little bits of meat and bone, eaten scooped up in our hands.

The next day, on the way back to Pakistan, I realised that the sparrow had disappeared.

The more times I went into Afghanistan to cover the war the more I realised that there were many realities and the best I could hope for was a few fragments, never the big picture. But always within a few days of returning 'outside' to the comfort of Peshawar and the luxury of plentiful food and clean clothes, there would come an aching hollowness and I would spend all my time trying to get back inside. War was an addiction and I was badly hooked.

'No foreign editor is worth dying for,' said someone older and wiser who saw what was happening to me but I laughed, downed shots of the smuggled vodka we referred to as 'Gorbachev' and went swimming at midnight in the Pearl Continental pool to the outrage of the hotel management. The ragtag mujaheddin of the mountains with their plastic sandals and Lee Enfield rifles were defeating the powerful Red Army with all their tanks and helicopter gunships and these were glory days.

That was before Jalalabad.

Jalalabad was different. By then it was March 1989 and the Russians had finished withdrawing their troops from Afghanistan. After years of guerrilla warfare the pressure was on the mujaheddin to show that they could capture and control a town. 'It's time to fish or cut bait,' said an American diplomat with a southern twang at the weekly 'Sitrep' and we knew it was battle on. Kabul was the ultimate prize, but snug in its nest of tall mountains, the city presented too difficult a target. So the royal winter capital of Jalalabad was chosen as it was only fifty-eight miles from the Pakistan border and thus logistically easy. There were no secrets in Peshawar though plenty of misinformation and rumour. Everyone knew that the Pakistani military advisors were working on a plan. We all wanted to be the first one there.

One evening when I was in Islamabad the phone-call came. 'It's starting.' Quickly I dressed in my mujaheddin gear of shalwar kamiz, rubbed permanganate powder mixed with earth into my skin to darken it, tucked my hair into a flat wool *pakol* cap, and wrapped a woollen shawl around my shoulders. By then, as a fully paid-up member of the War Junkies Club I also had a mud-spattered US army jacket. I grabbed my small rucksack and jumped into my little Suzuki car weaving my way though the camels and arms trucks up the Grand Trunk Road to Peshawar to meet with the group of guerrillas I was planning to travel with. They had bad news. The border had been closed by ISI and no journalists were to be allowed across.

The commander was a friend and willing to take the risk so we left immediately, crammed in the back of a jeep, up the Khyber Pass, a twenty-five-mile journey through narrow gaps in craggy mountains decorated with pennants of the Khyber Rifles and other frontier forces familiar from British history. The mountains were barren and not spectacularly high but it was always a thrilling drive, recalling the various British misadventures starting in 1839 when British troops marched up here on the way to the First Afghan War which ended in disaster in 1842, and back again in 1878 for the Second when they were again forced to withdraw. Each time hundreds of men had been killed just getting through this pass, controlled then as now by the murderous Afridi tribe famous for smuggling and complete untrustworthiness. Many of these men were buried near the Masjid mosque at the top of the pass. Nearby, at the Torkham border post, ISI were out in large numbers. An officer jumped in the back and shone his torch on our faces. I had my head down, my shawl covering me as much as possible.

'You're not a mujahid!' he spat, hauling me out, 'you're a Britisher!' As my mujaheddin friends zigzagged across the border towards battle, I was unceremoniously taken back to Peshawar in the back of a police van. I was furious, crazed and desperate to get to Jalalabad. It was little comfort to find that none of the journalists were getting in. Famous war correspondents were pacing about hotel lobbies, shouting at their fixers and interpreters and waving wads of dollars. ISI had told the mujaheddin that they would be fined $2000 if a journalist was found with them so most were refusing even to try.

That night I visited all my friends and contacts, pleading to be taken across the border. Speed was of the essence and the usual ways of going by foot or donkey along smugglers' paths over the mountains would take too long. Then my friend Azim came up with an idea. He had a fleet of ambulances that were going back and forth to ferry the wounded and I could hide under the floor. He lifted up one of the floor cushions and I curled in the space while he piled blankets and medicines on top of me. It was perfect.

We left before daybreak, last in a convoy of three ambulances. It took us about two hours back up the Khyber Pass to reach Torkham. I held my breath as I heard the doors being opened but we were waved straight across with only a cursory glance into the back of the ambulance. The blankets under which I lay were saturated with disinfectant so by the time we got into Afghanistan and I could emerge into daylight I was high on the fumes.

The men driving the ambulances were delighted by the success of the plan, laughing at how we had fooled the Pakistanis. The air always seemed lighter and cleaner the moment one crossed the border and the scent of the pines and spruces of the Spinghar Mountains began to clear my head.

In the first ambulance was a boy called Naem with the stubbly beginnings of a beard who picked a pink flower, which he shyly offered to me. 'It must be orange blossom season in Jalalabad,' he said as we sat on the ground looking down across the vast plain. 'My mother told me that before the war every year at this time poets from all over the country would gather here to read poems dedicated to the beauty of the orange blossoms.'

He told me that he was working as a medic rather than a fighter because his father and elder brothers had been made *shaheed* in the war and so he was looking after his mother and sisters, but he really wanted to fight. It didn't seem odd to me. It was too far away to smell the oranges but in the distance I could just make out the green trees of Afghanistan's garden city and remembered the famous oil painting of Dr William Brydon arriving slumped over his exhausted horse at the gates of the garrison, the only survivor of 16,000 British fleeing from Kabul back in 1842 including women and children.[4] He had been allowed to live by the Afghan forces in accordance with the orders of their commander Akbar Khan, son of the former ruler Dost Mohammed whom the British had unseated, to 'annihilate the whole army except one man who would reach Jalalabad to tell the tale'. The doctor's report recounted in chilling detail how his fellow officers and their families and orderlies had been mown down by gunmen on mountaintops as they fled the ninety miles through narrow snowy passes. So many were killed that when the British Army of Retribution marched back this way a year later they wrote of their gun carriages crunching over the bones and skeletons. These plains had seen so much death, and sitting on that hilltop, listening to the far-off sounds of war, the hum of planes and pops and crashes of tank-fire and rockets followed by puffs of grey smoke on the horizon, I felt the familiar rush of adrenalin.

We stopped for a while at an earth-walled mujaheddin post in Ghaziabad, about twenty miles outside Jalalabad, for a glass of green tea drunk with boiled sweets in place of sugar. There were hundreds of men with Kalashnikovs milling around, eyes rimmed with black kohl for battle, many chewing *naswar*, opium-laced tobacco, which they then spat out noisily. The news from the front was not good. In the first few hours the previous day, the mujaheddin had captured several government outposts, southeast of the city, including

---

[4] Although Dr Brydon is generally remembered as the only survivor, in fact a few hundred Indian soldiers and camp followers did stagger into Jalalabad or back to Kabul a few days later, while some of the British women and children and married officers were taken hostage on the fifth day by Akbar who took them to Bamiyan where they were rescued by the Army of Retribution nine months later.

Samarkhel which was headquarters of the feared Eleventh Division, and it had been easier than expected. 'They just fled,' said one commander who had taken part. But as the fighting had progressed to the perimeter of Jalalabad airport, the regime had sent in reinforcements from Kabul. The Afghan airforce that the Americans had confidently pronounced useless now the Russian pilots had left was flying skilfully, and it was looking bad.

Ahead we could see columns of smoke rising and hear the dull rumble of bombing. Sher Ali, the medic in my ambulance picked up a clutch of bullets from the floor. 'See,' he grinned. 'That was last time.' He pointed to a string of holes along the rear door. He wasn't smiling for long. As we neared a small stone bridge over the Kabul River which flows through the centre of Jalalabad, the whine of aircraft suddenly grew louder and the sky darkened as a bomber-jet hummed low like an enormous grey moth over our heads. Our ambulance screeched to a halt off the road and we all jumped out and scrambled down the stony slope. For a moment everything seemed to stop. My heart was thudding so hard I could not hear anything outside, just a voice in my mind praying for survival. Then there was a loud explosion and scraps of dust and rubble flew all around us and the plane was gone. There was an eerie moment of complete silence then a stray dog started whining and cluster bombs were dropping sending up mushrooms of smoke and seeming to bounce towards us. Then I saw. Almost in slow motion on the road in front the first ambulance had been hit and exploded into orange flame. No one could have survived. Still tucked behind my ear was the pink flower that Naem had given me only an hour or so earlier.

I was horrified but not as much as I should have been. All I could think of was getting to the front. When the other ambulances decided to turn back, I was incredulous. 'It's too dangerous,' said Sher Ali, 'we have to look after you. Mr Azim would be very angry.'

'But you're ambulances!' I protested, 'you're supposed to go to dangerous places and pick up the wounded.'

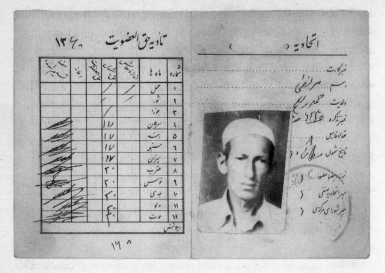

There was no persuading them. We headed back toward Pakistan at high speed. In the end after furious arguments they let me off back at the mujaheddin post where I begged everyone coming through to take me to the front. Eventually a group of fighters arrived from Peshawar under the command of Rahim Wardak, whom I knew, so they agreed I could go with them.

At Samarkhel we stopped and walked around the captured government post, half-eaten meals testimony to the speed with which the forces of the regime had fled. There were dead bodies in a cornfield lying on their backs like broken puppets. A red food-ration book was lying by the side of one and I picked it up.

We were getting nearer to the noise of battle and close to the airport we came upon an exodus of people on donkeys and foot. There were hundreds, thousands of them. Mostly women with children, a few belongings bundled up in scarves. Many were bleeding and wounded or dragging half-dead people on carts behind them. It was clear what was happening. The 200,000 civilians of the former Moghul city that had once been a place of palaces and gardens were being caught between the mujaheddin rockets coming into the city and the Afghan airforce bombing of the roads. It was what commanders like my friend Abdul Haq, who had been against the battle, had predicted would happen. In those few days 10,000 people were killed, the biggest single death toll of the whole war.

I was scribbling non-stop in my little notebook. I had a great story. But the refugees, seeing a western woman, presumed I was a doctor. I was surrounded by people, then dragged to one side of the road. A weeping woman was crouched over her young daughter laid out by a clump of witch's hair. Her eyes were open, a pale limpid green but there was a film over them and a waxiness to her face. I guessed she must have been about seven. The woman lifted up a cloth. The girl's insides were hanging out of a hole in her stomach.

'What happened?' I asked, pen poised, not looking too closely.

'She was hit by a rocket while fetching water. Please, you take her in your jeep to Peshawar. If she dies it is too much for my mind. Her father had been killed and her brothers have not come since the fighting began two days ago. Now it is just us. Please by the grace of Allah help us.'

I made notes then started to walk away. I had to get to where the action was. I wasn't getting the point that it was all around us.

The woman pulled at my sleeve. There was a heady perfume in the air, not from the orange blossom which was still only in bud, but from crimson and yellow narcissi growing nearby and often sold in the bazaar in Peshawar. The flowers were meant to signify hope and the coming of spring.

'Her name is Lela,' she said, 'please you can help us.'

'I'm sorry. I am not a doctor,' I said as I got back in the Pajero with the mujaheddin who had been signalling impatiently. We drove off leaving the woman staring disbelieving after us, her arms in the air in a gesture of supplication. It was a picture that would stay frozen in my mind and later sometimes come to me in the unlikeliest places, ice-skating under the Christmas tree of the Rockefeller Center and seeing a young girl with head back and green eyes shining as her mother twirled her round and round.

It turned out there wasn't really a front, just a mess in which everyone was trying to survive and turning on each other, and for which later everyone would blame everyone else, the commanders saying they had never wanted to fight and were not equipped or trained for such a frontal assault. The previous year General Zia had promised Jalalabad as a Christmas present to Congressman Charlie Wilson, a frequent visitor to Peshawar and fervent supporter of the war against the Communist Russians. But Zia was dead now after an explosion brought down his plane, so you couldn't blame him.

The Soviet ambassador in Kabul, Yuli Vorontsov, told me a few months later that 'the amount of ammunition spent in Jalalabad was four times that spent in the battle of Stalingrad because unlike the German and Soviet armies the Afghans are getting it for free and so are not economical'.

In the midst of it all as we were crouching down trying not to get hit by bullets that may well have been from our side, I felt the man next to me stiffen. I followed his gaze and saw an ISI colonel we all recognised from Peshawar. Rahim Wardak, the commander, was furious and strode towards him, said something and walked back. The ISI man looked stunned so I asked Rahim what he had said. 'I asked him "How do you who have never won a war, dare try and order us who have never lost one?"' he replied. Later, much later, I read that Osama bin Laden was also there in that battle and was so shocked by the needless slaughter of both civilians and mujaheddin that he became convinced that it was part of a US conspiracy implemented through the Pakistanis to discredit and end the jihad.

Whatever your point of view you couldn't be part of Jalalabad and not be affected.

War wasn't beautiful at all. It was the ugliest thing I had ever seen and it made me do the ugliest thing I had ever done. The real story of war wasn't about the firing and the fighting, some *Boy's Own* adventure of goodies and baddies. It wasn't about sitting around in bars making up songs about the mujaheddin we called 'The Gucci Muj' with their designer camouflage and pens made from AK47 bullets. It was about the people, the Naems and Lelas, the sons and daughters, the mothers and fathers. I had let someone die and I knew however far away I went there would be no forgetting.

I had never gone back to Afghanistan after that. The world had used and forgotten Afghanistan and it gave me an excuse to pretend I had forgotten too.

Kabul, October 12, 2001

Dear Christina

This week I listen to the bombs falling on the airport and military command just a few miles away and though we are scared by the bangs which shake our flat, we believe they will not hurt us and we come out and watch the flashes in the sky and we pray this will be an end to our suffering.

Now it is good that after all this time the world has turned its face towards Afghanistan. Right now I want to laugh a lot because in other countries of the civilised and progressive world no one knew about our problems before those attacks on America and now we are all the time on the BBC.

Many people have left but my family is staying, praying for change. The market is still working – we Kabulis are tough – and there is food in the market but we have stocked up in case it runs out. Already there is no oil. At night there is no light. We eat by candles and moonlight.

This week a bad thing happened. For a long time my mother mostly just sits silent in her room because she has a cough that does not go and is nervous after all the fighting thinking her sons will be conscripted – also I did not tell you before that in 1993 when the rocketing was very bad, she was not well and we children went with my uncle to live in Pakistan. That was the worst time because we knew there were rockets and bombings every day between Hekmatyar and Massoud and we didn't know if our parents were alright. We do not have a telephone. The only way to get messages was if someone went to Kabul.

Anyway on Tuesday my brother persuaded her to go with him to his tailor's shop because he had some spare material for winter shalwar kamiz. So she lifted her burqa to look at the material and a Taliban from the Bin Marouf in the bazaar saw her and came and slapped her and called her bad insults. Under their laws if a woman shows her face the punishment is twenty-nine lashes. Now she is always crying again.

You cannot imagine how an educated Afghan girl lives or how even when we go out for something in the market, the Taliban, in particular Pakistani Taliban, tease us a lot. They insult us and say 'you Kabuli girls, still coming out on the streets, shame on you', and worse. Now think, Afghanistan is my motherland and a Pakistani Talib treats me like that.

You might wonder why I am not married at my age. My father lost his job in the Foreign Ministry when the Taliban took over because they knew we were supporters of the king and now he makes some few Afghanis bringing oil from Pakistan to sell, so I must help my parents by teaching to earn some money. It is not much. When things are better they will arrange me a marriage – I think that's odd for you. Anyway it's hard to find love in this situation, we are so tired. What is a wedding when there can be no music and all the women even the bride must wear burqas? I look in the mirror and I see a face that does not remember a time before war, and I would not want to bring a child in this city of fear.

The Taliban say this is a war on Afghanistan. Some of our friends say we must now support the Taliban against the outside but how can we support those who lock us away?

We listen secretly to the BBC and hope that Mr Bush and Mr Blair mean what they say.

I hope they do not come and bomb and forget us again. Maybe when you watch the bombs on television you will think of me and know we are real feeling people here, a girl who likes to wear red lipstick and dreams of dancing, not just the men of beards and guns.

Marri

3

Inside the House of Knowledge

'How can you have a minister for railways?' asked the Pakistani,
'you don't have any trains in Afghanistan?'
'You have a Justice Minister,' replied the Afghan.

Mujaheddin joke

As I stood at Hamid Karzai's doorway in Quetta's Satellite
Town a week after the attack on the World Trade Center, war
in Afghanistan was once again imminent, but it was reawakening
long-buried ghosts from the past that worried me, not the future. By
then I had been a foreign correspondent for fourteen years and knew
that conflicts often seem more dangerous from a distance than when
one is there. I rang the bell. The Karzai house was salmon-pink and
high-walled and the front step piled high with dusty sandals. Tribesmen with Kalashnikovs stood guard, for Hamid had become chief of
the Popolzai and was a prime Taliban and al Qaeda target, particularly
since September 11th. Two years earlier, on 14 July 1999, his father had
been assassinated on the road behind the house, shot dead by a man
on a motorcycle while he was chatting to a neighbour on the way
back from evening prayers.

Though I had never gone back to Afghanistan after Jalalabad, I
had seen Hamid in Pakistan several times, whenever I returned to
cover one of the periodic removals of an elected Prime Minister by

the all-powerful military, always laughing as we recalled our days of mud-crabs and ditchwater. It was a story he loved to recount to other people, telling them, 'she was part of the jihad'.

The resistance had finally ousted the Communist regime in 1992, three years after the Russians had left and the ill-fated attempt to capture Jalalabad. Hamid had been made Deputy Foreign Minister in the mujaheddin government. But he had quickly become disillusioned and resigned in May 1993 as the leaders turned on each other, and fighting between the forces of Hekmatyar and Ahmad Shah Massoud destroyed much of the capital and killed thousands of civilians.

One evening in 1995, over dinner in Islamabad, Hamid said he had something to tell me.

'Remember the Mullahs Front?' he asked. 'Well those same guys on motorbikes are now running Kandahar!'

I looked at him in astonishment. 'The motorbiking mullahs are the Taliban?'

'They are good honest people, you remember,' he replied. 'Besides things have been so bad, you can't imagine. People go to bed not knowing if they'll wake up. They are the only hope.'

He explained that the key members of the Mullahs Front were all on the Supreme *Shura* of the Taliban and he had moved to Quetta and was travelling around trying to raise funds for them. Bor Jan, the house-proud commander with his bucket-shower and pots of geraniums, was now Mullah Bor Jan, the commander-in-chief of the Taliban forces. As they swept across the country capturing Helmand, Herat, Jalalabad and eventually Kabul, I would later hear him described as the Rommel of the Taliban. Abdul Razzak, the Airport Killer, was his deputy and a member of Mullah Omar's ruling council in Kandahar. Mullah Mohammed Rabbani, the important man who had come to greet Hamid in the orchards of Argandab, was regarded as Mullah Omar's number two and was also part of his inner cabinet as well as commanding forces in Loghar province. Mullah Ehsanullah Ehsan, the man who had so clearly disapproved of me and had boasted of his father burning down cinemas and girls' schools, was also on the ruling *shura*. Ratmullah and even young Abdul Wasei, the former raisin-cleaner who had guarded my showers, were commanding units.

Little was known about the Taliban at that point but what I had heard made me uncomfortable. In Kandahar, which they had captured in October 1994, they had closed girls' schools and told all women to give up work and stay home, and were doing the same in Herat. Yet Hamid seemed convinced that they simply wanted to establish security in the country then would invite back the king. He reminded me that our friends in the Mullahs Front had been royalists. He himself had given them $50,000 and arranged for the king's son-in-law and military commander General Abdul Wali to fly over to Pakistan to meet with them on the border at Torkham.

But within a year of my dinner with Hamid, both Bor Jan and Mullah Mohammed Rabbani had died mysteriously. The speculation was that they had been got out of the way because of their pro-monarchical sympathies. Bor Jan had been killed when his pick-up hit a land-mine in the Silk Gorge during the final advance on Kabul. After the capture of the capital in September 1996, Mullah Mohammed Rabbani had been appointed head of the six-man *shura* in charge of Kabul then suddenly disappeared, supposedly shot while walking in the street.

Abdul Razzak, who had also acquired a Mullah title, was the only one of the three motorbiking commanders to remain on the ruling council and had become Governor of Herat. From there he opened the western front against General Dostum and went on to lead the Taliban forces into Mazar-i-Sharif in May 1997 where he met his death, amid fierce fighting, as his men were driven from the city. Abdul Wasei was said to be heading one of the units of the feared moral police. Mullah Ehsanullah Ehsan[1] had become Governor of

---

[1] He was also killed in 1997 in the fighting for Mazar-i-Sharif.

the State Bank and was also commanding an elite force of 1000 crack troops.

As for Hamid, he had fallen out with the Taliban and become one of their strongest critics. He explained that first they had been taken over by ISI, then, 'others had started appearing at their meetings, silent ones I did not recognise. I realised they had been infiltrated by terrorists, people like Osama bin Laden who were thoroughly corrupt and I did my best to tell the world.'

If anyone could offer insight into what had been happening in Afghanistan that had led to the World Trade Center attack it was him, and the pile of shoes outside his door suggested I was not the only one to think it. I was ushered into a downstairs room where he was sitting cross-legged on the floor holding court with a group of commanders, tribal elders and a former headmaster, and immediately provided with a glass of tea and a dish of sugared almonds. For as long as I had known Hamid he had been clean-shaven and I was surprised to see he was growing a beard. It was streaked with silver and made him look older than his forty-four years.

'I'm very upset,' he said, after greeting me warmly then telling me off as usual for having tried to talk to him on the phone, which he insisted was bugged by ISI. 'I knew something like this would happen. If people had listened to us in London and Washington two years ago all those lives would have been saved.'

A few days later he invited me to dinner. Once again the house was full of men. Under pressure as head of the tribe to take at least one wife, Hamid had got married the previous year to a woman doctor, the daughter of a friend of his father. His mother also lived with them, but as always in Pashtun houses, even an enlightened one, the women were nowhere to be seen. During dinner he was less garrulous than usual and the realisation dawned on me. Gesturing to his beard, I said, 'You're planning to go inside, aren't you?'

He said nothing. Later, as we said goodbye, I asked, 'If you go can you take me with you?'

'Let's see, ma'am,' he replied, which I knew meant no.

'It will be just like before,' I pleaded. But I knew it wouldn't. Nothing was like before. The Taliban were a different enemy and we were living different lives.

The next day I got a message from the hotel reception to say a Mr Karzai had rung. When I called back, his assistant Malik said he had gone to Karachi and was uncontactable. A few days later I called again and Malik said he was in Islamabad, still not reachable. Malik was not a good liar. Then I heard that Abdul Haq had led a force inside to fight the Taliban and I knew where Hamid had gone. I supposed if I felt guilty for having travelled with the mullahs on motorbikes and thought they were the good guys, he must have felt more so. The next time we spoke was by satellite phone and he was in the mountains of Uruzgan, north of Kandahar, home territory of Mullah Omar.

There seemed little point in staying in Quetta. I had received another letter from Marri in Kabul, even more moving than the first, but I doubted that she could smuggle any more out as the Americans had begun bombing Afghanistan. The start of the bombing had sparked off riots in Quetta, Taliban sympathisers burning down banks and cinemas showing the latest Antonio Banderas movie, and stoning the Serena hotel where all journalists and UN workers were staying. In the mosques, mullahs were issuing fatwas to kill all Americans and British. One morning we woke to find that an anti-aircraft gun had been mounted on the roof and local police had locked us in, meaning all we could do was sit in our rooms watching the green flashes on CNN that were Pentagon film of bombing raids. The lobby of the hotel was full of ISI agents and on the rare occasions we were allowed out, after signing a paper saying we accepted 'all life risk', they followed us everywhere. Conversations had become meaningless.

One day in a refugee camp I met a widow whose eleven-year-old son Abdul was a student at a *madrassa* called Haqqania and she told me that she had not been allowed to hug him since he was eight. A cart of green apples pulled by a small one-eyed donkey passed as I asked her why she sent him there, and she pointed at it and said simply, 'I have four children and they have never tasted apples.' The *madrassas* provide free board and lodging. Thousands of these religious schools had sprung up in Pakistan's border areas since the start of the jihad, larger versions of Abdul Razzak's camp in Khunderab, where education consisted of sitting at low tables rocking back and forth intoning page after page of the Koran in Arabic, a language incomprehensible to Abdul and his schoolfellows, most of who were Pashto-speakers. But there was little other schooling available for refugees, the billions of dollars of foreign money that had poured in during the war against the Russians going on weapons rather than books.

Haqqania was not just any *madrassa*. Often referred to as the 'Jihad University', its full name was Darul Uloom Haqqania – the House of Knowledge of Haqqania – and the school had a particular claim to fame. Not only had it conferred the title of Mullah on the man who had once been plain Mohammed Omar, but its prospectus – a thin white book entitled 'Mission and Services Rendered' – proudly boasted 'ninety percent of personnel of Afghanistan's Taliban Movement are students of Haqqania'.

This school in Pakistan's North West Frontier Province was the academic fount of the Taliban policies that Marri was writing about in her letters and which Khalil Hassani had described in such chilling detail in the garden of the Serena Hotel. I knew that were I ever to understand how the jocular mullahs on motorbikes had turned into menacing figures who chopped off women's fingers for wearing nail varnish and considered kite-flying a heinous crime, I needed to enter the House of Knowledge for myself.

*   *   *

As a Western woman it was never going to be easy to get into a male *madrassa* where students were taught from an early age to regard communication with such a species as the fast route to eternal damnation. The Haqqania view on females was summed up by its spokesman Maulana Adil Siddiqui who had publicly stated: 'It is biologically, religiously and prophetically proven that men are superior to women.'

But my plans to visit Haqqania could hardly have started less auspiciously. The rector, Maulana Sami-ul Haq, was a fundamentalist cleric, who, as a close friend of both Mullah Omar and Osama bin Laden, was leading criticism of the Pakistan government's decision to support America's war on terrorism – though as he himself privately conceded they had not had a lot of choice. When President Bush said to General Musharraf, 'you're either with us or against us', to choose the latter would have implied Pakistan becoming a target itself. Anyway Pakistan was now 'on side' so Maulana Sami-ul Haq had been placed under house arrest and was not meeting with western journalists. However, in the way things work in Pakistan, his late father had been the close friend of the late father of one of my friends, so on the day he was released from house arrest, I was telephoned with the address of a basement flat in Islamabad and told to be there at 3.30 p.m. 'British time' – in other words, punctually.

Islamabad is an artificial capital that was ordered by a general and designed by a Greek. The buildings are white and in keeping with its sterile environment, the city has no street names but an Orwellian address system of letters and numbers starting from Zero Point and including a wide thoroughfare leading to the oft-closed parliament called Constitution Avenue, which locals call Suspended Constitution Avenue. In the more upmarket F and E sectors, the houses tend to be modelled on the White House with tall columns and wedding-cake tiers but our meeting was in a basement flat in the city's slightly down-at-heel G8 sector. I arrived with my friend and colleague from the *Sunday Telegraph*, photographer Justin Sutcliffe, at the appointed hour to find a dark red corrugated-iron gate between us and the apartment. There was no doorbell and banging on the gate elicited no response. The gate did not seem to be locked so after standing there for a while, Justin tried pushing it. The stone pillars either side started to shift ominously and the top of one fell off. Horrified, we quickly balanced the bricks back together but a large crack had appeared in the wall. A few minutes later a jeep drew up with the Maulana inside. His driver jumped out to open the gate and Justin and I looked at each other in panic. There was a loud crash and the entire wall collapsed to the ground. We had gone to meet one of the world's most anti-western clerics and had destroyed his front wall.

Sami-ul Haq standing by his garden wall.

Fortunately Sami-ul Haq was a mullah with a sense of mirth. 'So the foreign terrorists have arrived,' he giggled, his long orange henna-ed beard waggling merrily and eyes watering under his heavy black-rimmed bi-focals as he waved us in past the rubble. 'This must be what they mean by collateral damage.'

A politician who had served as a senator during the military regime of General Zia ul-Haq in the 1980s, Sami-ul Haq was sixty-three but his apartment was as unkempt as that of a student. It was just one room with a bed and a camping stove on the floor surrounded by unwashed dinner plates and pans, opening onto a grimy bathroom, and I remembered that there had always been a whiff of personal scandal around his name. He did not seem embarrassed, tying an orange turban round his head with an impressive twist then fixing his brown eyes on me intently.

'We have met before,' he stated as he rummaged under the bed and unearthed a two-thirds-full bottle of flat Pepsi, which he began pouring into teacups. I did not recall and thought it odd that a man who ran a school which had endorsed a call from Osama bin Laden to kill all Americans should be serving American fizzy drink, but it seemed wiser to start what might be a fraught conversation more diplomatically. As he handed out the cups, I asked the maulana what it was like to be known as 'The Man who Taught the Taliban'. 'Every teacher is proud of his students, particularly when they humiliated one of the world's superpowers and are not bowing before the other superpower,' he replied. 'The Taliban are not dangerous people, they are just misunderstood.'

If anyone knew the Taliban he did. The large number of Taliban with the surname Haqqani such as Jalaluddin Haqqani, the army chief, were all graduates of Haqqania as were the Prime Minister, many ministers and judges, and the Governors of Kabul, Kandahar, and Jalalabad. But he insisted, 'I am their teacher not their commander. And actually like all pupils, they don't always listen to me. I've been advising them not to be harsh, to be lenient. For example I tried to stop them destroying the giant Buddhas of Bamiyan earlier this year but they went ahead.'

The maulana was being modest. It was well known that he was in regular contact with Mullah Omar whom he had first met in 1996 and had awarded him Haqqania's first-ever honorary degree as he had not done the necessary three years study to become a mullah. 'He phones me for advice about decisions on *Shariat* – Islamic law,' he admitted. 'He's a very pious and humble man with no formalities who sits on the floor.'

It was these Islamic rulings I had wanted to talk to him about. I had scoured the Koran and could not find anything that suggested kite-flying or chess should be banned, while on women's rights the holy text seemed positively progressive[2], stating, 'to every man what he earns and to every woman what she earns'. During the early years of Islam, women played an important and full role in society, leading armies and ruling countries, and the Prophet's wife Khadijah had been his greatest influence. Older and richer than him, it was she who initiated the marriage proposal and who always encouraged him in his great mission.

Sami-ul Haq smiled patiently as if pained that I could not understand the Prophet's real meaning. 'Islam doesn't ban anything which is beneficial to mankind. If kite-flying was simply a pleasure it would be alright but unfortunately there can be gambling on kites and it can be harmful because people fly them from the rooftops and may fall off and get hurt.'

'Chess is also notorious for gambling,' he added, shaking his head. 'And these things have no purpose, time is better spent reading the Koran.' Seeing I was about to interject, he added, 'Purposeful games which do not involve any gambling are allowed, for example the Taliban have not banned golf. The Taliban also have a cricket team but no one except Pakistan will play them. You English play Zimbabwe but you will not play the Taliban.'

I would clearly never understand why golf and cricket were purposeful but not chess so I asked on what basis girls had been banned from going to school. 'It's just a question of having things ready. Until their separate education system is evolved the girls must sit in

---

[2] See for example in *The Koran*, Chapter (Surah) 16, verse 97 or Chapter 33, verse 35.

their houses. So far the Taliban have not even managed to set up an education system for men so how could they for females?'

'Why should women be beaten if they do not wear burqas?' As I spoke, I suddenly remembered where we had met. It was at an interminable party of politicians in Islamabad where the Johnny Walker and Russian vodka had flowed from gallon bottles with only 7-Up to mix, the men had danced with PIA airhostesses, and no food had been served until midnight by which time everyone was barely capable of standing. But Sami-ul Haq did not miss a beat. 'In Islam women must wear a certain type of dress where there is no vulgarity and no body parts are projected or remain naked,' he replied.

Sami-ul Haq's influence in Afghanistan did not start with the Taliban. It was from Haqqania in 1979 that the call for jihad against the Russians first went out, and his graduates included two of the seven mujaheddin leaders, Mohammed Nabbi Mohammedi and the late Yunus Khalis, the two whose fighters went on to become Taliban. Haqqania was said to be the most popular *madrassa* in Pakistan and for budding Islamic warriors a place there was as valued as getting into Oxford or Cambridge for a British schoolchild.

'More and more boys are applying because they are so fed up with the injustices of the West,' he said, 'last year we had more than 5000 applications for 400 places.' He currently had 3000 students aged from five to thirty-five, though he said there was no upper age limit. They were mostly from Pakistan and Afghanistan as well as some from Uzbekistan, Kazakhstan and Chechnya, and Haqqania had affiliated *madrassas* in the British towns of Sheffield, Birmingham and Bury.

Was it true that the founder members of the Taliban were all his graduates, I asked? 'Yes,' he nodded, a proud smile cushioning out his spongy features. 'After the withdrawal of the Soviet Union there was no central administration in Afghanistan and lots of infighting between warring factions. In Kandahar there was so much lawlessness

JAMIA
DARUL ULOOM HAQQANIA,
AKORA KHATTAK
N.W.F.P PAKISTAN

Introduction
Mission & Services Rendered

http://www.jamiahaqania.org.pk
email:haqqania@nsr.pol.com.pk

AIMS AND OBJECTIVES

The main aims of establishing Darul Uloom Haqqania were
as under :-

1.   To spread the light of knowledge in the world.

2.   To spread the teaching of Quran and Sunna and
        provide correct guidance to understand Islam.

3.   To provide the society with scholars, learned people,
        writers, reformers and men of wisdom.

4.   To work for the enforcement of Islamic Laws in the
        country.

5.   To provide religious and intellectual guidance to the
        Muslims.

6.   To preach and spread the message of Islam.

7.   To help in establishing a net work of religious
        schools in the country.

8.   To edify Islamic values and safeguard Muslim
        culture and civilization from corrupting influences.

The Haqqania prospectus.

and moral degeneration that a commander married a boy and took
him out on his tank and showed him to the people saying this is my
bride. They had debased the jihad. In those circumstances my students
had no choice but to react.'

'There were only about thirty of them in the beginning and they
had no idea of forming a government. They didn't even have a name.
They were just *taliban* – religious students who came out on the
streets to overpower gangsters. They didn't even have vehicles, just
motorbikes. Ninety percent of the areas they captured were not by
force but because Afghans were so fed up with the moral degeneration
that wherever they went people welcomed them and handed over
their guns.'

He personally, along with other *ulema*, or religious scholars, had toured *madrassas* all over Pakistan in 1994 encouraging students to join the movement. In the early days when the Taliban were fighting to capture the border town of Spin Boldak, many of their recruits came from the *madrassa* of Abdul Ghani in Chaman, just the other side of the border. Abdul Ghani was deputy leader of the Jamiat-e-Ulema Islami (JUI), one of Pakistan's leading religious parties, which had been a coalition partner in the government of Benazir Bhutto at the time of the creation of the Taliban and wanted to introduce *Shariat* or Islamic law in Pakistan. The JUI leader Maulana Fazlur Rehman, who at the time was chairman of the Parliamentary Foreign Affairs Committee, was a graduate of Haqqania, though there was little love lost between him and Sami-ul Haq who ran his own break-away faction of the JUI known as JUI(S).

Subsequently any time the Taliban had been in trouble, such as after their defeat in Mazar-i-Sharif in 1997, one phone-call from Mullah Omar to Sami-ul Haq and he would close his *madrassa* and send his students to help.

Yet he insisted, '*Madrassas* don't teach fighting. Islam is a religion of peace. You will not find anyone carrying a gun at Haqqania. My students have been forced to fight by circumstances, because of being occupied by foreign powers. It's like when the Americans went to Vietnam and the Vietnamese struggled against them. They had no religious *madrassas* so why did they fight? If you go through history it's the same, the French Revolution, the Chinese Revolution. People revolted against the tyranny of rulers. What would be the British reaction if some part of Britain were occupied by a foreign power? You would fight. We call it a jihad, you call it a fight for freedom.'

We argued for a while about the war, and he questioned whether his friend Osama bin Laden really had the technology and resources to have carried out the World Trade Center attack. 'Where is the evidence?' he asked, and I knew with a sinking feeling he was going to proffer the same theory that had been repeated to me several times a day ever since I had arrived back in Pakistan. 'The real criminals

Maulana Sami-ul Haq in Islamabad, 2001.

are still sitting in the State Department and the Pentagon. This has been done by the Jews to blacken the name of Muslims and so the Americans can get a foothold in this region.' Almost everyone I met, from rickshaw drivers to university professors, had categorically insisted to me that 4000 Jews had failed to turn up for work at the World Trade Center the day of the attack and claimed the whole thing had been masterminded by Ariel Sharon and the Israelis because they were worried that the Bush administration was not offering them enough support.

Sami-ul Haq's view was slightly different however. 'The Americans want to set up a puppet government in Afghanistan to counter China,' he said. 'I met General Musharraf a couple of weeks ago and I could see he was under great pressure both from Bush but also his own greed in wanting to continue in power. He told me, "We cannot afford to have America as our enemy." I replied, "We cannot afford to have them as our friend." Our history is a history of betrayals by the Americans. As for the British, we Pashtuns have not let you set foot on Afghan soil for almost 300 years and now you want to avenge these defeats.'

I laughed, not wanting to be drawn into an argument, as I needed to broach the subject of visiting his school. 'Women are not allowed on the campus and I'm afraid my students don't like Westerners,' he said apologetically as if he personally couldn't understand this, 'and there's a lot of rage at the moment. You'll be stoned or maybe killed.'

I replied that I would wear a burqa to make sure 'no body parts protruded' and was willing to take the risk. Laughing, he agreed that we could come to his house on campus in two days' time, and, if the mood was 'calm' and we promised not to destroy any of the architecture, his son Rashid would show us around the *madrassa*.

On the appointed day, Justin and I set off with a driver at dawn on the Grand Trunk Road, which goes from Islamabad to Peshawar and is part of the Delhi to Kabul route along which so many invading armies had marched over the centuries. The morning light was pearly pink, dust trapped in fingers of sunlight spreading across the fields where a small boy in a red cap was leading some buffalo towards a rice paddy as if painted in by an artist to complete the scene. Either side of the road, not far out from the capital, were hundreds of small brick kilns where children as young as seven worked fourteen-hour days making bricks for a few rupees, or in many cases for nothing because they had been sold by their families to the kiln owners, and would never go to school.

I felt a familiar wave of excitement as the road curved around a rocky outcrop and in front of us I saw the old arch leading to Attock Bridge over the green waters of the Indus River. On the other side was an archway between two stone towers on which was written Welcome to NWFP – Gateway to the Frontier. At this point Afghans would always say 'from here starts Afghanistan' for they do not recognise the border marked by the Durand Line drawn by the British in 1893 which for the first time split the Pashtuns, one of the world's largest tribal societies.

The line was named after Sir Mortimer Durand, Foreign Secretary of British India who supervised the arbitrary division. It was agreed to by the then ruler of Afghanistan, Abdur Rahman, after a combination of arm-twisting and a substantial increase in his annual purse from Britain, but according to the Afghans it was never meant to be an international boundary, simply an agreement of delineating zones. Running about 1000km from one mountaintop to another, cutting through dozens of Pashtun tribes from the Afridi to the Waziri (though they have always remained free to cross back and forth), it was described by Sir Olaf Caroe, the last British Governor of Frontier Province, as 'a line beyond which neither side would exercise interference'.

For the British, finding themselves unable to subjugate the Pathans, as they called the Pashtuns, the idea was to create a buffer zone between the Raj and Afghanistan as part of their 'Forward Policy' to block the Russians in their attempts to gain access to the warm-water ports of India. Shortly after drawing the Durand Line, the British established the so-called Tribal Areas in which the Pashtuns were left to govern themselves under the eye of a Political Agent, a policy Pakistan continued after Independence. While on the map this Pashtun belt south of the Durand Line is officially part of Pakistan territory, in practice the Tribal Areas are a no-go land of mud-baked forts and feuds in narrow valleys and mountains where the word for stranger is the same as enemy, only these days the Pashtuns are armed with Kalashnikovs and rocket launchers rather than Lee Enfields.

Many times I had heard Pashtuns say, 'I have been a Pashtun for five thousand years, a Muslim for one thousand four hundred and Pakistani for only fifty.' In fact almost all of them seemed to consider themselves Afghans and openly advocated the concept of Pashtunistan – a greater Afghanistan reaching to Attock as it once had. The hundred-year agreement on the Durand Line expired in 1993 which was one of the reasons that Pakistan was so desperate to have a government of its choosing in Kabul that would recognize this border.

Back in 1989, I had once driven over Attock Bridge with Homayoun

Assefy, cousin and brother-in-law of the former king Zahir Shah, who was working as a lawyer in Paris with an office just off the Champs Elysées. A sophisticated man whose manicured nails stick in my memory, he and fellow émigré Dr Shams, the kindly former managing director of the Afghan National Bank, were on their way to visit Jalalabad so that they could see their homeland before returning to Europe, and I was accompanying them. We did not make it all the way to Jalalabad because of fighting, and the Jalalabad oranges Dr Shams bought over the border to take home to his family turned out to be sour. But as we crossed the Indus early that morning when we were still full of hope about the trip, Homayoun had said, 'This is really Afghanistan. One day we'll take it back.' I turned to smile, then saw that he was deadly serious.

I recalled this conversation with sudden clarity as we stopped by the riverside under some willows and tamarisks, noisy with the chatter of green parakeets, and stared out over the emerald waters of the Indus. Conquerors from Alexander the Great to the Moghul Emperor Akbar had crossed this river using a bridge of made of small boats placed end to end, and a village of boatmen still lived on the riverside. Not far upstream was the confluence with the Kabul River, its muddy waters having travelled 250 miles from its source in the Hindu Kush just west of the Afghan capital, and for a while the two rivers run side by side without mixing. Just visible in the other direction were the impressive crenellated walls of Attock Fort, which was built between 1581 and 1586 by Akbar when he made Attock his base for military campaigns against Kabul. These days it was used by the Pakistan army, mostly it seemed to imprison politicians arrested in military takeovers and had recently been the location for part of the ongoing corruption trial of Asif Zardari, the husband of former Prime Minister Benazir Bhutto as well as the treason trial of Nawaz Sharif, the Prime Minister ousted in General Musharraf's coup.

*   *   *

Not far after Attock, as the tented expanses of the first refugee camps started to appear, we came to the dusty town of Akora Khattak. The sprawling campus of Haqqania was easy to spot just right of the road, with the white tower of its minaret, elegant as a swan's neck. It was a blustery day and behind an iron gate, I could see a few figures wrapped in shawls over their thin cotton shalwar kamiz scurrying across the courtyard and disappearing into an archway, the wind catching a blue plastic bag and a discarded paper which it whisked up and down behind them in an angrily spiralling dust-wizard.

Scrabbling in the bottom of my bag for my burqa and not finding it in time, only my hair was covered as we swung into the driveway of the rector's house. Fortunately there were no signs of angry mobs. The maulana was sitting in the driveway in a folding chair, wearing a long dark brown wool coat over his shoulders and listening to a radio, surrounded by a circle of men in turbans, and he was looking crotchety. He waved a bored hand to greet us then called, 'Osama, go and fetch tea and Pepsi for the foreign terrorists.' Seeing our expressions, he laughed, explaining, 'Osama is my fifteen-year-old son. I love asking him to get soft drinks for foreigners to shock them, particularly Americans as they have become O-sa-ma-phobic.' He pronounced the word with great satisfaction, emphasising every syllable. Then he turned back to his radio. The maulana was clearly not in the mood for chitchat, so after sipping our drinks and nibbling a sawdust biscuit, we asked Rashid if we could see the *madrassa*.

He led us first behind the house to a white marble grave in a small iron-railed enclosure overlooking fields strewn with weeds. 'This is the burial-place of my grandfather Shaikh ul Hadith Maulana Abdul Haq, the founder of Haqqania,' said Rashid, who was twenty-seven and one of Sami-ul Haq's eight children by two wives. 'He was a great activist against you Britishers.' I remembered what Sami-ul Haq had said the previous day about jihad being a freedom struggle. Maulana Abdul Haq so hated the British that he refused to let his son learn English and on founding the school had stated, 'We do not have the money, resources or ammunition to face the British. However we can raise an entire generation of youth that can become our strength and force the British out of our land.'

Near the grave was a small white mosque. This was the original school back in 1947 at the time of the creation of Pakistan, with just twelve students. Maulana Abdul Haq named it after Darul Uloom where he had studied in the northern Indian town of Deoband in Uttar Pradesh. The first *madrassa* of what came to be known as the deobandi movement, Darul Uloom Deoband was established in 1867 by Islamic scholars who had participated in the Indian Mutiny – the anti-colonial uprising that had been brutally crushed by the British a decade earlier.

Although Hindus and Sikhs had also participated in the uprising, the British blamed the Muslims and began dismantling institutions associated with the former Moghul Empire, particularly anything educational, and requisitioning mosques including Delhi's famous Jama Masjid for use as military barracks. Under siege and seeing education as the key to unifying Muslims and reviving threatened Islamic values, India's Islamic scholars divided into two camps. One group founded the Aligarh Muslim university, a progressive institution which was based on the Oxbridge colleges and where students debated in Urdu but also in English, wore fez but also ties, and played cricket. The other group created the deobandi school to train a new generation in a pure, some would say narrow, form of Islam, purged of all western and Hindu influences such as praying at the graves of saints, and viewing the Koran as a blueprint for everything.

In the last thirty years deobandism and the *madrassas* have become the fastest growing education system in South Asia, particularly in Pakistan. This may have been motivated less by parents wanting children to imbibe such strict Islamic values but more because of the complete collapse of the state system. Pakistan has one of the world's highest illiteracy rates with only one in four being able to read, a result of spending only two percent of the gross national product on education – one of the lowest levels in the world – compared to thirty percent on defence. Militant Islamic groups displayed much more foresight than the West in coming forward to fill that gap and as a result the number of *madrassas* in Pakistan rose from 900 in 1971 to 8000 by 2001 with perhaps as many again unregistered.

As Rashid led us somewhat nervously onto the main campus, we saw another reason for their popularity. 'These are the hotels,' he said, an odd word to choose for the four-storey dormitories with washing hanging on the terraces. For a poor family struggling to feed their children, particularly in a refugee camp, the free board and lodging offered by *madrassas* constituted a huge incentive to hand over their boys as wards. The dormitories were unheated and looked basic and dirty with just thin mattresses on the ground, but were positively palatial compared to life in a refugee tent. Moreover the school offered the chance one day to become a mullah or even a mufti – someone with the authority to issue fatwas or Islamic rulings. In a country where children are sold into slave labour, sewing footballs or making bricks, it was easy to see the attraction. All of this was paid for by donations from rich Muslims, often Arabs, though Sami-ul Haq insisted he had never received any money from bin Laden. Only the day before our visit General Musharraf had given an interview praising the *madrassas* as 'the biggest welfare organization anywhere in the world' which provided free education, food and accommodation for around one million children.

But for impressionable young boys, cut off from their families or perhaps even orphaned in the war, it was a strange hermetic life, getting up at 4 a.m. for the first of five daily prayers. Apart from a poster printed with a saying of the Prophet, and the inevitable one of a white-clad Osama bin Laden clutching a huge Kalashnikov, the dormitories were bare, none of the usual posters of pop-stars or stereo systems blasting loud music one would expect from 3000 mainly teenage students.

There did not seem many students about and Rashid explained that normally the classrooms would be full of boys in white prayer caps reciting the Koran, but the previous day had been graduation, 700 students each stepping up to a podium decorated with posters of bin Laden and receiving a certificate and a white turban from Sami-ul Haq. The highest commendations went to those who had memorized the entire 114 chapters of the Koran in Arabic. Now the pupils were either on holiday or had gone to fight in Afghanistan, it wasn't quite clear. 'You will think what you want to,' said Rashid.

As we turned a corner, two boys jumped out cocking their fingers at us as if they were guns and shouting 'Osama!' They stopped, embarrassed, and put their hands behind their backs when they saw Rashid and were about to flee, but I asked him if I could talk to them. They were wearing thin shalwar kamiz and plastic sandals like the ones issued to refugees and looked about eleven.

'Why do you like Osama?' I asked.

'He stands up for Islam against the West,' said the taller one.

'And he kills Americans,' added his friend.

'What do you want to be when you grow up?'

'Holy warriors,' they both replied. They did not use the word *mujaheddin* and I wondered if it was no longer a heroic word after the many years of infighting.

'Can you use a gun?' I asked.

'It cannot be difficult.'

'How will your mothers feel if you were to get killed fighting?'

'They would be honoured that we had embraced *shahadat*,' said the smallest one solemnly. *Shahadat* means martyrdom.

An older boy walked up, about eighteen, his bloodshot eyes rimmed with kohl and the pupils black with hatred. His name was Sultan Mohammed and he was from Jalalabad. 'We will not spare the Americans, we will rip them apart like old clothes,' he said angrily, almost spitting the words as he held up the hem of his kamiz and mimicked tearing it. Rashid was rocking back and forth on the balls of his feet, obviously anxious to go, and I wondered if he thought they were going to stone me. Here, as in the streets of Quetta, I had become an enemy just for being white and western, and hated above all for being female. It was an uneasy feeling to be hated by strangers so nakedly, particularly in a country I had once felt at home in. I was finding the front-line of this war in more and more places.

'Let's move on,' urged Rashid. But I could not see any stones around, only dusty weeds and I was intrigued by these young boys who rather than wanting to be pilots, engine drivers or astronauts, longed to die in combat, so I asked him what subjects they studied.

'Islamic ideology, *Shariat*, Islamic economics,' he replied. The only literature was the Koran and the *hadith*, the sayings of the Prophet, and the form of teaching was rote learning. The most respect was given to those who could remember the most *hadith*, no easy task as there are said to be hundreds of thousands of them.

'And are there class discussions?'

'What is there to discuss?' asked Rashid. 'What is written is written.' No foreign languages were taught apart from Arabic, nor any science, and there were no signs of any computers though Rashid told me that he was in charge of Haqqania's website.

I asked the boys some basic sums, and they looked at me blankly, giggling. They had never heard of dinosaurs though they were keen to boast of Pakistan's nuclear bomb, and though they told me they learnt astronomy they did not believe that man had walked on the moon, shaking with laughter at the idea.

'How could that be?' said one. 'He would fall off.'

It was like going back in time and hard to associate with the teachings of the Koran in which *ilm*, the Arabic word for knowledge, is the second most used word after God. I remembered a friend who worked for the UN in Afghanistan, telling me about going to a talk at a school in Herat given by the mullah who was the Taliban's Minister of Education. The minister told the boys, 'If you want to be an engineer then go and work three months in a garage. If you want to be a doctor, go and work in a butcher's.' He ended by deriding Western education, saying, 'I went into the classroom of a foreign school once and it was written on the board that the sun is so many thousands of miles from the earth. Tell me this, who had the ruler long enough to measure it?'

Travelling with mujaheddin in the late 1980s, such village mullahs had often been the butt of their jokes. Community servants who earned a living through bonesetting and selling religious amulets to protect against the evil eye, they were not particularly respected, living off *zakat*, a percentage of the local crops, in return for their services at the mosque and funerals. Yet these were the kind of people now ruling Afghanistan. I was thinking about this as Rashid led us into a building and up a flight of stairs to see the auditorium where the call for jihad against the Russians first went up. The surrounding walls were covered in framed calligraphed scrolls bearing lists of graduates. The names were in Arabic but Rashid pointed out Mullah Kabir Haqqani, the Prime Minister; Noor Mohammed Saleih, the Chief Justice; Jalaluddin Haqqani, the commander-in-chief of the Taliban forces; Maulana Hasan Rahman, Governor of Kandahar and Maulana Sadar Azim, Governor of Jalalabad, as well as Fazlur Rehman, leader of the Jamiat-e-Ulema Islami (JUI), and Nabi Mohammedi and Yunus Khalis, the two mujaheddin leaders. 'Look,' he pointed out, 'there's Mullah Omar.'

Next he took us to the Library of Fatwas, a long basement room of shelves full of heavy bound volumes with gold lettering on the spines. 'Many of the fatwas have been issued here at Haqqania,' said Rashid proudly, 'more than a hundred thousand.' The deobandi form of Islam as preached by the Taliban seemed far more puritanical than even the Wahhabi sect, the austere Saudi Arabian faith that was the inspiration of bin Laden and which fiercely opposes anything seen as *bida,* the Arabic word for any modernization or deviation from the Koran. Wahhabis ban movie theatres and women from driving but deobandis seem to regulate every aspect of personal behaviour, issuing a quarter of a million fatwas over the last century.

My friend Akbar Ahmed, Chair of Islamic Studies at the American University in Washington DC and former Pakistan ambassador to London, has made it his life's mission to increase understanding between the Muslim world and the West, even producing a movie on Jinnah in which the founder of Pakistan was played by British actor and horror-film veteran Christopher Lee, much to the fury of his countrymen. He explained it to me the following way: 'While bin Laden's kind of thinking is coloured by his own exposure to the West and reaction against it, deobandism is a kind of scholarship of exclusion, an attempt to draw boundaries around Islam which the Taliban have taken to extremes. The Taliban have no contact with the West, they haven't travelled and it's not part of their thinking. But running over televisions with tanks and hanging spools of tape from lampposts is their attempt to keep out this corrupting influence and within that system of exclusion it makes sense.'

There was another factor. While the *madrassas* in India had always preached non-violence, those in Pakistan were mostly concentrated in rural areas and refugee camps in the Pashtun belt of Frontier Province and Baluchistan as well as among the Pashtun community in Karachi. Consequently they have been heavily influenced by Pashtunwali, the violent and highly conservative Pashtun code of behaviour where every insult must be revenged with interest and girls are locked away in purdah from the age of seven. The result was the very crude form of deobandi teaching as preached by the Taliban.

It made for a frightening combination, particularly as the Pashtun way of life seems to have changed little since 1898 when Winston Churchill wrote in *The Story of the Malakand Field Force*: 'The Pathan tribes are always engaged in public or private war. Every man is a warrior, a politician and a theologian. Every large house is a real feudal fortress, made it is true only of sun-baked clay, but with battlements, turrets, loopholes, flanking towers, drawbridges etc.

Every village has its defence . . . Every family cultivates its vendetta; every clan its feud. Nothing is ever forgotten and very few debts are left unpaid.'

To try and understand more about Pashtunwali I went to see Iftikhar Gilani, a silver-haired lawyer and politician whom I had first known as a close friend of Benazir Bhutto. Appointed Law Minister in her first government of 1988–90, he had become disillusioned by the corruption and switched sides to the Muslim League where it was just as bad so had switched back again. For the time being there was no parliament at all as General Musharraf had dissolved it; so he was seated on his lawn, wrapped in a warm shawl, reading an airport thriller and enjoying the late afternoon sun at his house in the countryside outside Islamabad. I joined him there for hot tea and samosas which melted in the mouth in a spicy mix of meat, chopped leeks and potato, watched by curious grey herons that tiptoed delicately round the lawn. It was a bucolic scene overlooking a green valley, yet just the other side of the road was the highly guarded entrance to Pinstech, Pakistan's nuclear development programme, the world's first Islamic bomb.

In the brief democratic periods between military regimes, Iftikhar had been member of parliament and senator for his hometown of Kohat, an old British garrison town surrounded by the tribal agencies of Kurram, Orakzai and Darra Adam Khel, the arms factory of the Frontier where numerous small forges turn out painstaking copies of guns, right down to the serial numbers. He was also a Pashtun and one of the most eloquent people I knew. If anyone could explain Pashtunwali to a westerner, it was him.

'First and foremost a guest is a guest,' he said. 'If my guest is harmed even if he has committed a crime then it is my responsibility to harm that person even if he is my relative.'

There was a Baluch story that illustrated this. A man arrived at a house and threw himself at the feet of the khan saying he was being pursued by a band of horsemen. The old khan granted him asylum, invited him to join them for dinner and sent a servant to lead him to the guest room.

The khan's son went to his father and said, 'Father, that is the man who killed my brother and your son just two months ago.'

'Yes my son, but now he is a guest in our house. He has asked for asylum and I have granted it.'

The son was furious so grabbed his brother's dagger, crept to the guest's room and stabbed him in the chest, as he had stabbed his brother.

The next morning the guest's body was found amid shouts and lamenting.

'Who could have done this?' cried the Khan. 'Who could have brought such dishonour on our family?'

The boy threw himself at his father's feet, admitting what he had done.

The old khan took the dagger and plunged it into the heart of his son.

This sounded unbelievable to me but Iftikhar insisted, 'Every day this happens. A person kills someone in Kohat then goes into the tribal agency for protection. The only difference these days is that the maliks often charge money for giving asylum.'

So if Osama bin Laden was going to take refuge anywhere this was surely the perfect place?[3]

'Yes,' he said.

I asked him what he thought of the Taliban and why they preached such an extreme form of Islam. 'Talibs used to be figures of fun,' he said. 'Pashtun is a very egalitarian society with no caste or class system. It's not like Sindh with its waderas or Punjab with its feudal

---

[3] In August 2002, the bodies of three Pakistani tribesmen were found near the border, their hands, noses and ears chopped off and US dollars stuffed in their mouths to show what happens to informants in tribal areas.

lords. In my sixty-one years of life, the only class that I can say we have always looked down on in Pashtun society is the Talib. When I was a child the Talibs were used for begging. They would come round the houses with begging bowls and cry out "I'm a Talib," and we'd say "poor darling" and give them bread.'

Referring to the Taliban as 'poor darlings' was not just a recognition of their straitened circumstances. There was a more sinister side. The *madrassa* boys were not only separated from their mothers and all females at an early age but were taught to stigmatise women and that the mere sight of an ankle or a varnished fingernail would lead to damnation. In Pashto, women are referred to as *tor sari* which means black-heads until their hair turns grey and they become *spin sari* or white-heads, and they are seen as something to be covered, locked away and beaten.

'We're talking about a society where in my village a boy and girl kissing is an unpardonable crime seen as worse than murder,' said Iftikhar. 'The inevitable result is sodomy. It's the done thing in Pashtun society because of women being shut away in houses. A good-looking boy would have dozens of attempts made on him. I was a very handsome youth and had lots of problems but fortunately our family name and standing protected me. These Talibs have no such protection and it starts with the kind of people who run these seminaries. We used to say, "Oh my God, he's a Talib," and that meant he's a sissy or he's available.

'Over a period of time they must become very angry people. And very frustrated, mostly against women, coupled with the hurt of a childhood trauma you can never get rid of and never, never talk about. It must leave a permanent scar.'

Kabul, October 24, 2001

Salam Christina

I do not think there will be a way of getting this letter to you because it is too much danger but I am happy to write. I do it secretly, my father would be angry if he knew as already we are in trouble.

We had to move this week from Microrayon to a small house the other side of town, near the mountains behind which are the Shomali Plains. Maybe you have heard of them, terrible things happened there, the Taliban abducted many women. I heard of one young girl they found crying in a mosque, all her family had been killed and she was left without clothes.

We moved in a rush, some of our neighbours told us the Taliban were coming to raid our flat because they know of our support of the king and our friendship with Karzai. My heart was thumping with fright. We hid two nights in a relative's house then we heard of this place and moved. It is better for my mother's nerves because we are not so near the bombing though of course we still hear the B52s, they are flying in the day now, not just at night. In Microrayon it was like 1992 again when we were on the first line and there was so much rocketing we could not go to school. The Americans say they are trying to help us but some of the bombs are hitting innocent people. My brother told us today of a family he knew where the mother and baby were asleep

*in the bedroom and a bomb fell and killed them leaving just
the father and thirteen-year old daughter and small children.
The father is in shock and the girl Haziza is looking after
everything.*

*There is fear now, what will happen here in Kabul? More
people are leaving the city, every day we see families putting
all their things on top of taxis and leaving to Pakistan or to
villages. They say the Pakistani border officials are charging
lots of money – 500 rupees each person. Our family is in
Loghar province, it is not so far from here but they have
little.*

*We could not bring everything when we moved but today
our neighbours sent some boxes and inside were black and
white photographs of myself and my sister and brothers when
we were young. It seemed so long ago. There was one in a
garden, full of flowers. Christina, can you think it is so long
since we had flowers in Kabul! When I was a girl the air
smelled of flowers. And another picture at the zoo. We used
to go to the zoo at weekends, there were big elephants and
lions and monkeys and snakes. Now all the animals are
dead, I think there is just one lion left. I do not know what
he eats. There is no food for the people. My brother says in
the streets he sees children searching the rubbish.*

*The new house is better but the rent is very expensive –
thirty lakh afghanis a month – and I do not know how we
will pay it and I have lost all my pupils as it is too far for
them to come. Now we must spread the word here so we can
start classes again but slowly as no one knows who they can
trust.*

*On Radio Shariat they said the Taliban has brought in
6000 soldiers to protect Kabul but no one has seen them. My
mother cries that they will take my brothers but no one
wants to fight. We heard some Arabs were murdered, one*

near Pul-i-Khishti mosque. Can it be true? What will happen to us? Will the Americans come?

Marri

4

The Royal Court in Exile

'We have not come here in pomp and show;
we have taken refuge in this place from unfortunate events.'

HAFIZ

IT WAS A STICKY JULY NIGHT, the eve of Princess Homaira Wali's wedding and she was wandering restlessly in the moonlit garden of her father's palace in Kabul when she heard the rumbling of tanks. The pale twenty-year old with dark glossy hair and the spirited ranginess of the wild horses she loved to tame, was King Zahir Shah's eldest grandchild, and her wedding was to be the society event of the summer. The scent of roses hung heavy on the night air and the princess had been thinking about how her life was about to change for as a married woman she would no longer be able to sneak off from her bodyguards to go alone to the movies or drive her car around town playing The Beatles.

'We had come back from the king's palace where we had all been watching the new Candice Bergen film in the private cinema and everyone had gone to bed,' she recalled. 'I couldn't sleep, it was too hot and I was excited because it was in the middle of my wedding – we had had the first ceremony two days earlier, the civil ceremony,

Princess Homaira as a young girl in Kabul.

and were due to have the main reception with all the guests two days later. It was a clear night with a big full moon and, about 1 a.m., I went out to the garden for some air. Suddenly I could hear the sound of tanks. It seemed odd, the annual military parade was due so sometimes there would be tanks practising early in the morning but this was too early.

'I went back in the house and upstairs to the second floor and from there I could see over the walls of the palace and all these little heads sticking up from tanks moving nearer. Instead of going past they were stopping and pointing their guns towards the house. There had been rumours that Daoud [the former Prime Minister] was planning a coup but my grandfather had always insisted "Daoud's my cousin, he would never stab me in the back", and had refused to do anything.'

It was a foolish claim for the whole history of Afghanistan's mon-archy was one of treachery and intrigue, cousin murdering cousin, brother murdering and blinding brother. One of Zahir Shah's predecessors, Abdur Rahman employed foodtasters to test even his tea, and used to keep horses saddled by the door of the palace so he could leave at a moment's notice for fighting in any part of his kingdom, as well as fast mules for carrying treasure if he had to flee. By the head of his bed was a cupboard with glass doors in which his best rifles were kept and under his pillow were two loaded revolvers. As a further precaution he would stay awake working until 4 a.m. then sleep in the day on the grounds that any treachery was usually carried out at night.

When Abdur Rehman died, his eldest son Habibullah who succeeded him immediately occupied the Arg, the large fortified complex that included the treasury and arsenal, fearing one of his brothers would try to seize the throne. The estate had both inner and outer walls and along its tree-lined roads guarded by stone lions were dotted various domed and colonnaded sandstone buildings that had served as guest houses, audience chambers and harems. It was in one of these palaces that Homaira's family were living when the tanks rolled in.

'I knew something was going on so I quickly woke up my husband and father,' she continued. 'My father, who was His Majesty's military commander, went to the balcony and saw the tanks so phoned his headquarters but as he lifted the receiver the line went dead. Then the lights went out. My father and husband ran down to the office to get the guns which was obviously useless, how could you fight off a coup with some revolvers and one machine gun? I had my own pistol, which I always carried.

'Father told us to sit on the steps in this kind of glass conservatory full of plants and canaries in wooden cages that was before the main entrance to the house, but I'd seen too many *Columbo* programmes so I said "No" and took my mother and younger sister and girls we used to look after and told them to lie down in the corridor leading to the bedrooms which had only a couple of windows. I saw my father and husband coming up the stairs with guns, and then the tanks started firing and I couldn't see them anymore, there was so much dust. They shot at my bedroom, my father's bedroom and my sister's bedroom and we couldn't breathe. Then we heard another shell from inside the house and all the glass breaking and the sitting room caught fire. My mother rushed to put on trousers in case they hanged us.

'Our plan was that if they captured us we would kill each other. The main thing was not to be captured alive because who knew what might happen. I was to kill my mother and sister.

'I had learnt to use my father's pistol at the age of five and had my first gun when I was seven so I was used to shooting and we all felt anything was better than torture. Anyway my father said, "I think it's me they are looking for," so he started to go and my little sister grabbed his legs begging him not to. He bent down to pat her head and push her away, and as he did, machine gun fire sailed over his head. It would have killed him if he hadn't been leaning over. They arrested him and took the rest of us into the drawing room, which was full of broken glass. I could see three tanks outside and Daoud in his white Toyota looking with binoculars and he saw us.

'Around 7 a.m. they took us to the king's palace where my grand-mother and aunts and uncles and cousins were in the dining room, about twenty-three princes and princesses surrounded by soldiers. There were helicopters overhead. That's how I spent my honeymoon, sleeping under the dining room table – very romantic. We were kept there for about a week not knowing what was going to happen, whether we were going to be killed or what had happened to my father.'

Finally, one morning at 4 a.m., they were taken to the airport and put on a plane from the state airline Ariana. Homaira's nine-year-old cousin Prince Mostapha held her hand as they walked to the steps. Before boarding they were searched and the gold chain with a minia-ture Koran, which Mostapha wore round his neck, was ripped off by a soldier. When the young prince kicked out in protest, the soldier knocked him to the ground with the butt of his rifle. Mostapha grabbed a handful of earth and put it in his pocket.

They were flown to Rome where they joined the king who had been in Italy recuperating from an eye operation, and somewhat mortifyingly, was in the midst of taking a mud bath at a spa on the island of Ischia when he was informed of the coup. Homaira had hoped her father, General Abdul Wali, would be on board but in fact he was in solitary confinement in Kabul Central Prison being tortured so badly that his femur was smashed, leaving him with a permanent limp, and it would be three years before she saw him again.

Ever since that hot July day in 1973, the royal family had been in exile in Rome, living in borrowed homes on the generosity of other foreign rulers. Largely forgotten, they became part of an *ancien régime* left adrift in a country far from home. All that remained other than Mostapha's pocketful of earth, which he put in a silver pot that he kissed and placed under his pillow every night, praying for a return to his homeland, were the photograph albums. There were a few family snapshots relaxing in the palace gardens or the princesses in traditional costume and headdress, but mostly they contained black and white news pictures, showing the king riding in open Rolls-Royces or stepping off planes to be greeted by Mao Tse Tung, Dwight Eisenhower, John F. Kennedy, Jawaharlal Nehru, Marshal Tito, General de Gaulle, all figures of a bygone age. The king had grown old and frail, spending his days painting, reading French novels, playing chess, photographing animals and landscapes, and listening to Indian sitar music.

It was in Rome that I met Homaira, by then a woman of forty-eight, though she seemed much younger and never stopped talking or laughing except to answer her constantly ringing mobile phone. I had gone to interview the king because the Northern Alliance had broken through Taliban lines at Bagram and were only twenty-three

King Zahir Shah with John F. Kennedy.

miles outside Kabul, and with American planes blasting away at Taliban positions, it looked as though the capital might fall any day. From State Department officials in Washington to shopkeepers in Kandahar, suddenly people were talking about Zahir Shah as the 'only hope' for peace and stability in Afghanistan. But while I was having a pre-interview coffee with his son-in-law General Wali, a message had come to say His Majesty was suffering from lumbago and would have to postpone our appointment, so Homaira had offered to show me around.

It was a glorious blue and gold autumn day, and Homaira was the perfect guide to a city I had never visited, weaving in and out of traffic like a native in her old Volvo, often narrowly avoiding pavements in her enthusiasm to show me the Colosseum or the track used for chariot races. As she drove round the majestic monuments and fountains decorated with chariots and gods that seemed to grace every street, she sang along to Robbie William's cover *Mack the Knife* on the car stereo.

Yet as home as she seemed in Rome, even looking the part, effortlessly handsome in leather jacket and tailored trousers, Homaira confessed that she considered arriving there as the end of everything she had loved. Growing up as a princess in Kabul may not have been the fairytale lifestyle that the title suggests but she described a blissful childhood with a surprising degree of independence. The eldest daughter of the king's eldest daughter, the exquisite Princess Belquis, Homaira had no brothers and was a confirmed tomboy. 'During my grandfather's reign, girls went to mixed schools, to the cinema, listened to foreign groups like The Beatles, went swimming, wore short skirts, but even then I was different,' she laughed. 'I learnt to ride at the age of two and a half, to use my father's pistol at five, and was the first woman in Afghanistan to drive a car, going all over town with my pistol in my belt, though I always had a guard. I loved movies and often slipped away to the Park Cinema. I accompanied my grandfather everywhere.'

The Arg was sprawling rather than grand and the king did not wear a crown nor ride in a carriage. But even so Homaira had grown up used to being surrounded by ancient tapestries and oil paintings that had been gifts to her ancestors from other monarchs, and to travelling around in one of her grandfather's prized collection of Rolls-Royces or her uncle's Thunderbird as well as going on elaborate expeditions hunting deer and quails with hundreds of retainers.

Suddenly the entire family was crowded in one flat. Everything they owned had been left in Kabul – the only thing they got past the guards before boarding the plane was a miniature painted by the king which Homaira's husband had slipped out of its frame and hid under his shirt. It now hangs in her parents' apartment in Rome. The royal family had no property or bank accounts abroad and initially the king refused to accept any help. He sold his cufflinks, watch, camera and the carpets he had taken with him as gifts for his doctors and used the proceeds to rent a small villa in Quartimiglia just outside Rome.

'There were twenty-four or twenty-five of us in a four-roomed villa,' recalled Homaira. 'People were saying we had lapis lazuli castles but we had nothing, only the clothes we had left in. No money. We were living on one egg a day.'

Although several offers of financial support came in, the king was determined not to be dependent on one person or country. Eventually accommodation and a monthly allowance were arranged with contributions from King Fahd of Saudi Arabia, the Shah of Iran, and President Anwar Sadat of Egypt. It was an unfortunate choice as over the next few years the Shah was deposed and Sadat assassinated. After that, King Fahd picked up all the bills.

Life in Rome demanded both a sudden adjustment to a new life, as well as an exposure to all sorts of new freedoms. In the first year Homaira gave birth to a daughter, Mariam, then less than two years later, shocked her family by announcing that she was leaving her husband even though it had not been an arranged marriage. 'I thought it was love,' she smiled sadly. 'My mistake.' It was the first divorce in a royal family where kings were notorious for taking many wives. Her parents took away the two-and-a-half-year-old Mariam and refused to give her back unless Homaira returned to her husband. 'I could not do that. I even went to court but they wouldn't give me a divorce and custody because they wouldn't recognise my marriage as it had been halted in the middle so we would have first had to get properly married which of course was impossible.'

Desperate for money and distraction, she looked for work. 'Horses were all I knew, so I got a job in a stables in Rome, mucking out,' she explained. There she met a Scotsman who persuaded her to go to England where she found a job working for champion show-jumper Carolyn Bradley in her stables in the pretty Cotswold village of Broad Marston. No one knew she was a princess. A few years later, after Bradley's unexpected early death, she took a job as a photographer's assistant in England, then moved back to Rome where her daughter, by then thirteen, was finally entrusted to her care.

'So you see I am the black sheep,' she said, winding up her story with a quizzical smile, the ashtray in front of her overflowing with butts. We had been talking all day, driving round the city, stopping only for lunch in a trattoria where Homaira told me she had a surprise. I closed my eyes as instructed, opening them to see Zia Mojadiddi, an old friend to whom I had been introduced by Hamid Karzai and who now lived in San Diego among the large exiled Afghan community. Zia was a radio-journalist and I had spent many an hour at his house in Peshawar as he patiently explained his country to me, often with Hamid interjecting, and the two of them arguing about long-ago tribal battles. We had not seen each other for eleven years.

By the time Homaira finished her tale, we had moved on to espressos in a steamy windowed café where dusk had turned to night and the crowd transformed from middle-aged women with big coiffured hair and designer shopping bags to young men in leather jackets clasping ruby-lipped girls in tight-waisted dresses, sipping Negronis. The café was on a piazza of apartment blocks in the northern suburbs and across the road was the Fleming Hotel, a drab 1970s-style block full of Japanese tourists wearing cameras and name badges trailing in and out of the lobby and into coaches.

Outside on the square, six or seven carabinieri sat impassively in squad cars, flicking cigarette ash onto the road through half-open windows, for the Fleming had become the meeting place of the royal court in exile. For a while Homaira and I sat and watched a group of olive-skinned men in dark suits and dark glasses huddled in yellow alcoves, scheming and smoking. Among them was her cousin Mostapha.

A plump-faced man of thirty-eight with black sideburns and a balding head, Prince Mostapha Zahir was the person most of the dark suits were waiting to see. As the king's spokesman, he was the closest most people would ever get to the eighty-seven-year-old former monarch, and was relishing the attention. The prince's chest seemed to puff out peacock-fashion as he paced back and forth across the dingy lobby, one mobile phone constantly glued to his ear and another in his hand. 'One for commanders and one for other people,' he explained. 'I've had calls from twenty-seven provinces, eighty-five satellite calls from commanders. The Taliban are collapsing and everyone wants to surrender to His Majesty.'

Occasionally he would deign to sit with one of the groups for a few minutes and there would be a flurry of papers and business cards as they presented their case before one of his phones rang again and he would stride off. Among those waiting for a word of princely approval were an oil executive from Dubai hoping to build a pipeline across Afghanistan to bring gas from landlocked Turkmenistan to Pakistan and on to Europe, an exiled academic living in Geneva with a plan for a school of fine art, and a bright young lawyer from San Francisco whose father had edited the *Kabul Times* and who wanted to help draw up a constitution for the new Afghanistan.

Talking to some of them, I found myself drawn into all the intrigues of a long-forgotten court that after almost thirty years in exile suddenly saw power once more within its grasp, advisors and relatives surfacing, many of whom had never worked, forming cliques, reliving feuds, and plotting against the others in the rush for ministries and ambassadorships. 'Do not believe anything he says,' whispered one advisor after seeing me talking to someone else from the king's office, 'his uncle killed my uncle.'

General Abdul Wali had described his father-in-law's court in Kabul to me as 'like Europe in the Middle Ages', and at the Fleming Hotel, apart from the modern suits, that was exactly how it appeared.

Watching it all with a sceptical eye was Homaira. 'My grandfather never wanted this,' she said. 'He was happy here in Rome. He had a simple life, going for walks and every day driving downtown for a cappuccino in Café de Paris in Via Veneto where he would read *Le Figaro* and *Paris Match* and smoke a cigar and sometimes go to the

French bookshop. Believe me, he never talked about restoring the monarchy. He always said there must be someone better than me to run the country. But no one ever emerged.'

We were debating whether to go back to my hotel or have a late supper in a nearby Iranian restaurant when Homaira's phone rang. It was the king asking us to go over there if we didn't mind that he might be in his pyjamas.

'Now?' I asked in surprise. His house was an hour's drive away. 'It will be midnight!'

'It doesn't matter. He doesn't sleep much these days. He watches CNN all night. He's very upset about the bombing.'

We set off on a motorway heading north and took the turn-off to Olgiata, a private estate of villas surrounded by high privet hedges that is home to footballers, film-stars and Cicciolina, the porn-Queen, and so discreet that even the lampposts are painted green to blend in with the pinewoods. To reach the king's house we had to go through three checkpoints, the last of which was a concrete roadblock where we had to leave the car. 'My grandfather's life has changed dramatically since September 11th,' explained Homaira, shaking her head. 'He hates all this.'

There was good reason for the Italian police to be vigilant, particularly with journalists. Only two days before the World Trade Center attack, Ahmad Shah Massoud, the legendary Panjshir commander and leader of the Northern Alliance, had been killed when two North Africans presenting themselves as Moroccan journalists walked in to interview him with a bomb inside their camera. The king himself had survived an assassination attempt back in 1990, again by someone posing as a journalist. A Portuguese Muslim called José Paulo Santos de Almeida had carried out an entire interview then picked up a Kandahari dagger that he had brought as a gift and said, 'Now I'm going to have to kill you.' He stabbed the king three times in the head and chest, obviously intending a mortal wound to the heart, but the dagger was stopped by a tin of Café Crème cigarillos inside the old man's breast pocket, leaving him lying bleeding on the cream sofa but still alive. 'The funny thing is,' said Homaira, 'his doctors had pleaded with my grandfather to stop smoking and he refused, but he used to smoke huge *Romeo y Julieta* Havanas and he had just swapped those for the small cigarillos. Now he refuses to give up the cigarillos, saying they saved his life.'[1]

Zahir Shah's security had been stepped up at that time, but it was since the war on terrorism was launched that his house had been turned into a prison. Considered a prime al Qaeda target, the king was under round-the-clock guard, no longer allowed to travel downtown to the café on Via Veneto or even go for his daily walk around the estate. Carabinieri with Uzis were everywhere, outside the front gate, in a Portakabin in the garden, and even inside the house and I was body-checked before entering. Searchlights swept across a lawn denuded of trees and bushes, and helicopters flew over every hour. The Japanese family living next door found it so disruptive that they had moved out.

Inside, a slight man with a grey walrus moustache was sitting on one of the two cream sofas and rose to greet us. The former monarch was not wearing pyjamas as threatened but dressed impeccably in a dark suit with a grey shirt, silk Hermès tie, and shiny black Italian shoes, and was extremely courteous. He held out a pale elegant hand marked with liver spots, and apologised for all the police. 'I'm a prisoner in my own home,' he said in French, which used to be the language of the court in Kabul.

A Filipino butler brought green tea in china cups and a silver dish of tiny buttery *pasticcerie* decorated with chocolate and cherries, and

---

[1] The Portuguese man, who was subsequently released from Italian prison for good behaviour and then disappeared in Africa, had a suitcase full of Korans and later claimed in an interview with Portuguese weekly *Expresso* that the assassination had been ordered by bin Laden whom he had met while fighting in Afghanistan.

I looked around the room. The four-bedroomed villa was not particularly palatial. Apart from the old red, green and black Afghan flag draped over the banister, it looked barely lived in, like a rental property one does not stay in long enough to make one's own, with wipe-clean wooden floors, a few plants, a modern CD player and some coffee-table books. The only personal touches were some of the king's landscape photographs and several framed black and white engravings of robed and turbaned ancestors including Ahmad Shah Abdali.

Unlike the ambitious Ahmad Shah, Zahir Shah had never wanted to be king and was only nineteen when the throne was thrust upon him, just four years after unexpectedly becoming crown prince. He was born into a side-branch of the Durrani dynasty in November 1914, a time of particular turbulence in Afghanistan which prepared the ground for many things that were to happen later. His father General Nadir Shah was commander in chief of the forces of King Habibullah, who was said to have taken a wife or concubine from each region as a way of keeping all the different ethnic groups under control, and had more than thirty-five sons. When Zahir Shah was five, Habibullah was assassinated, murdered in his sleep while on a hunting trip to Jalalabad. Nadir Shah was arrested in the initial round-up but then released and again made commander of the Afghan army by his distant cousin Amanullah, one of Habibullah's sons, who had taken the throne and many believed had plotted his father's murder, spurred on by his ambitious mother.

Once King Amanullah had quelled various tribal revolts around the country, in May 1919 he declared war on the startled British, provoking the Third Anglo-Afghan War, with the aim of securing complete independence and recovering the lands between the Durand Line and the Indus that had been part of Afghanistan. The advantage of surprise meant that Nadir Shah's forces at first scored several victories, particularly as many Pashtuns in the Khyber Rifles and Frontier Scouts deserted to join the Afghans. But then the British

King Habibullah.

escalated the war and sent RAF pilots[2] flying First World War war-
planes over the high mountains of eastern Afghanistan to drop bombs
on Jalalabad and Kabul.

It was the first time the country had been bombed, and after one
bomb hit the tomb of his grandfather Amir Abdur Rahman, an
outraged Amanullah sent a cable to Lord Chelmsford, the Viceroy
of India, complaining: 'It is a matter of great regret that the throwing
of bombs by Zeppelins on London was denounced as a most savage
act and the bombardment of places of worship was considered a most
abominable operation while now we can see with our own eyes that
such operations were a habit which is prevalent amongst all civilised
peoples of the West.'

Just as the Taliban were to find years later, Amanullah's forces

[2] One was to become famous during the Second World War as Bomber Harris
who, as commander-in-chief of RAF Bomber Command, developed the controversial
saturation technique of mass bombing, devastating Hamburg and Dresden.

had no chance against this lethal new weapon. But nor did the British have any eagerness to take on these martial people in their impenetrable mountains once more, particularly so soon after the First World War when the British units stationed in India had lost most of their experienced men. Both sides initiated peace moves and the result was the Treaty of Rawalpindi, which ended the control Britain had long exercised over Afghanistan's external affairs. An Afghan delegation immediately travelled across the Oxus to Moscow and entered into an agreement of mutual assistance with the Bolsheviks. The Treaty of Friendship was the start of the Soviet-Afghan relationship, sealed with a gift of planes, pilots and telegraph operators, and over the next few years the Russians laid phone lines to link Herat, Kandahar, Kabul and Mazar-i-Sharif.

Calling himself a 'revolutionary king', Amanullah was a fervent admirer of Ataturk, whom he hoped to emulate by trying to forge a modern nation from Afghanistan's warring tribes and ethnic groups. As a first step he began building a national army, bringing in Turkish military advisors, much to Nadir Shah's irritation as their advice such as reducing pay only demoralised the troops. An arrogant man, Amanullah had no time for critics so in 1924 his cousin was relieved of his command and dispatched to Paris as ambassador, then shortly afterwards retired to the South of France because of ill-health.

Afghan rulers have a tendency to be out of step with the times. While the Taliban yearned to turn the clock back to the medieval era, in Amanullah's case he was much too far ahead. In December 1927 he travelled to Tehran and Istanbul from where he embarked on an eight-month Grand Tour of Europe visiting all the major capitals from Rome, Paris, Berlin, Brussels to London where he and his doe-eyed queen Soraya were entertained so lavishly that he became obsessed with westernising Afghanistan. On his return he announced the opening of co-educational schools, instituted a minimum age for marriage, scrapped the veil for women – dramatically removing that of the queen in public, and insisted that everyone in Kabul wear western dress in public including a European hat. His opponents began a campaign condemning him as anti-Islamic and spreading rumours that he had brought back from Europe machines to make soaps out of dead bodies.

Eventually, in 1929, tribesmen in Jalalabad, angered more by new taxes than by modernisation which had little effect on them, began a revolt. It quickly spread and when Amanullah sent his army to crush it, most of his soldiers joined the rebels, leaving Kabul open to invasion. As the tribal forces advanced from the east, Amanullah abdicated in favour of his eldest brother Inayatullah and fled in his Rolls-Royce to Kandahar, discovering that it was hardly the best vehicle for cross-country travel on mud roads when he got stuck in the snow.

Inayatullah's reign was to last just three days. Bacha Saqqao, an illiterate Tajik bandit-leader in the north whose name meant 'son of water carrier', saw his chance amid all the confusion and captured the throne. Amanullah's attempt to gather tribesmen and retake Kabul failed dismally and he fled again, this time to British India from where he went by ship to Italy. On his Grand Tour the previous year, King Victor Emmanuel III had somewhat foolhardily presented him the Order of Holy Annunciation, one of Italy's highest honours which among its privileges allowed the recipient to call himself the king's cousin, so had little choice but to give him asylum. Amanullah lived there till his death in 1960.

As soon as he heard what had happened, Nadir Shah sailed back to India and joined forces with some of his brothers in Peshawar, setting up base in Deans Hotel. The Pashtuns loathed being ruled by a Tajik, particularly as Bacha Saqqao had formed a government of Tajik friends and relations most of whom were also illiterate and spent their time engaged in murder and plunder, so the brothers were easily able to enlist an army of Pashtun tribesmen. Their first two attempts on Kabul failed, largely because the tribesmen were too busy settling blood-feuds between themselves but they collected a third army and gathered support within the capital by launching an underground newspaper, *Islah*, which later went on to become the official state newspaper. On 10 October 1929, after only nine months in power, Bacha Saqqao was overthrown.

Most Afghans expected Nadir Shah to restore his deposed cousin Amanullah to the throne. Instead, he declared himself king then executed Bacha Saqqao by firing squad. Finding that the Tajiks had emptied the treasury and needing what little money he had to buy off Amanullah's supporters, he let his tribal army loot Kabul and they left with their booty.

With no army, no money and no one he could trust to help him govern, it is not surprising that he became an autocratic king. In January 1931, Richard Maconachie, the British Minister to Kabul, sent a despatch back to London that could have been written today: 'Throughout the country the advantages of anarchy seem to have been better appreciated than its drawbacks and the tribes are asking themselves why they should resign the freedom which they had enjoyed the past year and submit again to a central authority which would inevitably demand payment of land revenue, customs duties and bribes for its officials and possibly the restoration of arms looted from government posts and arsenals.'

Kipling wrote, 'trust a snake more than a prostitute and a prostitute more than an Afghan', and Afghan history involves so much killing and betrayal, that I could see why the shy, studious Zahir Shah might not have rejoiced in suddenly becoming crown prince. He had spent most of his youth in Paris, where he had lived with the family of a member of the French Chamber of Deputies and studied at Lycée Pasteur and Collège de Montpelier, acquiring a lifelong passion for the works of Molière and Dumas as well as an interest in parliamentary democracy, often going to the gallery of the chamber to watch debates. After his father became king, he returned to Kabul to attend military college, and on 8 November 1933 was at the Arg attending a ceremony at the Dilkusha or Heart's Delight Palace, which had been designed for Habibullah in 1900 by a British architect. Nadir Shah had recently reopened the high schools and was handing out awards to the best students. To the prince's surprise, the king called 'Zahir, come to me, my son', and held him so close that he could smell Tabac, his father's favourite cologne. 'My son I am so proud of you,' he said. 'You have been a good son to me.'

Arm-in-arm, father and son then walked together across the lawn onto the podium to the sound of a military band. As they took their seats, three shots rang out. To start with the prince did not realise what had happened; then he saw the crimson drops of blood on his father's glasses as he sank into his chair. Zahir flung himself at his father's feet until one of his uncles, his father's youngest brother Shah Mehmud, slapped him, saying, 'Zahir, this is no time to cry. It's time to save your country.'

At 4.30 p.m. that afternoon the Kabul cannon sounded over the city to announce that a new king had been crowned. Successions have rarely been smooth in Afghanistan and the prince's uncle must have been tempted to take power himself. As it was he controlled things for the first two decades of Zahir Shah's reign. For the new young monarch it was a difficult time. Used to living in the West and spending his days painting miniatures and reading French classics, he had little idea of how to govern this country of warring tribesmen.

'I never wanted to be king,' he told me, and by all accounts his forty-year reign was not a glorious period in Afghan history. 'The most difficult thing in Afghanistan has always been to keep a balance between the tribes, keeping them in harmony and out of trouble.

'The other big problem historically is our geo-strategic position. In the north we have the Soviet Union or now the newly emerged Central Asian states, in the east China, in the south Pakistan and in the west Iran. Afghanistan is a very small country but very proud. Yet these neighbours all try to interfere. Take the Taliban, for example, they were not really Afghans but Pakistanis and Arabs. Because of these foreign hands, pursuing our independence and freedom has always been enormously important to our people.

'Of course we have been helped in that by our peculiar topography which is so mountainous as you British know only too well.' We laughed with the shared respect of hundreds of years of warfare with much bloodshed on both sides. 'Ours is an impenetrable land with many, many hiding places where people can hide for years then regroup. Look at bin Laden, one of the world's most famous faces yet the most powerful army on earth cannot find him. In our mountains and valleys it is like looking for a needle in a haystack.'

He referred to the famous retreat from Kabul in 1842 in which 16,000 British troops and their families were killed, and continued, 'Our terrain is so difficult that when you British sent in conventional armies with all their batteries and cannons to fight Afghans sitting on the tops of the hills and cliffs who knew the land, every rock and every stone, it was an easy pick. It almost became like a hunt. That is the problem when outsiders come into our country.

'We have always kept a balance so if one power intervened another came to our rescue. That's why my most difficult decision was during the Second World War when the Allies gave Afghanistan a forty-eight-hour ultimatum to give up our neutrality and support them and hand over the German diplomats or like Iran be invaded. We had always fiercely safeguarded our neutrality and had remained neutral in the First World War so I called a *loya jirga* for the people to decide and the *jirga* decided we should stay neutral whatever the threats. It is a matter of principle for Afghans that when you have guests in your country they should be protected so we would not hand over the Germans or their archives but we asked them honourably to scale down their mission.'

Only when he reached middle age did King Zahir Shah start taking any significant decisions on the administration of his country, and after convening another *loya jirga* in 1963–4, he introduced a kind of constitutional monarchy with freedom of speech, the right to form political parties, guaranteed primary school education for girls and boys, and allowed women to vote. 'We had human rights, equal rights, women's rights, women in government,' he told me. Ariana airlines employed unveiled women as airhostesses and receptionists; there were female announcers on Kabul Radio and a woman delegate sent to the United Nations, much to the fury of religious leaders.

But he was a very cautious man, a procrastinator, disliked by the Americans who described him as 'furtive'. A cable from the US political attaché Charles Dunbar to the State Department after the unveiling of his new constitution, referred to him as 'the foremost obstacle to economic modernisation'. Disillusioned with the lack of real reform, in 1965 a group of student activists and writers formed the country's first Communist party, the People's Democratic Party of Afghanistan, which quickly split into two groups: *Parcham*, the Standard (or Flag), under Barbrak Karmal and *Khalq*, the People, under Nur Mohammed Taraki. As the economic situation worsened, student demonstrations and strikes as well as clashes between religious and Marxist parties repeatedly brought the capital to a halt, and a three-year drought meant that by 1971 there was widespread famine.

'Looking back I realise it was a mistake allowing the training and education of young Afghans in the Soviet Union,' said the ex-king. 'They were inexperienced, so easily indoctrinated in Communism, then came back and found themselves rejected by the people of Afghanistan and reacted by themselves rejecting everything.'

Moreover an unwise clause in Zahir Shah's new constitution had made a powerful enemy of his cousin and former Prime Minister Prince Mohammed Daoud Khan. Article 24 prohibited any member of the royal family from holding a government ministry, which meant that the only way for a royal to exercise any power was to seize the throne. When Daoud sent an emissary to sound out American reaction to a possible coup, it was made clear that Washington cared little who was in power in Kabul.

On 17 July 1973, Zahir Shah's reign ended abruptly when Daoud took advantage of his absence in Italy to seize the palace and take over with just a few hundred troops. Some of the former king's advisors, including Homaira's father, believed Zahir Shah should have mobilised his own forces rather than abdicate but, a lifelong pacifist, he said at the time, 'I wanted to avoid a bloodbath.' Having assumed power at the time when Hitler was ruling Germany and Mussolini Italy, perhaps he realised he was of a different era.

In his villa in Rome, the king lived on almost forgotten and kept a low profile, mostly staying in, playing chess and cards – 'He cheats terribly,' said Homaira. Meanwhile as the years passed, back in Kabul one after another of the successive inhabitants of the royal palace were brutally killed.

First, in 1978, Daoud was murdered with most of his family in a coup, battling inside the Arg until the end as air strikes were launched against him by his own military. His successor Taraki, one of the PDPA's three founder members, set about trying to replace Allah with the Communist party, changing the Afghan flag with its green stripe representing Islam for a solidly red one, throwing thousands of professionals and clergy in Pul-i-Charki jail, and introduced a personality cult with himself as the 'Great Teacher'. Most Afghans were horrified but the first real response came from Herat where approximately a hundred Russian advisors and their families were publicly hacked to death, prompting Moscow to send in planes and tanks to pulverise the city, killing thousands. In October 1979, Taraki was found dead, suffocated by a cushion.

His replacement, Hafizullah Amin, managed to survive an ambush as he arrived at the palace and at least two KGB-sponsored coups before, on Christmas Eve 1979, an elite Soviet battalion secured Kabul airport for a massive airlift of troops which Amin apparently thought were coming to help him. But to the north, thousands more were crossing the Oxus river and on December 27th, the first tank-shell hit Amin's headquarters. After surviving a farcical attempt to poison him, he was 'disappeared' and Barbrak Karmal, the final member of the founding trio, installed as President, backed by 85,000 Russian troops. Moscow's claims that it had been invited in by the Kabul regime were treated with derision and worldwide condemnation.

Karmal survived until 1985 when he was sent to the Soviet Union for 'medical treatment' and never came back.

He was replaced by Mohammed Najibullah, the man known as the Ox for both his hefty size and stubborn nature, and who survived in power even after the last Russian troops left in 1989, defying Western predictions of his imminent downfall. Of all the killings that have taken place in the Arg, Najibullah's was perhaps the most grisly. Removed from power in 1992 when the mujaheddin finally took Kabul, he lived under UN protection until the Taliban captured the city. Taken to the palace from where he had once ruled, he was castrated in his old bedroom, tied to the back of a Toyota Land Cruiser and dragged round and round the compound, then hung from a traffic post outside for all the city to see.

Occasionally as things got desperate in Afghanistan, such as during the mujaheddin infighting after the Soviet withdrawal, someone would revive the idea of bringing back the king. But there were implacable opponents both inside and outside of the country. Iran, having got rid of its own monarchy, the Pahlavi Throne, had no intention of seeing a kingdom restored in its neighbour, while Pakistan still dreamed of a friendly government and feared a return to the Durrani dynasty would lead to renewed calls for Pashtunistan and a greater Afghanistan. Many Afghans, particularly members of the Northern Alliance, were vehemently against Zahir Shah's return. 'What did he do in the jihad?' asked Dr Abdullah Abdullah, a leading Northern Alliance member who went on to become Foreign Minister, when we discussed the matter. 'Zahir Shah can come and Zahir Shah can go. It creates noise but it doesn't matter.'

The king himself had almost given up hope of returning to his homeland though he told me that like his grandson Mostapha, he kept a jar of Afghan earth by his bedside. 'It is sand from Kandahar where the monarchy has its roots.'

But in November 2001, with the Taliban's days numbered and many fearing a return to the mujaheddin infighting of the 1990s,

Afghanistan was running out of options and once more the king's name was being raised. Compared to what had followed, Zahir Shah's reign began to be spoken of fondly as a golden era in Afghan history. Average life expectancy in Afghanistan was only forty-two years so few had actually lived through it. In Quetta's Satellite Town I had seen flags and posters being prepared calling for the king's return, though typically with all things Afghan, there were rival king offices on different streets, each denouncing the other. Francesc Vendrell, Special Envoy for Afghanistan for the United Nations, which was also mooting the Zahir Shah option, explained, 'The king is a kind of dream of a peaceful and stable past. He was the only leader who did not harm the Afghans.'

This partly explained why there were so many people hanging out at the Fleming Hotel hoping to secure an appointment with His Majesty. The US State Department and the British Foreign Office had sent representatives to Olgiata, and Lakhdar Brahimi, the UN mediator, had just been to tea. Even the Northern Alliance had sent a delegation and the US Congress had authorised $400,000 for a new office. The Sandhurst-educated General Wali and his military advisors were involved in coordinating the Afghans on the ground helping guide Americans bombs onto Taliban and al Qaeda targets, and a royal website had been launched.

Homaira said the king had started leafing through old photo albums of Kabul again, after years of leaving them untouched, though he was depressed at the number of buildings that he knew had been destroyed, particularly the Kabul Museum, the Dar-ul-Aman Palace, and the experimental farm he had founded which grew seventy-six different kinds of grape and thirty-five kinds of orange. If the Taliban fell, the whole family were planning to go back. But they were wary. They had made such plans once before when the Taliban first emerged and described themselves as 'the king's soldiers'. The king had been so excited that he began packing and sent for new suitcases – 'He said the old ones were too scruffy,' said Homaira.

**BATHROS GHALI
SECRETORY GENERAL,
UNITED NATIONS,
NEW YORK, N.Y. 10017.
U.S.A**

The Afghan people has endured unprecedented hardship and misery, during the past 14 years, resulting in 1.7 million killed and producing the world's largest refugee population. Over 2 million people are physically disabled and psychologically traumatized the country littered with 10 million mines. Now the miseried have transformed to fratricide and disintegration of Afghanistan. The Afghan people highly appreciate the assistance of the American Nation in it's struggle against Communism. The salvation of the Afghan nation lies in the political process initiated by the **EX**-King of Afghanistan **H.E.**Mohammad Zahir Saha who enjoys the support of the majority of the people of Afghanistan.

Sincerely Your's,

_____

Address_____

His Majesty Mohammad Zahir Shah founder of the Constitution and father of Democracy in Afghanistan

A mild man who rarely raises his voice, Zahir Shah was clearly infuriated by being taken in by the Taliban, and by what they had done to his country after claiming to take power in his name. Homaira said the only time she had ever heard him curse was over the destruction of the Bamiyan Buddhas. The king looked pained when I asked him about this. 'From Alexander the Great to the Nazis it is astonishing what people will do for power,' he told me. 'We went backwards instead of forwards, it was unbelievable.'

He seemed to be flagging so to lighten the mood I asked his favourite memories of his country. 'I miss everything,' he said, 'I miss the mountains, the lakes, valleys, everything. But it's the small things I most remember. One of my fondest memories is going to a

King Zahir Shah and Queen Homaira (third and fourth from left) on their visit to London in 1971.

remote part of southern Afghanistan where few people venture because the people are so proud and I was walking in the forest and a small boy came up to me and took his coat off and said, "Father, Father why don't you come and sit down on my coat and have a rest." Then he pointed to a little house on a hill with smoke coming out of the chimney and said, "Father, we have simple food and a fire, please come and eat with us tonight?" I said, "Thank you very much for your kindness, I would love to but son, I'm sorry, time does not allow me."'

He said his most enjoyable trip had been that to Britain in 1971. 'Given the past experience between Afghanistan and England, all our wars, I wasn't too sure but I got the warmest reception I had ever had. The Queen for whom I have the greatest respect was the kind of personality who always made things easy for her guest. At the beginning she said to me, "Your Majesty there are lots of Afghans waiting to welcome you." When we rode out onto the Mall, I saw they were Afghan hounds!

'The Lord Mayor hosted a dinner for me at the Guildhall which was very tricky because the trumpets kept playing and I wasn't sure what I was supposed to do, or when. But it was a good trip which went a long way to thaw relations.'

Two years later, the king was back in London for an operation on his eye after which he went to Ischia to recuperate. 'An Italian Foreign Ministry official came up to me looking worried and was so nervous he just kept stuttering, saying "c . . c . . c . .". He couldn't say the word coup,' he recalled. 'At the time my feelings were numb but when he said the name of who had done it, my cousin Daoud Khan, I thought, well, he was a capable person and would at least rebuild the country. I was also very tired, you know the feeling of when you have lived in the same house too long, so I abdicated.'

I asked him if he subsequently regretted this and he fell silent. 'If I had known all the terrible things that would happen in my country, I would have taken a different decision.' He gazed into the distance with the terrible sadness of a man who clearly bears the weight on his conscience of one million of his countrymen dead, another one and a half million disabled, four million refugees, and a nation of children who have known nothing but war, and I wished I had not asked the question.

If Zahir Shah were to become king again, the scenes at the Fleming Hotel suggested that the succession battle might be bloody. The king had eight children by his wife Homaira, a cousin whom he married at sixteen. Two of their sons had died and Ahmad Shah, the crown prince, was a reserved soul who lived in Washington and spent his days writing Pashto poetry, with no interest in power. His other sons Mir Wais, Shah Mehmud, Shah Wali Shah and Nadir Shah seemed equally unenthusiastic. 'I can't imagine anything worse than being king,' Shah Wali Shah told me, a thin wire of a man who looked like an artist with his metal-rimmed spectacles and long grey ponytail. With what seemed to be exasperation, General Wali told me; 'They are a very quiet family. They shouldn't be the royal family, they just want to keep to themselves.'

While Zahir Shah's sons may not have had any interest in reclaiming the throne, his ambitious grandson was clearly desperate for a chance. Yet Mostapha had barely lived in Afghanistan, having gone from Rome to England where he was educated at Harrow Day School and Ealing College, then to university in Canada. 'What does he know of the country?' was what everyone said.

In his villa in Olgiata, watching the bombing on CNN and waiting for a signal to pack his French novels, Hermès ties and old astrakhan hat in his new suitcases, the king seemed impervious to all the machinations around him. 'At my age there is nothing that can happen to me. I just want to see a happy Afghanistan,' he said as his police guards escorted me away into the night. 'If my people want me then I will be king again.' He looked very old and frail and I suddenly remembered something General Wali had said earlier as we discussed Afghanistan's future: 'History sometimes repeats itself and if you use the same ingredients you would probably end up with the same result.'[3]

[3] The family subsequently returned to Kabul in April 2002.

Kabul, 13 November 2001

Salam Christina

Kabul is free, can you believe it! The Northern Alliance arrived at dawn from the Shomali road and we came out of our houses to welcome them and give them sweets and biscuits and throw glitter. They came on their tanks and in trucks and on foot and there was no fighting, the Taliban just left like thieves in the night.

My brothers went to follow the soldiers though my mother did not want them to in case there is fighting. It is hard to be a woman, my sister and I wished so much we could go too. One of our neighbours said he saw some dead Taliban on the main road, their trousers pulled down. That is a very bad thing.

We took our radios from their hiding places and listened all day waiting to hear about the new government which we hope will be very friendly, especially to women, and reopen the schools and give us back our jobs. Radio Afghanistan has been taken by the Northern Alliance and there was already a female announcer on the radio and also songs by Farhad Darya, a very beautiful singer who was banned by the Taliban. Do you know they smashed instruments and hung them from posts but now I pray all that is over.

My brothers have come back without beards! They say everyone is shaving them off. Our new neighbours have small children and they are laughing – their father has brought them a pink and green paper kite and it is flying high in the sky. How long it is since we heard laughter – now imagine, that was banned too.

I am so happy. I think we'll celebrate every year on this date – I marked it on the calendar with a big red circle. Now I can hear Indian music playing along the street.

This is a sweet night

Marri

5

The Sewing Circles of Herat

When your face is hidden from me, like the moon shadowed on a dark night, I
shed tears of stars and yet my night remains dark in spite of all those shining stars.

Epitaph on the poet Jami's tomb, Herat

WE SAW THE BROKEN MINARETS long before we saw Herat.
We didn't realise what they were at first. 'Look, there's a
factory,' said Justin, pointing surprised into the distance. The tall
brick stacks sticking up from the desert-floor did look like Victorian
factory chimneys in one of those industrial towns of northern Britain
though with jagged tops and leaning in different directions as if
slightly drunken. But then a patch of green came into view, a long
oasis of pine trees in the flat gravelly landscape beyond which lay the
Paropamisus Mountains, and we realised we were nearing the fabled
Persian city.

I wound down the car window expecting to breathe pine-scented
air but choking dust forced me quickly to close it. It seemed a long
time since we had given a hundred *rial* to a hunchbacked man to
push our luggage in a wheelbarrow across the no-man's-land from
the Iranian border. Waiting for us the other side was an imposing
figure in a woollen cloak and Russian bear hat who introduced himself
as Ayubi, scooped up a handful of earth which he kissed theatrically,

and said 'Welcome *my* Afghanistan'. He emphasised the word 'my' and we looked at him in awe. On his left hand he wore a large silver signet ring encrusted with turquoise and jet stones, and his eyes were full of life and fire and sadness. He exuded so much power that all the men with guns who had been circling us, rather too interested in our bags, slunk away at a single glance.

'I have instructions from Tora Ismael to escort you to Herat,' he said, speaking in formal Dari, the Afghan dialect of Persian which is spoken in the half or so of the country which is not Pashtun, and led us to a Toyota pick-up spattered with dried mud. Tora Ismael was Ismael Khan, a Tajik warlord who was the most important muja-heddin commander in western Afghanistan and had swept back into town the previous week, one day after the Taliban had left. Ayubi was his head of logistics. I smiled, enjoying the idea of being escorted by this impressive man to whom everyone seemed to bow, and feeling like one of those British envoys in the Great Game whose accounts I had read about being conducted to the courts of Afghan kings and chieftains (in some cases later to be horribly stabbed to death).

'Are you a pilgrim?' a man at Tehran airport had asked me two days earlier as I fought my way to the front of the queue for a plane-ticket to the holy city of Mashad in eastern Iran from where we would cross the border, and I nodded happily, thinking that yes, in a way I was. It was twelve years since I had last trodden the soil of the land once known as Khurasan, thirteen since I had last been in Herat, and it had been a long struggle to return.

As we squashed into the back of the jeep, two gunmen sharing the front seat next to the driver, Kalashnikov barrels sticking up between their knees, Ayubi explained it was an emotional journey for him. He had been living in Mashad (he later gave me his address there as Ice Factory Road) and had not seen his home city since September 1995 when the Taliban captured it. Ismael Khan and hundreds of his commanders had fled to Iran but Ayubi had fought to the end and been caught. For all his fierce appearance he had a poetic

Only five of the original twenty or thirty minarets still stood.

turn of phrase like the warrior poets of old. 'They beat me fourteen times but eventually I escaped and got to Mashad where my body was so broken I was in hospital for two months,' he said. 'My family thought I was dead. Now my heart beats like the wings of a bird to see my home again.'

The sign at the border to Herat said 123km but it seemed much further as the road had long ago disintegrated into scree through a combination of being bombed, driven over by tanks, and lack of any maintenance. Ahead of us lay a discarded glass Coca-Cola bottle and a burnt-out tank. It felt like driving into a wasteland. After about an hour we suddenly found ourselves on a 5km stretch of tarmac which was just long enough for me to sit back and naively say, 'Oh good, the road has been resurfaced,' and then it was back to ruts and gravel which Ayubi thought was very funny. 'Dear Christina, by the time you come back to Herat I promise you all roads will have tarmac,' he said expansively, 'even to the most small places.' After a while we drew behind an overloaded truck of Japanese televisions. The Taliban had fled from Herat the previous week, two days after abandoning Kabul to the Northern Alliance with barely a shot fired, though they were still defending their stronghold of Kandahar in the south, and the Heratis were obviously already shopping.

Like the television truck, our pick-up was rocking as much as a ship on a rough sea and by the time the minarets came into view we were in a kind of stupor induced by bumping all afternoon across the desert in a trail of dust. We had had nothing to eat but a packet of hard vanilla biscuits and, between the clouds of grey blown up by other vehicles, there was nothing to see but a few small groups of camels or the occasional lone figure swathed in cloths and turban, rifle over the shoulder, standing gazing into nowhere, like the illustration of an Afghan tribesman in a Victorian book. Justin and Ayubi fell asleep, jerking awake again every time their heads banged against the window. Once, I noticed the ruins of an old fort just off the road and wanted to investigate but the driver laughed, saying the area was land-mined and that if we stopped, we would be robbed by bandits or attacked by Taliban. Spontaneity had become a dangerous pursuit in Afghanistan.

As the light faded to pale apricot and the dust rose, the figures took on a ghostly appearance and the whole journey began to assume a surreal hue. Once, some years before on the other side of the world in Zambia, a man in a government office where I was trying to buy a map had questioned what I was doing there. He did not seem to understand the concept of foreign correspondent, instead asking me, 'Are you an explorer?' I told the official that I tried to go and find unreported places and people to write about. For a moment he looked confused, then he nodded vigorously, 'Ah, I see, you are an old-fashioned voyager.'

Back in Afghanistan, that's what I felt like, an old-fashioned voy-

ager, though I suspected the road to Herat was worse than it had
been a hundred years before. Robert Byron, Peter Levi, Eric Newby,
Bruce Chatwin and almost every British writer that has travelled in
Afghanistan all waxed lyrical on the quality of light, describing arriving
in the country as like 'coming up for air', and of air as 'crisp and light
as champagne', and so it was. 'Here at last is Asia without an inferiority
complex,' wrote Byron in his classic *The Road to Oxiana* of arriving
in Herat in November 1933, shortly after the assassination of Zahir
Shah's father, King Nadir Shah, the country then as now in turmoil.

But I didn't feel elated or champagne-high. Instead I felt strangely
disconnected as though watching what was happening from outside
on some grainy film. I had only ever been in Afghanistan in war and
kept expecting to hear the boom-boom of cluster bombs and loud
throbbing of gunships filling the sky and see people with panicked
faces running toward us as they had at Jalalabad.

Going back is a hazardous endeavour. I was scared that I had
remembered Afghanistan as more than it was because what I was
really remembering was being young and fearless with a sense of
everything in life still to come. Over the years I had edited out the
death and destruction, keeping only the snow-capped peaks, orchards,
streams, wild-eyed warriors on motorbikes with marigolds sticking
out of their guns, crossing rivers on inflated goatskins and sleeping
under stars. But as if the past had been waiting for me, now I was
back in the country, I vividly recalled the afternoon dust-storms that
matted the hair, clogged the mouth and caked the perspiration on
the face, and endless journeys on destroyed roads through grey
deserts, head pounding from lack of food or drink and excess of
music. The driver had been playing his favourite Pashto tape ever
since we crossed the border, a monotonous nasal whine, but after so
many years of music being banned by the Taliban, I did not have
the heart to ask him to turn it off.

It was dusk as we drove through the city checkpoint and into
Herat, waved through cheerily by the men of Ismael Khan whose

merriment looked as though it might have been enhanced by artificial substances. Nearer now, and out of the dust-storm we could see that the minarets were more than one hundred feet tall which was why they had been visible from such a distance and there were five of them, four in a square and another some distance away. One was slightly fatter than the others and looked as if it had had a large bite taken out of the side. The minarets were in the old part of the city and we headed for the new part, drawing up at the Mowafaq, Herat's only hotel, and a place one had to be careful how to pronounce. Just in front was a busy crossroads with a traffic island where the Taliban used to hang their victims and according to the driver had bodies hanging there as recently as two weeks before. The name of the crossroads was Gul, which means "Flower' in Dari and Pashto. As we opened the doors of the car, women in faded blue burqas clawed at us for money, but were cuffed away by our guards. Knowing these must be war widows, I wanted to protest, but Ayubi winked at me and slipped them some notes, then bowed to us in farewell.

'I have to report the successful completion of my mission to Tora Ismael,' he said, 'now you will rest and I will come for you to present you to him.'

I started to ask what time, in my British way, but he had wrapped his cloak around him and was gone, striding off with people clearing the way in front.

On the steps of the hotel a polite young man in a pinstriped suit several sizes too big addressed me in perfect English. 'Excuse me, are you Britisher?'

'Yes,' I replied, stepping back. He had come so close he was almost touching me.

'You are the first real Britisher I have met. Do you mind if I ask you a question?'

'Not at all. Go ahead.'

'Can you please tell me how many positive adjectives are there in the English language?'

Ayubi.

Since the Taliban had ridden into town in their tinted-windowed jeeps six and a half years before, patrolling the streets with their Moral Police, it would have been impossible for this man to speak openly to a Western woman. Now he finally had the opportunity and his first question was on a point of grammar. To my shame I didn't have a clue.

We both stood there silent for a while, dissatisfied by the encounter. In my bag I had a bundle of pens to give to children and I wondered whether to offer him one, but it didn't seem quite appropriate.

'Oh well, I was extremely honoured to meet you,' he said eventually and walked away.

The lobby of the Mowafaq was dark and foreboding, the dusty glass reception cubicle empty apart from a black Bakelite telephone that was not connected to anything. But the worn red carpet up the stairs and the rubble-filled swimming pool out the back suggested the hotel might once have had pretensions of grandeur. A small man with a permanently surprised expression, who looked like a young Charlie Chaplin with a tuft of black hair, thin black tie and white shirt, but without the moustache or bowler hat, appeared from the back and led us upstairs to the restaurant to be registered in a large ledger. The restaurant was busy with turbaned men who were scooping up rice with their hands and looked too big for the small white plastic tables, like a feast of Henry VIII and his cohorts on picnic furniture, and it was lit by pink and green neon strips which kept flashing on and off with the vagaries of the power-supply.

It was *iftar*, the time of the day during Ramadan when the fast is finally broken, first with a palm-date, then a large meal, and the men were noisily slurping from plates of rice and meat. The restaurant had a printed menu card with various dishes so we sat down at one of the tables overlooking the traffic island and started making our selection.

'A lamb kebab and *qabli* rice, please,' I said in Dari to a sullen young boy who had come to take our order.

The boy looked up from his feet then laughed. Presuming he was not comprehending my accent, I pointed at the item on the menu.

'No,' he said. 'Eggs.'

'What about what they are eating?' I gestured towards the men in turbans.

'Finished. Eggs.'

The ancient Greek historian Herodotus had referred to Herat as 'the breadbasket of Central Asia' but things had clearly changed. The illuminated glass refrigerator case in the dining room contained only a pot of pink jam and some rusted cans of Russian peas and the shops in the bazaar had nothing but Iranian mango juice, and we were ridiculously delighted when one day we came across a boy selling a wheelbarrow of American food parcels, dropped from the sky in between bombs in yellow plastic packets marked 'A Gift from the People of the United States'. Inside were sachets of peanut butter

*Begging for nan: a quarter of all Afghan children die
before they reach the age of five.*

and strawberry jam, pop tarts and boil-in-the-bag herb rice. It was
hard to imagine what an Afghan might make of this.

That first night, the eggs arrived pale and wan and swimming in
oil, a fly trapped in the white. Across the room the turbaned men
were gnawing on chicken bones, soaking up the last juices on their
plates with bread then gobbing noisily into a rusty spittoon. After a
while they all got up, slung their guns on their backs and left, looking
well-sated, in order to get home before the nine o'clock curfew. The
timing of curfew was random as none of the mujaheddin on the
checkpoints had watches but we knew it had started because there
was a guard post just in front of our hotel and every time a car or
bicycle approached, men jumped out into the road, thrusting their
Kalashnikovs in front and shouting 'Kalash!' in a fearsome way.

The pink and green lights of the restaurant flashed twice then went
off, pitching us into darkness, and there seemed to be nothing to do
but fumble our way up the stairs to our rooms and sleep. The door

to the terrace was ajar, a moonbeam stretching across the corridor and the old man employed to sweep the floors with a brush of birch twigs gestured to me to follow him outside. By night, the destruction and the colourlessness of the landscape were not visible and the brilliance of the moonlight in the clear air highlighted the domes and the minarets. I caught my breath the way one does in front of a work of great art or listening to a sublime pianist play Schubert *Impromptus* and the old man who had never seen or heard such things grinned, satisfied.

Back in Afghanistan. I went to bed with all the excitement of a child on Christmas Eve, not caring that the bombing had blown out the glass from the window of my bedroom and the plastic sheeting which had replaced it let in a stream of freezing wind. Sleep did not come readily. Apart from the flapping of the plastic, there seemed to be a colony of wild dogs on the pavement below, and cries of 'Kalash!' echoed throughout the night.

The next morning, woken at 4.30 a.m. by the call for breakfast before the day's fast began to find that the basin had iced over, I went back out to the terrace. In the dawn sun the minarets seemed to be sparkling. There had once been four or five times as many and, although they looked plain brick from a distance, they had been covered by turquoise, grape-blue and opal glazed tiles in intricate designs and formed part of a *musalla* or religious college so spectacular that Byron wrote on seeing the ruins, 'there was never such a mosque before or since'. Only a few pieces of faience on the towers remained, and it was these that were catching the light, a small reminder that back in the fifteenth century, while Europe was undergoing its own Renaissance, Herat had been a city of great wealth and splendour. I shared the excitement of Byron who felt he had discovered the long-forgotten capital of the Oriental Medicis.

In the other direction I could see a huge baked brick citadel of thick walls and turrets, dominating the city on a large mound that was thought to contain the ruins of the fortress of Alexander the

Great but had never been excavated, and the whole surrounded by a dry moat. It looked like the sort of fairytale fort a child might draw, but over the centuries its ramparts had frequently been used to display the heads of enemies and few places in Central Asia had seen so many bloody battles. Both Genghis Khan and later Timur (or Tamerlane as we know him in the West from Timur-i-lang or Timur the Lame because an arrow wound had left him with a limp) had fought beneath its massive walls in their bids to conquer the world. Genghis Khan is said to have wiped out all but forty of the city's 160,000 inhabitants.

Herat's location as both an ancient crossroads of trade caravans and part of the traditional conquerors' route to India had always attracted invaders, and in the nineteenth century a series of young British officers passed through on Great Game reconnaissance missions, fearing that the Russians would use the route to invade India from the west. The first of these was Captain Charles Christie,[1] who entered the gates of the great walled city in 1810 posing as a horse-dealer but was in fact an agent for the East India Company trying to find out the plans of Tsar Nicholas. Spending a month there, impressed by the fertile valley surrounded by vast deserts, he was dismissive of the citadel, writing, 'on the whole it is very contemptible as a fortification'.

His view that the citadel had no hope of holding out against a modern European army was to be proved right more than a century and a half later when the Red Army swept into town. No city suffered more than Herat under the Soviet occupation. In protest to the Communist takeover around a hundred Russians were killed in an uprising in 1979 led by Ismael Khan who was then a major in the Afghan army. Publicly hacked to death, their heads were paraded on spikes around the city. A furious Kremlin sent in tanks and helicopter gunships which for three days pounded the city, pulverising buildings,

---

[1] Christie claimed to have been only the second European to enter Herat. He was killed two years later in a Russian attack while seconded as a military advisor to the crown prince of Persia, Abbas Mirza.

destroying one of the minarets and leaving a hole in another, and killing an estimated 24,000 people.

If the Russians were hated by the Heratis, the Taliban were despised. When the Taliban took the city in 1995 not a single Herati was drafted into their administration. The Heratis and their liberal history in which a woman had played such a key role in the city's cultural heritage, as well as their large Shia minority, were anathema to the uneducated village mullahs of the Taliban. To put the Heratis in their place, they referred to them as 'strangers', banned speaking of Persian, closed the city's historic female bath-houses which were the only places where hot water was available, forbade visits to the many shrines of Sufi saints, and whitewashed over a mural in the Governor's office showing five hundred years of Herat history. The painting had been the lifework of artist Mohammed Sayed Mashal, his gift to the city he loved, and he died shortly after its destruction. Although the official cause of death was lung disease, most Heratis believe he died of a broken heart.

Now these latest invaders were gone and standing on the terrace, looking across all these centuries of history and bloodshed in the pale winter sunshine, I suddenly caught the scent of pines that I remembered from my last visit when Herat was still under Russian occupation.

Down below, the sunrise had brought on the day, bringing everyone out as suddenly as if a switch had been flicked. Pony traps with red tasselled bridles jingled by as well as large men wobbling along on small bicycles and the occasional pick-up full of gunmen. On a verge by the road a man was setting up an old box camera, placing a stool for his clients to sit solemnly in front of a painted backdrop of a Tyrolean meadow full of gaudy pink and yellow flowers. A traffic policeman with a white jacket, a peaked cap and a hand-held Stop sign had even appeared at the traffic island and seemed to be laughing though everyone was ignoring his frantic signalling.

The hotel was on the corner of two wide treelined avenues, Blood-bank Street and Cinema Street. I chose to explore the latter, though the cinema had been demolished by the Taliban. A crowd of beggar women and children quickly collected in my wake, tugging at my clothes. Looking for a place to escape, I ducked into a gateway just along from the hotel. A path led to a white colonial-style building with a sign saying in English and Persian *Literary Circle of Herat*.

I stared at it, intrigued. First settled five thousand years ago, Herat has always been regarded as the cradle of Afghan civilisation, so renowned as a centre of culture and learning that one of its leading patrons of arts in the fifteenth century, Ali Sher Nawa'i, claimed, 'here in Herat one cannot stretch out a leg without poking a poet in the ass'. Babur, the first Moghul Emperor, descended from Tamerlane on his father's side (and Genghis Khan on his mother's), visited his cousins in Herat in 1506, only a year before it fell to the Uzbeks. In his memoir *The Baburnama*,[2] a sort of personal odyssey which tells of what he calls his 'throneless years' wandering Central Asia in search of a kingdom, having lost his own tiny Ferghana, he wrote of the city being 'filled with learned and matchless men'.

Herat's golden era was under Queen Gowhar Shad, wife of Tamerlane's youngest son, Shah Rukh. The name of Herat's most important queen is almost unknown in the West but she used her power as wife of a ruler whose empire stretched from Turkey to China to find and promote the best architects to carry out such grand projects as the ruined *musalla*. She also sponsored painters, calligraphers and poets, usually in the romantic language of Persian even though the Timurids themselves were Turkish-speaking. One of her protégés was Abdur Rahman Jami, widely considered the

[2] Written in Chagatai Turkish, the language of the Timurids, rather than Persian, the lingua franca of Central Asia at that time, it became a sort of handbook for Moghul rulers and was widely copied, but the original version was last seen during the reign of Emperor Shah Jahan.

greatest-ever Persian poet with his prolific outpouring of *ghazals* and couplets. Her court artist Bihzad is regarded as the master of Persian miniatures for his intricate depictions of hunting scenes and chivalrous encounters between tall princes and reclining maidens in intense colours such as deep lapis blue made from powdered jewels. One of the first miniaturists to sign his paintings, he headed the Herat Academy from 1468 to 1506 and became so famous that many miniaturists tried to emulate his style, signing their work 'Worthy of Bihzad', though Babur was characteristically frank, writing, 'he painted extremely delicately but he made the faces of beardless people badly by drawing the double chin too big'.

Over the years the city had been sacked so many times that it was hard to imagine any of this artistic spirit had survived. The door of the Literary Circle was open and I walked in, unsure what I would find. The building seemed to rumble in protest as overhead planes flew low, American bombers heading south to Kandahar where the Taliban were threatening to fight to the last after Mullah Omar had announced that he had had another dream that he would stay in power. The rooms were bare and deserted but I noticed a pair of scuffed black sandals outside a door on the left. Inside a man in a black polo neck who looked like a young Robert de Niro was sitting at a desk moodily staring into space. He introduced himself as Ahmed Said Haghighi, the society's president, and invited me to sit down.

I asked him how the Circle had survived the onslaught on culture of the Taliban years and he smiled wearily. 'It was not just those years,' he said. 'Here in Herat we've been fighting a war on culture for hundreds of years. Ever since the death of Queen Gowhar Shad you could say.'

'How old is the Literary Circle then?'

'It was founded in 1920 by the poets of the city to make known the rich culture and heritage of Herat. We used to have literary evenings when people would come and read their works but we've always been opposed by governments. Many times the doors of this place have been shut down. The Communists locked up many intellectuals and when the Russians came in 1980 they wanted to turn this into an institute of propaganda so many of our members fled to Iran. But the Taliban was the worst time. First they tried to turn us into a propaganda voice, then they came and padlocked the door and publicly whipped our members so we were forced to become an underground movement, meeting in members' houses to secretly read stories and poems.'

On the shelves were piles of stapled papers that looked like a monthly journal. 'Yes, we call it the Eighth Orang, it means throne in English, after a poem called *Haft Orang*[3], the *Seven Thrones* written by Jami, the most famous poet of Herat, during the most turbulent years of the Timurid Empire. We thought if he could write such a work at that time then why shouldn't we in our difficult time.'

I was surprised that they had been able to get it past the head of censorship. 'The Taliban were stupid,' he replied. 'They didn't realise what we were writing. We used symbolic language as in any totalitarian state to convey our messages. Some writers used devices such as the discourse of birds and animals.'

He fell silent and I wondered if I should leave. There was not even a paraffin heater in the room and in the sub-zero temperature my feet felt like blocks of ice, but then he started speaking again without looking at me.

'In other cities, where there had been fighting between factions and lots of crime and insecurity, when the Taliban came they were greeted with relief. But we had not had those problems. So to us they were simply a bunch of illiterate religious fanatics who did not speak our language and had come to make life difficult for us. Barbarians who hung people from electricity poles and crossroads. One day I counted eighteen people hanging. Can you imagine seeing that?

[3] This is also the Persian name for the constellation Ursa Major.

'It was particularly hard for our female members. They closed the girls' schools and banned women from the university, initially saying this was temporary while they worked things out. But then they captured Kabul and started turning girls' schools into mosques, banned our language and stopped paying women teachers, so we knew. For a while we waited, hoping they would be defeated but when it became clear that they were going to retain control of Herat we sat around discussing what we could do to stop the culture of our city dying and to help our girls. There was only one thing we could think of.'

'What was that?' I asked. Haghighi studied me for a moment as if trying to make his mind up about something. I shifted in my seat and found myself pulling forward my scarf which was always slipping off my hair, already feeling uncomfortable to be stared at so openly in a land where men usually do anything to avoid a woman's gaze. He pushed his chair back from the table and got up.

'Come with me.'

His brusque tone brooked no possibility of asking where we were going and I found myself following meekly as he walked quickly along the road back past the hotel, across the Flower traffic island with the laughing traffic policeman, past Aziz barber's shop which was busy with men shaving off their beards, and down a small mud-walled alleyway. Some way along by a doorway on the left was a blue sign. *Golden Needle, Ladies' Sewing Classes, Mondays, Wednesdays, Saturdays.*

'This is what we did,' he said. I stared uncomprehendingly. 'The one activity which women could do and involved lots of coming and going was making clothes,' he explained. The innocuous plaque masked an underground network of writers and poets, who had become the focus of resistance in this ancient city, risking their lives for literature and to educate women.

Three times a week for the previous five years, young women, faces and bodies disguised by their Taliban-enforced uniforms of

The entrance to the Golden Needle.

washed-out blue burqas and flat shoes, would knock at the yellow wrought-iron door. In their handbags, concealed under scissors, cottons, sequins and pieces of material, were notebooks and pens. Had the authorities investigated they would have discovered that the dressmaking students never made any clothes. The house belonged to Mohammed Nasir Rahiyab, a forty-seven-year-old literature professor from Herat University, and, once inside, the women would pull off their burqas, sit on cushions around a blackboard and listen to him teach forbidden subjects such as literary criticism, aesthetics and Persian poetry as well as be introduced to foreign classics by Shakespeare, James Joyce and Nabokov.

Mr Haghighi banged on the door and it was opened by a small boy who showed us into a long windowless room with cushions on the floor, a board at one end, an oil painting of a man at a desk, and some glass wall-cases containing a few books including a Persian-English dictionary, some volumes of Persian poetry, and a book in English on Poisoning. Professor Rahiyab came and sat down with us beneath his own portrait, and a flask of green tea and a dish of pistachios were brought even though it was Ramadan. 'I don't go to the mosque,' he explained with a shrug. He was a shy soft-spoken man who only became passionate when talking about his beloved Russian writers and he showed me his bust of Pushkin, which he used to keep hidden, only taking it out for the classes.

While lessons were underway his children would be sent to play in the alleyway outside. If a Talib or any stranger approached, one of the children would slip in to warn him and he would then escape into his study with his books while his place running the class was quickly taken by his wife holding up a half-finished garment which they always kept ready.

Only once were they almost exposed when the professor's daughter was ill in bed and his son had run to buy bread so there was no one to raise the alarm when a black turbaned Talib rapped at the door.

Literary Circle President Ahmed Said Haghighi
in the classroom of the Golden Needle.

'Suddenly he was in the courtyard outside. I just got out of the room in time and my wife ran in and the girls hid their books under the cushions. I realised that I had not cleaned the board or hidden Pushkin. I sat in the other room, drinking tea, my hand shaking so much my cup was rattling. Fortunately the Taliban were such ignorant people they did not know what they were seeing.'

In a society where even teaching one's own daughter to read was a crime, the Sewing Circle was a venture that could easily have ended in more bodies swinging above Gul Crossroads and I asked the professor why he had taken such a risk.

'If the authorities had known that we were not only teaching women but teaching them high levels of literature we would have been killed,' he replied. 'But a lot of fighters sacrificed their lives over the years for the freedom of this city. Shouldn't a person of letters make that sacrifice too?

'We were poor in everyday life,' he added. 'Why should we be poor in culture too? If we had not done what we did to keep up the literary spirit of the city, the depth of our tragedy would have been even greater.'

To lessen suspicion, Professor Rahiyab never openly criticised the regime and carried on quietly teaching his male students at the university, even though the Taliban had decimated his syllabus, forcing him to replace most of his literature classes with lectures on Islamic culture and Shariat and insisting the only books he use were those which he said were 'brought from the mosque'. Literary Theory was reduced from ten hours to two hours a week, European Literature scrapped altogether, and Islamic Culture increased from four hours to fourteen hours. 'I had an extremely long beard,' he added, rubbing his close-shaven chin with a wry smile.

Inspired by the *Golden Needle*, hundreds of similar courses were held all over the city, mostly in central places where there were lots of comings and goings so a few more would not draw too much attention. Some of the Literary Circle's writers even disguised themselves in burqas to go to women's houses to teach. A Unicef official later told me that an estimated 29,000 girls and women in Herat province received some form of secret education while the city was under Taliban control.

'A society needs poets and storytellers to reflect its pain – and joy,' said Professor Rahiyab as we got up to leave. 'A society without literature is a society that is not rich and does not have a strong core. If there wasn't so much illiteracy and lack of culture in Afghanistan then terrorism would never have found its cradle here.'

One of the professor's students at the *Golden Needle* was a feisty twenty-three-year-old called Zena Karamzade, and Mr Haghighi arranged for me to meet her in the public library, next door to the Literary Circle. She arrived with her friend Leyla Razeghi, two shapeless figures in burqas who could have been anyone until they disrobed to reveal attractive young women with strong faces and fair complexions, and I wondered how women in burqas ever identified each other. The library was even bleaker and colder than the Literary Circle, again no heater, a long white room furnished with just a table and chairs, its tall green-painted windows looking out onto the bare branches of winter trees. 'How do you like our library?' laughed Zena, gesturing around. 'We call this the book graveyard.'

Almost all the shelves were empty except for a bookcase at one end of heavy religious volumes with gold engraved titles like the ones I had seen in Haqqania, and another with a few tattered foreign paperbacks including *Moby Dick*, a 1965 *World Almanac*, a book entitled *Book of the Eskimo* and one called *The Road to Huddersfield*.

'What happened?' I asked. 'It was the Taliban,' replied a white-bearded old man who came over and introduced himself as Zare Husseini, the librarian. 'I am sixty and I have worked here forty-one years,' he said. 'This was a good library. We had twenty-five thousand books and magazines and many people came here. But then last year the Taliban came and took the books. They came one afternoon in pick-ups and big trucks. It was the Governor of Herat, the head of censorship, and thirty Taliban soldiers. They told me all books 'contrary to the tastes and beliefs of Sunnis must be confiscated as well as any books containing pictures, any books published in Iran or in the West, and any political books, particularly from the Communist era. That didn't really leave anything so they began packing them all up. I was the guardian of these books but there was nothing I could do.

'I even helped them pack because they hit me with their Kalashnikovs.' His rheumy old eyes began to water and he shook his head. 'Later we heard they had burned them on an enormous pyre outside the city.

'That's what they brought in their place.' He pointed to the case of religious volumes. 'Nobody reads them,' he said. 'They are all written in Arabic which no one here speaks and on subjects like the jurisprudence of Islam which are far too theoretical.'

Herat Museum was also raided, removing statues, vases and jars said to date from Alexander's time, and ancient manuscripts. The only non-religious books saved by the library were a few boxes that Mr Haghighi's Literary Circle had managed to remove earlier when they were tipped off that the Taliban were coming. They buried them in the ruins of an old theatre in the garden next door as well as under the lavatories of an abandoned youth centre. It was these, including *Moby Dick*, that had been returned to the shelves.

While many of the historic handwritten books from Herat Museum were taken out of the country and sold in Pakistan, a representative from the Taliban Ministry of Culture was stationed on the border to stop new books coming into the country. 'They weren't very clever though,' said Haghighi. 'We managed to bring some in hidden among car parts.'

Zena had been a second-year medical student at Herat University when the Taliban came and abolished female education. 'I had always dreamed of being a doctor. If the Taliban hadn't come I would be practising by now. Instead ... well, if I was to tell you the whole story it would take many days but what I can tell you is we didn't live under the Taliban, we just stayed in our rooms doing nothing like cows in their sheds.

'We had no communication with the rest of the world or even outside our home, we couldn't listen to television or radio or see our friends. Even to go to a doctor we had to be accompanied by our husband or father who would speak for us or we would be whipped. There was just one dentist here in Herat who still treated women and when the Taliban found out they arrested him and beat all the patients.

'We could not have come to this library as the Taliban would have said what business do you girls have with these books? Even the shopping was done by men. Women were treated like parasites in this society.'

As Zena spoke her eyes burnt with injustice and her breath made clouds of steam in the cold air. Outside sparrows chattered in the trees, the last few autumn leaves floated to the ground, and rickshaw horns clamoured in the street. I wondered what it was really like to live a life where all this was reduced to small pieces seen through a mesh grille, and I asked their feelings about the burqa.

'The burqa existed before the Taliban but few women here wore it and in the first year of Taliban they did not make us,' replied Zena. 'But later they insisted and that was awful.'

'It was like being in a cage,' interjected her friend Leyla, who was smaller and rounder but with expressive dark eyes and who had, until then, been listening, nodding occasionally.

'No, it was worse than that,' argued Zena. 'We would breathe out carbon dioxide and not get enough oxygen in because it was a closed space with restricted fresh air coming through so after a while your lungs would feel like exploding and you thought you would suffocate. Also if you were walking with the sun in front it blinded you and you could totter and fall.

'We survived only in the hope that the schools would reopen or somehow the Taliban would go. I tried to keep my brain alive by doing mathematical formulae and would often stay up till 3 a.m. doing them secretly. It became an obsession as if the moment I stopped doing calculus I would die and I was terrified of running out of equations to solve. The only time we felt human was in the sewing classes. If I'd known at the beginning that the Taliban would be here seven years I would have committed suicide.'

It was Leyla, herself an aspiring writer, who had first heard about the *Golden Needle*. 'I knew Professor Rahiyab through the Literary Circle and we arranged that he would come to my house to give lessons to five of us. If anyone came we were to say he was my uncle. He told us about great writers like Shakespeare, Dostoyevsky, Kafka, James Joyce and Alexander Dumas and taught us things like philosophy of aesthetics. For those few hours it was like being in another world. Of course if we had been found out we would have been killed.'

With his encouragement the twenty-four-year-old had already completed two novels, one about forced marriage called *Mirage* and another called *Beyond Our Vision*, the story of a girl whose father dies in the fighting, leaving her to support the family. Both had been painstakingly written out in Persian script, the manuscripts worn thin and almost damp from being worked over and over as it was not easy to obtain large amounts of paper without raising suspicion. She had also written some thirty short stories of which seven had been published in the Literary Circle's journal. Published under male pseudonyms to protect her identity and based on one theme – life for women under the Taliban –her stories used metaphors to criticise the regime.

'I wrote one called *Habari Bosh* which means *The Good News* and was a monologue of a woman called Rusa writing of her frustration at not being able to study because of a sick relative and watching her brothers all go off to school and university while she is stuck in this dark closed-in sickroom.'

Yet it wasn't just the restrictions on their own lives that both of the girls were angry about: 'Herat was always known as the city of mysticism and knowledge, you might have heard of our great Queen Gowhar Shad, and we felt we had a duty to continue that tradition,' said Zena. 'But the Taliban managed to damage our culture so much.

'To give you an example, because women were at home all day with nothing to do, cosmetics became very popular even though they were banned by the Taliban. My friends or sisters would spend all day putting on make-up and get their husbands or fathers to bring materials to make clothes. They became obsessed by getting the latest lipsticks smuggled in from Iran or Pakistan. Girls also started getting married younger again, at thirteen because there was nothing else for them to do.

'Also, as any kind of games and get-togethers were all banned and local television was abandoned, many people bought satellite dishes or VCRs to watch foreign programmes. In our neighbourhood I think for every five houses, two would have satellite dishes even if they were very poor. People would not eat in order to afford a dish or video because there was nothing out there. Of course it was prohibited and when Taliban caught them they would be arrested, beaten black and blue and paraded round the city with the television around their neck but people carried on.

'The videos had to be smuggled in secretly and there were just a few which were passed around. Sometimes there were American movies, like I remember *Titanic* coming and everyone wanted *Titanic* hairstyles and clothes and there were secret tapes of the music and all the girls fell in love with Leonardo di Caprio. Even the men wanted the same floppy hair as him with their Taliban beards. But mostly people preferred the Hindi movies because the American ones were often violent and as they saw beating here on the streets every day they were fed up with it, while the Indian ones always had good endings where the oppressed person finally wins out so it gave us a good feeling. You can imagine the effect of people being indoors all the time and watching these films over and over again. Our young speak Hindi and know all the names of the Indian actors and actresses yet know nothing of history or of the great figures of our past. They probably have never heard of Bihzad or Gowhar Shad.'

I was surprised that so many people had got away with breaking Taliban laws in Herat but Leyla had an explanation. 'In some ways it was easier than in other places as here they were so hated no one cooperated with them so our secrets were not revealed. And the Taliban were so obvious here. They dressed differently and spoke differently to us.'

Zena and Leyla risked imprisonment and beatings to study literature.

The new Governor Ismael Khan was said to be anxious to restart female education and I asked Zena if she intended to go back to medical school once the university reopened for women. She shook her head. 'I cannot go through all those years of study now. The Taliban destroyed all our university records so we would have to start all over again and I am already twenty-four. Besides how can I be a doctor and treat people? I am too traumatised myself.'

I was sorry to say goodbye to these brave young women. They invited me to a dinner in a nearby hotel to celebrate the first open meeting of the Literary Circle with women and apologised that they could not stay longer or invite me to their homes. 'The Taliban have changed our customs so much,' said Zena, shaking her head sadly. 'Once we would have been proud to have had a foreigner to our home. But now my father would be very unhappy if he knew I was here. It is still early days after the Taliban. Who knows what will happen?'

They gathered up their burqas and slid the heavy folds of cotton draping from embroidered caps over their heads so that the grilles of tiny holes were over their faces, and left the library, their voices muffled as they bid me goodbye. Whereas the women in Iran had looked chic, almost sexy, in their fitted long coats and headscarves, this seemed to me a garment that could only have been designed by a man who really despised women. I stood at the door, watching Zena and Leyla walk away. Their shoulders had stooped and whole personalities seemed to have been subsumed into the blue shrouds and soon they were invisible among the other burqas shuffling along the pavement.

I first heard the name Khafash at the Literary Circle dinner. He wasn't there but everyone kept asking me if I had met him. He was a poet, they said, and from the way they spoke of him some kind of hero of the anti-Taliban resistance and he had an intriguing address. 'Go to Camel Stable Lane and everybody there knows him.'

Following directions for Camel Stable Lane the next afternoon, I found myself lost in a maze of mud alleys and dried-up canals behind the main road to the military base. It had been further to walk than I had imagined and the winter sun was already blotting into the horizon as I started asking for his house. A man installing a television aerial on a mud roof pointed me in one direction while a toothless fellow pulling a donkey bearing such a huge pile of grass that only its hooves and a small portion of its head was visible, pointed the opposite way.

Finally, after I was convinced we were walking in circles, a group of children who had been following me screeched to a halt in front of a red-painted door, chanting, 'Khafash! Khafash!' There was a gruff shout from somewhere upstairs and the children ran away. A small boy opened the door and summoned me up some outside stairs. At the top I was shown into a long room with plate glass at one end

looking out to the minarets. At the other end was a plywood wall
with a plastic gilt clock of the kind one often sees in Chinese restaurants while the in-between walls were lined from floor to ceiling
with shelves of books, mostly in Persian, including Sadi's *Rose Garden,*
Firdosi's epic *Shahnama, Book of Kings*[4] and the verses of Rumi and
Hafiz. In the centre a paraffin stove was clanking and billowing out
smoke, and seated cross-legged on a cushion next to it was Naser
Khafash.

My first reaction was disappointment. He was a short squat man
with a long grey beard and a bald head too large for his body and
did not look at all heroic, more like a holy man one might find
chanting at a Sufi shrine. I later found out he was fifty-five but he
looked much older. Waving away my apologies for arriving unan-
nounced, he gestured to me to sit down then taking my business
card with his left hand, frowned at it, while his right hand clicked a
long chain of amber worry beads back and forth between his thumb
and index finger. 'Ninety-nine,' he suddenly said, gesturing at the
beads, 'one for every name of Allah.'

I took that as a cue that my audience had begun so I asked him
how difficult it had been to work as a poet during the Taliban. His
answer was similar to that of Mr Haghighi though I sensed there was
little love lost between the two men. 'It was not just the Taliban,' he
replied. 'We have had years of suffering in this city. Only in the
Timurid era did our poetry have a one hundred and fifty years of
peace to blossom and tell tales of love and beauty. Since then it has
reflected only pain. But until the Russians came we did have theatres
and libraries and poets in the city. I would say we had about a

---

[4] The bible of Persian nationalists, the *Shahnama* took thirty-five years to write. Firdosi
was seventy-five years old in 1010 when it was complete and he presented it to Mahmud,
the ruler of Khurasan, expecting a handsome reward. Instead the sum was so paltry that
he gave it to a bath-house attendant in contempt and went into hiding, writing satirical
verses about Mahmud. Years later Mahmud repented his shabby treatment of the poet
and sent 60,000 dinars – one for each verse – on camels to his home town. As the camels
entered one gate, the poet's body was carried out of another.

LEFT The entrance to the Great Mosque in Herat founded by the Ghorids in 1200.

BELOW Glass from Sultan Hamidy's famous shop in Herat.

BOTTOM The shrine at Mazar-i-Sharif with doves flying in the foreground.

LEFT Fifteenth-century Persian miniature of Tamerlane besieging Herat: during the Timurid reign Herat was th[e] leading centre for miniatures.

ABOVE Dr William Brydon, painted by Lady Elizabeth Butler, was said to be the only survivor of the 1842 British retreat from Kabul.

In 1841 Afghan forces rose against the British Garrison in Kabul and attacked the house of Alexander Burnes, killing him, his brother and Lieutenant Broadfoot.

CENTRE Painting of a Kandahar lady smoking in her chamber.

ABOVE Amir Dost Mohammed became kin[g] for the second time in 1843 after his son's forces defeated the British in the First Afghan war.

British-backed King Abdur Rahman crushed over forty revolts in his twenty-one year reign (1880–1901).

RIGHT King Amanullah (seen here in 1929 while on a Grand Tour of Europe) scandalised Kabul by removing the veil of his wife Queen Soraya.

RIGHT King Zahir's eldest daughter Princess Bilquis (centre), her husband General Abdul Wali, and daughters in traditional dress in the gardens of the palace in Kabul *c* 1970.

ABOVE King Zahir Shah in exile in Rome in 2002, beneath a portrait of his late father King Nadir Shah.

ABOVE The Red Army entering Afghanistan, Christmas 1979.

RIGHT More than one million Afghans were killed during the Soviet occupation.

BELOW Mujaheddin, photographed by the author, on a captured Russian tank, Kandahar, 1988.

ABOVE Afghanistan is dotted with mujaheddin graveyards.

LEFT The old Afghan practice of severing the heads of captives was revived during the *jihad* against the Russians.

BELOW The traditional Afghan game of *buzkashi*, polo played with a goat – or a prisoner's head, as ball.

A young boy flies a kite in Kabul after the departure of the Taliban, February 2002.

Izatullah, one of Kabul's leading kitemakers, was jailed by the Taliban and all his kites burnt.

The author crossing into western Afghanistan after twelve years away, November 2001.

Women in Herat window-shopping for white shoes and shoes with heels that had been banned by the Taliban, November 2001.

The fourth-century, 170-feet high giant Buddha of Bamiyan before and after destruction by the Taliban in February 2001.

Refugee children in Maslakh camp, Herat, forced from their homes by the twenty-three years of war.

thousand intellectuals. Many of the enlightened ones then left. For the twenty years after the Russian invasion poetry was limited to verses created for consumption on the battlefield. Then for the past six or seven years of Taliban it became hidden literature and if they found one of those poems they would execute the writer. So most of our poets left the country and those who stayed were scared.'

Why hadn't he left, I asked. 'My father had gone to Iraq so I spent my childhood there. Then from 1979 for about seven years I lived in Iran. So I'm fed up with migrating and besides I felt responsibility to help those here.'

There was a knock on the door and Khafash stiffened then relaxed at the sound of his son's voice. 'He likes foreigners coming here,' he said as his son came in barefoot on the carpet carefully carrying a silver tray of black tea and glass dishes of sugary fudge.

His jumpiness was understandable. By electing to stay in Herat he was arrested seven times. For not only was he a poet but, like his hero Firdosi, also a prominent member of Herat's sizeable Shiite community and taught at a Shia school. The Taliban considered Shias as infidels and it was commonly believed that to be accepted into their inner group one had to have killed ten Shias. In 1999 Khafash was among the many people rounded up after an attempted Shia uprising in the city. 'They hanged the twenty-five people they thought were ringleaders and for forty-eight hours they left their bodies hanging upside down from the feet all round the city, near the old cinema and the hotel. Do you have children? The children of Herat have all seen bodies hanging. They took another hundred and twenty Shias to Kandahar prison and kept them there for sixteen months and they burnt our school and schoolbus and twenty-six Shia mosques. I didn't take part in the uprising but I did help raise money and find weapons and also culturally through my poems. Had the Taliban known this they would have treated me more harshly. Because I am an old man I was only held here for seven months.'

His real weapon against the Taliban had been his poetry. 'I am

Khafash in his room overlooking the minarets of Herat.

not strong physically. I am small and my heart not good. My poems were my only way to fight. I would come home from the school around 3 p.m. and sit up here every afternoon writing poems while there was still light and sometimes by lamp when we had kerosene.'

He was lucky to have his own room to write in, away from the living quarters down below. In most Afghan houses, the same room would be used for eating, sleeping and entertaining.

'When a poem was finished friends would help me copy them by hand or sometimes we could Xerox them. Then they would be circu-lated.' The most popular, he said, was one about the Amar bil Marouf, the much-hated moral police. 'These were the men who would go to streets at prayer-time and force shopkeepers to close their shops and herd them into the mosques with sticks, and would beat men whose beards were not longer than a fist or little boys if their hair was too long. To me this was a kind of Islam the Prophet Mohammed would not recognise so I wrote a poem that went like this:

I told you to say your beard is long
And under it are the plans of a Saudi
You moral policeman in the middle of the bazaar
Are as greedy as a long-tailed donkey in a trough.

'Little children would memorise the last two lines and when they caught sight of the bil Marouf, they would recite it behind their backs in Persian and run away and the police would get mad but they didn't know who was writing these things. It became a sort of anti-Taliban anthem.

'Often they suspected me but they never caught me with any of my poems. Look!' Laughing, he got up and went to the plywood wall at the end of the room. 'It's a false wall!' He pulled it open to reveal shelves stuffed with papers, all his poems, as well as a large television. 'And this is what I did with the most sensitive ones.' He took a torch from the shelf and unscrewed the battery compartment to reveal some rolled-up pages.

'Taliban have come to this place and never found anything. I always told them I was spending all my time on my book *Khatab* which is a translation of the prayers of Imam Sajjad in verse that I have been working on for the last fifteen years.

'Unfortunately not many of our people can read so I thought up different ways to get my poems to them. When Mullah Omar took the Sacred Cloak of the Prophet Mohammed from its shrine in Kandahar and crowned himself Amir-ul Momineem, I wrote a poem which had a kind of chorus line, "Congratulations for cloaking a pile of dung with an ass's skin". Then I had the idea to commission four busts of Mullah Omar, caricatures with a patch on one eye and beards made from sheep's wool, with this line inscribed underneath. At exactly 10 p.m. one evening, one hour after curfew, we placed them at four different corners of the city. They arrested all the poets in the city that night, as well as the dentists because it was such a good cast.

'They came for me at about 2 a.m. I had to swear I hadn't written the poem – it was either that or be killed – but even so I was kept under house arrest for five months and they beat my knuckles with sticks to stop me writing.'

He showed me his fingers. They were stubby and swollen.

'I am not by nature a brave man,' he added. 'For the last six years I never had a proper night's sleep and if I heard a car on the road I would break into a cold sweat and think it was the Taliban coming to get me.'

As we were talking the sky had grown dark outside and it was becoming hard to take notes. Khafash shouted for his son who came running with a kerosene lamp which he placed on the floor near me. The lamp gave out a gentle hiss and the room looked different in the flickering light, more sinister. In the shadows the poet's large head and eyes gave him the appearance of an owl on the lookout for prey. While in most cultures owls are regarded as wise creatures, in Afghanistan they have the opposite connotation and one of the worst things one could do to an enemy was to feed him owlflesh. There was a burst of automatic gunfire in a nearby street and I began to wonder about the wisdom of walking back to the hotel in the dark.

'I am very happy that the spell of the Taliban is broken,' he said as I got up to leave, 'I wrote this to celebrate.' He gave me a copy of the poem called *The Godly Sword* that he had written the day after they had left Herat. 'Begin taking out the ruthless and break the butterflies free' was one of the lines.

The city of Herat is dominated by the presence of the minarets but I had been there almost a week before I awoke to another dawn as clear as that first one and set off to see them. The sprawl of the city ended abruptly in wide open space and then there they were. As I walked towards them, my step quickening, I suddenly understood what Byron meant when he wrote; 'Strolling up the road towards the

minarets, I feel as one might who has lighted on the los
Livy or an unknown Botticelli. It is impossible I suppose to
cate such a feeling.'

For me part of that was loss. I felt as I had when stumbling upon
places in the Amazon where centuries-old forest had been burnt
down for mining or ranching, leaving just a few stumps sticking up
awkwardly from the scorched earth. The five minarets were as I had
seen from a distance – leaning at awkward angles, one on its own
with a jagged hole two thirds of the way up, then four forming a
square some way away. Apart from a small square building with a
ribbed dome near the first minaret there was absolutely nothing in
between.

This was all that was left of the centrepiece of the Timurid renaissance, the vast complex of religious college, mosque and mausoleum
that once had some twenty or thirty minarets all covered in brilliant
mosaic joined by walls and arches and bridges with heavy bronze
doors, founded by Queen Gowhar Shad in 1417. Everyone who passed
through, from Babur to the British Great Game players, wrote of
their 'extraordinary beauty'. Yet of the prayer halls, libraries and
colleges there were no ruins to suggest what had been there, not a
single brick. Only the five minarets remained, soaring skywards out
of bare fields of powdery earth like lone witnesses to the scene of
some great tragedy. In the field of the domed building there had
been a vain attempt at planting rows of trees but the seedlings had
withered and died and there were signs either side of the path warning
of land-mines.

As Byron wrote, things of that scale do not just disappear so
completely. The House of Timur collapsed largely because after Shah
Rukh's death in 1447, his many sons and grandsons, who had been
brought up to value beauty above anything, were far too intent on the
pleasures of wine and women to worry about anything as mundane as
running the empire or keeping out marauding Uzbeks. Visiting his
Timurid cousins in 1506, Babur explained their failure to meet him

as 'probably due to a hangover after having indulged in revelry and pleasure'. A year later the Uzbeks stormed the citadel of Herat, though they quickly lost it to the Persians who ruled until 1749 when it was captured by Ahmad Shah Abdali, the first of the Pashtun kings, after a nine-month siege.

Yet although the Uzbeks and Persians plundered the buildings, it was actually the British who destroyed them. In 1885, the Russians had attacked the Afghans south east of Merv and occupied northern Afghanistan and a Russian attack on Herat was expected any day to open the way to India, the great prize. The British, who were advising the Afghan king Abdur Rahman, insisted that all buildings on the north of town which could give cover to the expected invaders should be demolished. Hence, wrote Byron, 'the most glorious productions of Mohammedan architecture in the XVth century, having survived the barbarism of four centuries were now razed to the ground under the eyes and with the approval of the English Commissioners.'

The Russian attack never happened and just nine minarets and a mausoleum escaped the British demolition. Two later fell in an earthquake before Byron visited Herat in 1933. But he rhapsodised about the maze of flowers and arabesques in coloured mosaic decorating the remaining seven, which he likened to the fine patterning on a china teacup. There had been people too, Heratis picnicking or taking walks in their shadow, often carrying caged songbirds. Now the fields were eerily deserted, just a small donkey rolling in the dust, and the minarets had been so blasted by wind and sun, shaken by shelling and pockmarked by gunfire, that the only sign that there had ever been glazed tiling was the thousands of tiny pieces of faience in pale yellow, jade green, bright turquoise and cobalt blue scattered among the dry earth.

The first, solitary minaret, which had been one of a pair at the main gate of the path leading to the mausoleum, was the fattest and had two balconies supported by scalloped stonework beneath what had been the tower. The hole was about two thirds of the way up and two white doves were chasing each other in and out. Close to, I could see that the brickwork was diamond-patterned. When Byron saw it the diamonds were edged with Persian blue and filled with flowers and the bases of the minaret had white marble panels with inscriptions, but all that had gone. Instead at the bottom there was a white-painted skull and crossbones from Omar, the anti-land-mine agency.

Yet according to Byron this was the least beautiful of the minarets. He had seen two more in this first field that were far more exquisite and were all that remained of the four corners of the mosque or *madrassa* of Gowhar Shad. One of these fell in an earthquake in 1951 and the other was destroyed in 1979 in the Soviet bombing. The small domed building in the field was the queen's mausoleum and was situated in the centre of the great quadrangle of the college.

The other four minarets still standing were part of a second *madrassa* built by Sultan Hussein Baiqara, the last Timurid ruler. To get to them I had to cross a small bridge over a dried-up canal, past a man selling mandarins, piled in a pyramid on a table in front of one of those rusted shipping containers used to bring in arms and later by the Taliban to ship prisoners. For less than a dollar I bought a large bag to supplement our diet. A few opal tiles up the sides of these minarets were all that remained of the white network that Byron had written made it seem 'that one saw the sky as if through a net of shining hair'.

After Byron's visit, the minarets had not only endured another earthquake but also the Soviet invasion. This part of town had swung back and forth between mujaheddin control and Soviet control, the Green Line sometimes passing right through the centre of the min-arets, and at some point the Russians had mined the whole area to try and stop Ismael Khan's men coming back into the city. When I had come to Herat in 1989 the ruined *musalla* was a battlefield and I couldn't get anywhere near. Although the Russians had only destroyed one minaret, the constant shelling had caused them to shed their tiling to the ground almost like tears.

I crossed back over the bridge to the top field where Gowhar
Shad's *madrassa* had stood. It had obviously been a very different
kind of *madrassa* to Haqqania. The queen is said to have once visited
with her two hundred ladies-in-waiting on a tour of inspection and
the students had all been told to vacate their rooms. But one had
fallen asleep and woke to see a beautiful ruby-lipped woman in
front of him. When this lady-in-waiting returned to the others, the
'irregularity of her dress and manners' gave away what had happened
so Gowhar Shad immediately ordered all two hundred to marry the
students and provided each with a bed, clothes and an allowance.

'In the past people could only speak in rhyme here,' said a white-
bearded man who suddenly appeared beside me and turned out to
be the keeper of the mausoleum, the large key on a string round his
neck magically fitting the padlock to the domed building. 'Students
came from Turkey, Iran, India, all over.'

There were four tombs inside the mausoleum, all in strange dark
green marble and I wondered where it had come from. The largest
one in the centre was that of Gowhar Shad. Having outlived her
husband and, after years of trying, manoeuvred her favourite grandson on to the throne, she was over eighty when she was murdered
by one of Tamerlane's great-grandsons. On her tombstone was
inscribed *The Bilquis of her time.* Bilquis means Queen of Sheba.
The others were three of her sons, including her favourite Prince
Baisanghor who added a famous library to her college and hired the
best illuminators and bookbinders, then died from alcohol long before
his mother, and her least favourite Mohammed Juki to whom she
was so unpleasant that he is said to have died of 'mortification'.

Above the window in one wall of the mausoleum was a large hole.
'A Russian bomb,' said the keeper, 'these people need to rest after
all they went through but nobody respects the dead anymore in my
country.' He shook his head despairingly and I realised he was one
of the very few Afghan men I had met that was not wearing a gun.
'And nobody respects beauty,' he added. Along another wall were

piles of fragments of mosaic sorted by colour – cobalt blue, turquoise, jade, opal white, scarlet, yellow. 'Every day I collect more pieces,' he said, 'so one day this can all be rebuilt and Herat can get back its history. But I am afraid I am an old man and this is an endless task.'

Most of the pieces were no bigger than my thumbnail. Even the simplest flower designs comprising turquoise hexagons with cobalt blue petals around a scarlet centre on an opal background would surely be impossible to reconstruct from these tiny fragments.

The mausoleum obviously did not often get foreign visitors for the keeper was determined to show me everything and bounded up some crumbling steps, beckoning me to follow. We came out on a flat platform in front of the dome. Its turquoise ribbing seemed to be pulled up into the centre like the waist of a lady's crinoline and there was a marvellous view of the citadel which I would liked to have sat and enjoyed. But the keeper had already disappeared inside through a hole in the roof to show me the brick inner skin of the dome. The space between the inner and outer roofs was so low that I had to crouch uncomfortably as I followed him round, stumbling occasionally on a loosened brick in the near dark, expecting eventually to be shown something marvellous that would reward this effort. Instead we just came back out on the roof so I sat down and peeled a mandarin. The keeper refused one, lighting up a cigarette instead, and he was wise for it was so sour it brought tears to my eyes.

In my pocket were two pieces of faience, one of the dark grape blue and one of the bright Persian blue that I had picked from the earth. When the keeper wandered off to one side, I took them out and held them in my palm, moving it around so they glittered in the November sunlight. The deep blue was made from crushed lapis lazuli from the mountains of Badakshan and more intense than any colour I had ever seen.

MARRI'S DIARY
10 December 2001

They have chosen us a government in Bonn we heard on the radio and Karzai is to be its leader! My father and our family are very happy and we hope now his majesty Zahir Shah will come back and there will be peace again.

It is odd for our leaders to be chosen so far away. Most people here have never heard of Karzai they say he is too young and never fought in the jihad. My friends say this is a good thing for we have had enough of those who got themselves dollar accounts and Pajeros.

We hope he comes soon. The Northern Alliance commanders are driving round town with all their gunmen and posters of Ahmad Shah Massoud on their windscreens. Some like General Fahim fought with the Russians. We know they don't like us Pashtuns, they will try and punish us for all that went before, and we do not know if they will accept this government. My father says this Rabbani is like a snake and we remember what happened last time when he would not give up power as he was supposed to.

My brother tells us shopkeepers are putting up Massoud posters so they do not have problems with the Northern Alliance.

Many of our neighbours are going to the graves of their sons to pray. We have been lucky in all these years of war, we lost just one uncle murdered by the Russians when he was farming. They thought he was a mujahid and chopped up his body and put it in the well. Also one of my cousins lost his mind after going to the hospital and seeing so many terrible things there.

Today I talked with Farishta and Najeba about the burqas. We are waiting to see what happens. It's funny before the Taliban I had never worn one and I hated them, I couldn't see where I was going, the sound was all muffled. But now we have got used to them and in these cold days they give some warmth as we don't have coats. We decided the difference is we feel free – we're not wearing them by law. I think once we go back to work I will stop wearing it. How I pray for that day!

6

The Secret of Glass

The sand of the desert is lightly blown away by a breath;
still more lightly is the future of man destroyed.

Turkoman proverb

'WHICH IS BEST, Inglistan or Afghanistan?'
The question came as I was standing in one of the turrets
of the citadel contemplating the plains across which Genghis Khan's
hordes of wild horsemen had once come 'roaring like an ocean' and
the massive walls that had been besieged so many times in their seven
centuries of existence and imagining them impaled with the severed
heads of Persian attackers. It was in Afghanistan that I had seen my
first dead body, three Soviet soldiers lying in a pool of blood in a
field near Jalalabad, on their backs with legs bent as if flung there. I
had found myself strangely curious. Growing up in England, death
had been something kept from me, our only encounters strictly san-
itised. In Afghanistan the dead were impossible to avoid – I had seen
people with their brains blown out, killed by tank-shells, blown up
by land-mines, shivering with malaria or dying from tuberculosis. A
couple of days before, in the vast Maslakh camp outside Herat, I had
witnessed the burials of tiny children, their bodies stiff and doll-like,
dead of starvation and cold. I was not surprised to read a Unicef

report which said two thirds of Afghan children had seen someone killed, in many cases someone they knew. On one page was a child's drawing in black pencil of a little girl with fuzzy hair and one arm under which the child had written 'I hate the rockets because children have lost arms and legs'. On the ground next to the girl was her other arm.

Few places in this land of ghosts had seen as much death as the Herat citadel. We had bluffed our way in by showing a letter of permission for the prison, taking a likely chance that the guards on the gate would not be able to read. The citadel's latest occupants were Ismael Khan's men, instantly identifiable by their black and white Palestinian-style chequered keffiyehs over their heads like that worn by their leader, and though they had let us in, six of them were following us round, clearly suspicious that we were on some kind of British intelligence-gathering mission. We stopped by a large machine gun with a bunch of pink and white plastic flowers tied to the barrel.

'Which is best, Inglistan or Afghanistan?'

The question came again and the guard who had asked it had a jagged scar on his right cheek pulling down his eye.

'Well, Afghanistan is very beautiful and the people are very hospitable. You have beautiful mountains. Also the weather is very nice. But, England has roads, electricity, schools, hospitals, libraries, running water, trains, lots of food . . .'

The mujahid looked unimpressed. 'And how much fighting do you have in Inglistan?'

'Well, we don't really. I mean we had a civil war but that was more than 350 years ago and since then people in England have pretty much lived together peacefully.'

'What if someone was to steal your husband's gun? By Allah, then he would fight!'

He nodded towards Justin who was down below taking photographs they had said were not permitted. I could see it would be impossible to explain that Justin wasn't my husband.

'He doesn't have a gun.'

The men looked shocked, shaking their heads and repeating 'no gun' to each other. They all had standard-issue Kalashnikovs slung across their shoulders and wide belts of brass bullets on their waists except for one with a Russian army cap and a loopy grin who was carrying a hand-held rocket-launcher, which to my horror he kept dropping on the hard ground.

'How does he protect you then?' asked the grinning man.

'I don't need protecting,' I replied, trying to look fierce. 'Besides, my husband knows I am under the protection of Tora Ismael.' It was partly true. We had been brought to Herat by one of his emissaries.

The men looked suitably impressed and drew back a little allowing me to descend from the turret and explore.

The citadel was a strange building that seemed much bigger from the inside with the full width of the walls visible, than from the outside, where we had come across the entrance unexpectedly after wandering through narrow yellow-dust lanes of the bazaar in the Old City cluttered with shops selling smuggled electronics goods with unfamiliar brand-names, and crowded with men on donkeys or bicycles. On the dry mud verges just beneath the walls of the citadel by the fetid trickle of a moat in which a man was squatting, trousers down, were mounds of second-hand clothes. I had been told that one could pick up bargains of beautiful Italian wool overcoats and Russian fur hats and Red Army belt-buckles in Herat but all I could see were pink and purple Lycra tracksuits, Pakistani polyester shalwar kamiz and plastic sandals. One merchant had a pile of odd single shoes and I asked him what they were for. 'Those with one leg,' he replied.

Once inside the citadel, the walls were so thick I began to see how Tamerlane's son Shah Rukh could have employed 7000 men to strengthen them when he rebuilt it in 1405. Yet it had not been enough to save the Timurid empire from marauding Uzbeks or Persians, and in 1837 one of the oddest episodes in Anglo-Afghan history took place here. A young British player in the Great Game, twenty-six-year-old Lieutenant Eldred Pottinger of the Bengal Artillery, found himself organising the citadel's defence. Pottinger had dyed his skin and slipped into Herat in the guise of a holy man to find frantic repair works underway on the crumbling ramparts and the city buzzing with news of a Persian army, led by the Shah himself, marching from Tehran. Presenting himself and his expertise in modern siege-craft to the ruler Yar Mohammed, he was immediately put in charge of fortifying the citadel against the onslaught of the Persian army and their Russian advisors led by a general called Count Simonich. The siege went on for ten months until September 1838. Supplies ran so short that the Heratis slaughtered all their horses for food and tore down their houses to burn for fuel and only Pottinger's constant encouragement prevented them from giving up. By the time the Persian invaders desisted, apparently in the belief that British troops were arriving, the stench from the refuse and unburied dead piled up inside the citadel could be smelled from ten miles away.

The stench was still bad, but for all the carnage that had taken place there, the citadel seemed in better shape than most buildings in Afghanistan. Only the central area was in ruins, a jumble of bricks which

looked like the foundations of houses and the guards said was mined. I walked down a lane along one side of which were a series of arched alcoves stacked with boxes of ammunition, suggesting the Taliban really had departed in a hurry, and then back up onto a rampart looking down to a square in which a noisy crowd had gathered.

'What are they doing?' I asked the guards.

'Fighting with eggs. It used to be banned under the Taliban.'

'What do you mean, fighting with eggs?' I had never heard of such a thing.

'You boil the eggs then hit each other's egg to see whose smashes first. People bet on which egg will be strongest. It is much entertainment.'

From what I could make out the egg-game was a messier variant of playing conkers. It seemed a waste of food in a city with so little.

'This game is banned in Inglistan?'

'Not banned. I just don't think anyone has thought of playing it.'

The man with the scarred cheek could not contain his curiosity any longer.

'So in Inglistan, men don't fight each other even for fun?'

I thought about football hooligans or people coming out of the pubs on Saturday nights. Did they fight for fun? In Afghanistan, warfare was part of life even when the country was not at war, particularly among the Pashtun. One of their sayings was, 'Be tame in the city and rebellious in the mountains'. The Afghan scholar Louis Dupree wrote of visiting a village in the southeastern province of Paktia in 1962 and witnessing attempts by one tribe to steal some trees of another, sparking off a long-dormant feud. Within a week ten of the hundred men in the village had been killed.

'Fighting is our problem,' said one of the other men. 'We fight with everything. Afghans are world champions in fighting.'

It was hard to disagree. All the Afghans I had spoken to said they were fed up with war yet as a people there was no doubt they often fought for the enjoyment. All their legends revolved around fighting and so did their hobbies. It wasn't just the obvious ones such as bird-fighting, cockfighting and wrestling or *buzkashi*, the Afghan version of polo and pre-cursor to the western game, with a live goat (or

sometimes heads of Russian prisoners) used as a ball. Even activities that seemed peaceful, like boiling eggs, in Afghanistan involved some form of warfare.

Kite-flying was another unexpectedly martial sport. The ban on kite-flying had come to symbolise the lunacy of the Taliban and since they had fled the sky seemed to be awash with plastic or paper kites flown by small boys running on the flat roofs of houses. I had won-dered why the kites had no tails and why so many ended up trapped in trees and powerlines. Then it was explained to me that the point of kites was not to watch them soar and dive in the sky but to use them to fight other children's kites. Warrior kites. This was done by coating the string with a mixture of powdered glass and rice flour, and then flying the kite towards an opponent's to try to slash his string.

For children growing up in Afghanistan or for the four million born in refugee camps, war was not a vague concept but part of

everyday life – even primary school textbooks used pictures of hand grenades and bullets instead of apples and oranges to teach five-year-olds how to count. In a way it started from birth – when it was known that the arrival of a baby was imminent, men with guns would gather at the house ready to fire off bursts of five or seven shots for a girl and fourteen or more for a boy. In Pashtun custom the first thing the father of a newborn boy does is hang a rifle over his cot. I had never seen Afghan children playing a local version of cowboys and Indians or cops and robbers as they do in the West, and as I had seen in Palestinian and African refugee camps, because at the age when boys elsewhere might get a toy gun, Afghan boys got real ones and were taught by their fathers how to use them. There were always plenty of guns but the combination of US aid to the muja-heddin and Soviet assistance to the regime had made Afghanistan the world's foremost recipient of personal weapons by the mid-1980s. Those that could not obtain guns had slingshots or catapults which they learnt to use with deadly accuracy.

Inside the citadel, I suddenly felt overwhelmed by death and killing. Large stretches of the city below were still in rubble from Soviet carpet-bombing, first to wreak revenge on the city then to prevent shelter being given to the mujaheddin. Some houses had been rebuilt using the ancient bricks from Queen Gowhar Shad's *musalla* but much of it still looked like pictures of Hiroshima. Towards the mili-tary encampment there were some new ruins from the recent Ameri-can bombing. Out on the plains, entire villages had been flattened by the Soviets, virtually unreported, and beyond that were the hills where Ismael Khan's valiant men had played deadly cat and mouse with the Red Army. From our vantage point we could look right down into the small houses of the Old City with their walled courtyards, and after all that had happened it was odd to see normal life continuing. Children were pumping water from a well, a group of old men were on their knees on a flat roof scrubbing carpets with stones to make them look older and toddlers were throwing pebbles at a dog. Some men were just standing in that way people in Central Asia often do, as if waiting for something when there was nothing to wait for.

The card for Sultan Hamidy's famous glass factory described it as 'Handicrafts & Historical thinhgs Shop' and carried a small blue diagram which pictured it on the corner of 'North St. of the Big Mosque'.

It was not hard to find. Big Mosque was a literal but accurate

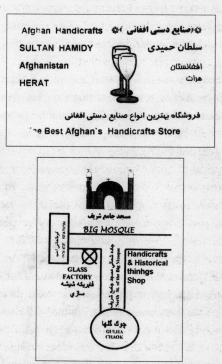

description of the Masjid-i-Juma or Friday Mosque where for eight centuries the people of Herat had gathered for prayers and important events in the city such as declaring a new ruler or motivating soldiers before they went off for war. Every inch of the walls was covered with stunning blue tiles decorated with golden arabesques and white-petalled flowers; the entrance was through an impressive archway with three tiers of pointed arched windows. We left our shoes with the old man sitting with his pile of sandals and tin of coins outside and stepped into a vast courtyard open to the sky with a marble floor which was icy cold underfoot even through thermal socks. Only the rich wear socks in Afghanistan, and I grimaced to see the worshippers walking barefeet. Near the entrance in a plastic case was a bronze cauldron at least three feet tall and wide, engraved with black markings, that had been commissioned by Tamerlane, and just off to the left a room which contained the tomb of Ghiyas-ad-Din, king of the Ghorids, who founded the mosque in 1200. A small marble shelf ran all the way along the west wall at about knee height and on it, in one of the prayer niches, a man had taken off his prosthetic leg and laid it by his side with his Kalashnikov while he prostrated himself. It seemed an odd place of worship where men leave their shoes at the entrance but not their guns.

It was too cold to linger long in the mosque so I scurried across the road to find sanctuary in Sultan Hamidy's shop. From the outside the windows were so encrusted with dust that it was hard to see what it sold. I supposed it was a long time since a foreign tourist passed this way. But inside, once one adjusted to the dim light, was an Aladdin's cave. Old British muskets hung from the ceiling along with wooden lute-like instruments called *tamburs* inlaid with ivory, as well as long Uzbek coats and antique silk scarves in bright pinks and emeralds. Glass cabinets contained a jumble of Bactrian lion heads, small limestone tablets covered with squiggly writing, flat squarish coins that looked like they dated from Greek or Roman times, Buddhist-style walnuts covered with ivory fashioned into dragon designs, Kandahari whistle-flutes, Persian seals and miniatures, and Russian pocket watches in silver cases carved with bears or trains. It was an inventory of Afghanistan's invaders.

By the windows was a series of cardboard boxes piled with candle-sticks, vases, dishes, water cups for birdcages and goblets twisted and sculpted into the strangest shapes and sorted into colours – bright mermaid blue, deep cobalt and jade green. I tried to pick out a set of six glasses but no two were even remotely alike, all different heights and shapes and thicknesses with strange bumps and bulges. They were layered with dust and when I took them to the doorway and wiped them with my sleeve they glittered in the sun as if tiny particles of dust were trapped inside the glass.

I was holding up one that I particularly admired when a papery voice behind me whispered, 'Do you know the secret of glass?'

I turned around to see an old man in white shalwar kamiz with a short waistcoat and a long white beard. His face was smooth and unlined yet his milky green eyes told of times long past. This was Sultan Hamidy, the owner of the shop.

'The secret of glass?'

'We once made glass for all over Afghanistan. All over Persia too. Kings and queens drank from Hamidy's glasses. We were the biggest glass factory in all Oxiana and Transoxiana. Look.' On the wall were framed yellowing certificates of awards won for his glassware in exhibitions in Tehran, Istanbul and Karachi.

'What happened?'

'War. Killing. Who is there to make glass when the men are all fighting? And who will buy glass when they don't even have a roof over their heads or bread to feed their children?'

The old man shook his head and turned in from the doorway as if the light was burning his eyes. 'Mine is a country where all the beauty has died. Look around you. This was a beautiful city of poetry and painting and pine trees famous as far away as your country. Foreigners loved this place. It was green and lush, the stalls were all piled high with pomegranates, figs and peaches bigger than your fist. Now it is brown and dry, a dead place.'

He walked back towards the depths of his shop and I feared

he would disappear. Instead he picked up something wrapped in yellowing newspaper from inside a drawer and handed it to me. It was a wooden pencil box varnished in lapis blue with the Herat citadel delicately painted in the centre surrounded by a border of tiny star-shaped red roses and gold edging in the style of the old miniatures. The price he quoted was the equivalent of six months' salary in Afghanistan and, I knew, far too much, but it was little to me and it seemed wrong to bargain over something so exquisite, so I took the box along with half a dozen of the turquoise blue glasses which he wrapped in straw in a box as if they were tiny kittens in a bed.

'You mentioned a secret,' I said after counting out several large bricks of tattered afghanis, considerably lightening the load in my rucksack.

'Each glass is individually made. We used to say a line of poetry for each one so that it would have its own soul. You see them there in the grains of sand trapped in the glass. Then when my first son Rahim was killed by the *dushman* [Russians] in 1979 I whispered his name into the glass as I blew it over the flame. Then we did the same every time a son or brother or neighbour was made *shaheed* but we could not keep up – you see how many glass pieces we have made but there were hundreds, thousands of dead. First we had no more customers. Then after a while we no longer had the workers or the materials. Our colours were from crushed jewels, you see the tiny splinters. Now the glasses just sit there, waiting to be found. This is the secret of Sultan Hamidy's glass.'

Back at the Mowafaq, Ayubi was waiting in the restaurant, wrapped in a soft woollen cape over a shalwar kamiz of embroidered white cotton. He had the same uncanny ability as Hamid Karzai of walking through dust and dirt without any of it clinging to him. I was horrified to find he had been waiting there for several hours.

'You should have let us know you were coming,' I said as he beamed as always at my pronunciation of '*haletun chetor e?*', Dari for 'How are you?'

'It is of no consequence. I am here to serve you. If I wait a day for you, it is like the tick of a clock. If I wait a week for you I am too happy. One month is not even a shadow across the moon. But now we must go, Tora Ismael is expecting us.'

We took a taxi to an avenue lined with stumps of trees and after some negotiation with the guards were allowed into the driveway of a large two-storey house with a terrace. This was the Foreign Ministry guesthouse and, as I got out of the car, I recognised the building. It was where I had stayed when I visited Herat in 1989 on a trip organised by the Najibullah regime. Even the pomegranate tree in the front garden where every evening a cuckoo sang was still there. It was the first time the regime had allowed journalists who had travelled with the mujaheddin to come and see the war from the other side and I had somehow ended up with a Canadian journalist who had never before travelled to the 'Third World' as he called it, stretching out the vowels and widening his eyes. He had a rucksack stocked with water filters, energy bars and vitamin pills and refused to eat any local food, once pointing out to me little white maggots in a bowl of mutton from which I had just eaten. The Canadian was horrified by children playing in dirty canals, which in those days had water, and terrified of straying near the Green Line, the shifting division between areas controlled by the regime and the mujaheddin which I was always trying to get to. We spent all week being shocked by each other and got little sense of the city. All I knew from snatched conversations with locals in the golden half-light under the arches of the covered carpet bazaar was that it was a place of fear.

The fighting at that time had been so intense that we ended up trapped in Herat for days and were finally sent by tank to the airport, stopping for most of a morning in a pine grove after a rocket narrowly missed us and a firefight crackled across the road up ahead. A former Governor of Herat had planted the pines, 32,000 of them, in the 1940s to escort the traveller out of the city so that they would leave with the scent and always remember Herat and though many had been chopped down, I knew the smell of pine would always bring back that day. When we eventually got to the aircraft, an old Antonov, it was like a furnace inside with no air conditioning. A large section of seats had been taken up for wooden coffins bearing dead soldiers back to the capital, requiring many passengers to stand. We were held up inside the plane on the runway for hours as the battle raged on around us, getting hotter and hotter with the stench of the dead bodies overpowering.

I was remembering all this and wondering if Ismael Khan was even in town or we would just wait outside the house all evening, a common occurrence in Afghanistan, when Ayubi suddenly whispered reverentially, 'Tora Ismael.' A Datsun pick-up with heavy chrome bumper bars and darkened windows roared into the driveway followed by two more packed with heavily armed mujaheddin, heads wrapped in black and white keffiyehs, their guns trained Top-Gun style on either side of the road. The gates closed behind them and out of the first car jumped Ismael Khan, legendary commander and the man whose forces had almost killed us that day at the airport.

He was instantly recognisable from the swashbuckling poster of him astride a horse that festooned the shops and buildings in Herat as well as the windscreens of all the Dubai-numberplated Taliban jeeps that had been purloined by the mujaheddin. On the posters he looked like Charles Bronson and even in real life, though his beard was white rather than jet-black and his eyes a little less soulful, he had something of the movie star about him.

He hugged Ayubi warmly, smiled a welcome to me and we found ourselves whisked into the house in his wake and taken to a side room where a man brought plates of almonds and small glasses of tea flavoured with cardamon. Every few minutes the man returned

Ismael Khan in Herat, November 2001.

with new glasses of tea until I had four in front of me and I wondered if we were going to be received.

Then Ismael himself came in, apologised for keeping us waiting and invited us to join him for dinner upstairs. 'You will not ask your questions while we are eating,' he said as he led us to a table covered by a flowery vinyl cloth on which were laid out a plate of scrawny chicken pieces, a large plastic bowl of pilau rice, lamb kebabs sprinkled with ground grape-seed and greasy chips. It was more food than we had seen for over a week.

Ismael sat at the head of the table. On his left was Haji Mir, his military commander for the south who briefed him on the latest position with the Taliban who were negotiating a surrender in Kandahar, their last stronghold, and he feared might flee north towards Herat. On his right was his newly appointed head of schools with whom he was discussing how to restart female education and whether boys and girls should be educated separately.

Ismael Khan was one of the most charismatic leaders that the resistance had thrown up. There was a famous story about him receiving a letter from the Soviet General Andrushkin in Herat warning Ismael that he had dealt with 'bandits' before and would make sure he suffered the same fate as the Uzbek bandit Ibrahim Beg who had resisted the Russians at the start of the twentieth century but been defeated. Ismael's reply was uncompromising. 'You Russians do not forget Ibrahim Beg after seventy years. I want you to remember the name Ismael Khan for two hundred years.'

Watching him gnaw on his chicken bones, the juices dripping into his beard, I could picture the relish with which he would have sent off the messenger on horseback, galloping across the plains to Andrushkin.

Of all the warlords who had emerged and prospered during the years of fighting, with the exception of the late Commander Ahmad Shah Massoud, Ismael was probably the least tainted. He was often described by journalists as having an elfin appearance despite his fifty-four years but his puckish eyes were clearly deceptive. Clean-living, religious, and according to his men, an inspirational orator, he could not have been more different in personality or appearance to the other prominent figure, General Dostum, the Uzbek warlord, based in Mazar-i-Sharif. There was no love lost between Heratis and Uzbeks and although the two men were working together in the Northern Alliance against the Taliban, they hated each other, Ismael blaming Dostum for his own capture by the Taliban. A former wrestler with a fondness for dancing girls and Scotch whisky, Dostum was more than six feet tall with almost no neck, and the glowering expression of one who liked nothing better than to go out and kill a few people after lunch. He was known to have crushed his enemies under tanks, and it was claimed by the Uzbeks that his laugh had frightened people to death. As Governor of Mazar, he had filled the grounds of his fort with peacocks, declared himself the 'Pasha of the North' and started his own airlines – Balkh Airlines – known as BA.

Ismael Khan had been less showy. He could also be ruthless, but during his three years as Governor of Herat after the fall of the Communist regime in 1992, he had sought reconciliation rather than revenge and was not linked to any massacres such as those that had occurred in Dostum's realm. His main weakness was that he adored power, calling himself the Amir of Western Afghanistan where he controlled five provinces and liking his men to refer to him as Excellency. The wording under his official portrait was 'The model of bravery and piety'. Every year he held an annual military parade in which his troops sat astride camels bearing Stinger missiles and loaded rocket-launchers, and special forces parachuted into the midst and skinned live snakes with their teeth.

Unlike Dostum who had initially fought with the Soviets, raising his 20,000-strong Uzbek militia under Najibullah, fighting mercilessly against the mujaheddin in the battles of Jalalabad, Gardez and Khost, then gone on to ally himself with – and betray – most of the mujaheddin factions, Ismael Khan had never switched sides. He came to prominence when as a major in the Afghan army, he led a mutiny in March 1979 against the Soviet advisors who had appeared in the city ordering shopkeepers to display red flags and photographs of President Taraki. When the Heratis rebelled and rampaged through the city attacking the Communist party headquarters and dragging Soviet advisors and their families from their homes, the Russians ordered the Afghan army to shoot. Ismael Khan and his men refused and fled to the hills where they started gathering supporters and preparing resistance, making contact with Burhanuddin Rabbani, one of the seven mujaheddin leaders in Peshawar, and like Ismael a Persian-speaking Tajik, as well as the Iranian regime which was to supply arms. His band of thirty men grew to five thousand called the Amir

Hanza Division, which he ran on strict army lines, dividing them into five regiments, each then organised into battalions of about two hundred men which in turn were divided into companies of about twenty-five.

Throughout the Soviet occupation there was more or less a stale-mate between the two sides with the citadel under Russian control but the Green Line cutting off areas of the city to them. The Russians saw nothing to be gained in trying to win the affections of the Heratis and viewed everyone as potential enemies and everything as targets, bombing villages and laying mines in farmland, while by night they barricaded themselves in as Ismael's mujaheddin took to the streets. So dangerous was it that one and a half million people, almost a tenth of the country's population, fled western Afghanistan to Iran.

Eventually in 1992, two years after the Russians had left, Ismael's men took Herat and he declared himself Amir of the West for the first time. Education was one of his priorities and he managed to disarm the population so that compared to other parts of Afghanistan beset by fighting between groups, Herat was peaceful. But he was seen as a weak ruler whose administration was riddled with corruption and nepotism, with his own family swelling the ranks. Soon customs officials were demanding $300, equivalent to a year's salary, for trucks to pass through the city.

By March 1995 the Taliban had captured the two south-western provinces of Nimruz and Farah. They then advanced on the former Soviet airbase of Shindand south of Herat but Ismael's troops were able to push them back, helped by Massoud who was then Defence Minister and sent in planes from Kabul to bomb the Taliban front-lines, as well as by the fact that the Taliban had no food or water or medical facilities in the inhospitable desert. The victory made Ismael Khan overconfident and a few months later he marched south and launched an offensive against Kandahar. But after their defeat the Taliban had spent the summer regrouping and training with ISI advisors and their numbers had been reinforced by thousands of new volunteers from the *madrassas* in Pakistan. At the same time Dostum had changed sides again and started bombing Herat. Ismael's men were not only forced to retreat but were completely overrun by the Taliban. They fled from the city to take refuge in the hills or across the border.

The commander belched and excused himself from the table to carry out his instructions, a secret mission, and I wondered if they were planning another attempt on Kandahar. Ismael Khan finished carefully peeling an apple that he ate without speaking, then pushed his plate away and turned his full attention on me. I asked him what effect he felt the Taliban had had on Herat and he shook his head sadly.

'Life under the Taliban was altogether a tragedy. A man can deal with hunger, poverty, cold and other hardships but dealing with an ignorant person is much harder. We were the captives of ignorant people and for Heratis that was probably the worst thing of all.

'Herat is different to other places in Afghanistan. The historical monuments you see here show that the people of this city are richer with respect to science, knowledge and culture and have a deeper awareness. The Taliban knew that the people of Herat were mad at them and remembered the uprising against the Russians and were worried that the same would happen. They thought they could stop it by spreading fear but they were wrong. The Taliban used to think that by killing people and hanging them in the city for all to see that the population would be scared. Not a week or two went by without a citizen of Herat being hung from lampposts. Yet every day a new slogan was painted on a wall demanding "Death to Taliban" or "Open our Girls' Schools". There was a constant flow of secret nightly papers and poems. Unlike in other provinces where many people worked with the Taliban, here people tried to have nothing to do with them.'

After one year of organising against the Taliban, Ismael was captured in a trap. 'I was betrayed by General Abdul Malik, one of

Dostum's deputies,' he said, bitterly. 'Like Dostum, Malik had been with Najibullah then joined the mujaheddin for a lot of money, twelve million dollars, so they say. I had been to Mazar to see Dostum to discuss joining against the Taliban, then General Malik came to Herat and sent a message arranging a breakfast meeting with me. The people he brought with him were Taliban and they pulled out their guns, arrested me and took me to Kandahar prison. Later he was also arrested but escaped to Turkey.'

Remembering Mullah Hassani, the Taliban torturer whom I had met in the orchard in Quetta and his bloodcurdling tales of torture in Kandahar, I asked about the jail.

'Physically they did not touch me,' replied Ismael, 'they did not beat or torture me. But I was kept with my hands and legs shackled, sometimes my neck too, chained to a pipe in a dark solitary cell for three years with no facilities. No books, radio, visits, news, nothing. Just a small piece of bread every day so that I did not die. The cell was so small that the few times I was unchained I could only take three paces. I wasn't allowed to speak to anyone, even my guard.

'Twice I tried digging a hole in my cell with my hands to escape but it was impossible. But among the guards were two former mujaheddin who offered to help me because they had fought in the jihad. They were Pashtuns from Kandahar and I did not know if I could trust them at first. But they seemed genuine and one of them, Hekmatullah, whose father had been a famous mujahid, got in touch with my son Mirwais in Iran and arranged a Land Cruiser and over months they planned an escape for myself and two of my commanders.

'Finally the day came. It was 2 March 1999. First they unlocked our leg shackles. Then at about 4 a.m. when everyone was sleeping they came for us, opened our cells and left bundles of clothes on the floor so that it would look as if we were still sleeping, then led us to the Land Cruiser which was in the parking lot. It was like a movie. We were sure someone would spot us. In the car Hekmatullah's father was waiting and he gave us black turbans and flowing robes so that we would look like Taliban. We had to sit there for hours in the carpark waiting for the sun to come up and Hekmatullah's shift to end. He told his colleagues that he was going for a steambath and then he came with us. We had a white Taliban flag on the car so it was easy for us to drive through the checkpoints but then we drove into the Dasht-e-Marg desert from where we would get across the border and got competely lost driving round and round in circles until it was late at night. Finally we came across a goatherd who said he knew the way but then we hit an anti-tank mine which hurled the car into the air. We were lucky none of us were killed but my legs were broken in the impact and so were Hekmatullah's. The car was completely destroyed and we lay there in pain as Hekmatullah's father walked off for help. Eventually he found some of my men and they came and rescued us. We got to Iran about 10 p.m. that night – it had taken us almost two days.'

Hekmatullah had taken a huge risk and some of his family were to pay the price. Several of his uncles were arrested. The fingernails of one were ripped out and the eye of another.

After a year of planning, Ismael returned to Afghanistan to launch a new offensive on the Taliban but it had made little progress, partly because of the difficulties of obtaining supplies. 'No one was interested in helping us,' he claimed. 'We had to get our bullets one by one.' Everything changed after the attack on the World Trade Center and the subsequent American bombing campaign which wiped out the Taliban military encampment in Herat and many of their tanks and vehicles. In the end the Taliban fled with barely a shot fired and Ismael and his men were able to ride into the city the next day and claim it as their own. It was clear that he would have preferred a battle to wipe them out once and for all. 'The Taliban have not been defeated,' he pointed out. 'They have just gone back to their tribes as mujaheddin but they are Talibs in their hearts and will come back again under a different name.'

Ismael had had six years in jail and exile or on the run to think about what he would do if he were ever governor again and I asked about his plans.

'My city is in ruins,' he replied. 'But it is not just physical problems we must deal with. Our young have known only war, a man of thirty in my city is illiterate after twenty-three years' war and knows nothing but how to fight. Both with the Russians and the Taliban, hatred and violence became the language and we must reinstil the value of words.'

It sounded impressive spoken in his soft, wise voice. But he made no secret of his dislike of the new government and a few days later held a meeting in the Big Mosque where his supporters all declared him Amir of the West. Back in the nineteenth century, Herat and Kabul had been ruled by bitterly opposed members of the same dynasty and I wondered if the same thing was happening again. He had already named his son Mirwais as intelligence chief and at the Mowafaq, the bearded men were complaining that a potato-seller had been put in charge of a police station and a man with no experience made head of the hospital just because they had been good mujahids.

By the tomb of a Sufi saint called Khwaja Altan, the Rolling Mullah, because he rolled all over Herat, a blind old man was sitting chanting and I met two small boys looking for snakes. I could not help thinking of Ismael's men skinning them alive with their teeth.

A few nights later, I was in the Mowafaq restaurant when there was a sudden crack of gunfire outside followed by burst after burst of artillery. The lights went off and everyone ran to the roof. The sky was lit up with red and green tracer bullets, exploding rockets and white streaks of anti-aircraft fire, and spent cartridges were cascading down around us. 'Get inside, get inside!' shouted the old sweeper man. The peace had always seemed rather fragile in Herat and at first we thought it was a battle and maybe the Taliban had come back. Eventually it became clear it was a celebration though no one seemed to know for what. The rumours were endless – Ismael had captured Mullah Omar and brought him to Herat, Osama bin Laden had been killed in a cave at Tora Bora, Ismael had captured Kandahar. The firing went on for more than an hour.

The next morning Ayubi came to see us and explained that the Taliban had surrendered and the firing was to greet the return of prisoners from Kandahar. He looked more serious than usual and after the long exchange of greetings, he took me aside.

'Miss Christina, I would like to use your satellite telephone to call Mashad to find out if my wife has had her baby,' he said. I looked at him in astonishment. He had never mentioned that his wife was expecting.

'When is it due?'

'It was due the day we left Mashad.'

That was about twelve days earlier. 'Why didn't you tell us? We would never have brought you to Herat if we had known.'

'No, it was my service to Tora Ismael to bring you.'

It turned out he already had seven children and two wives which explained why he could be casual about another arrival but when he got through to Mashad and discovered that his wife had given birth to a little girl the previous week, he could not stop smiling.

'Now, I will never forget you,' he said, 'because you have been the messenger of this good news.'

'We must celebrate,' I said, wondering how. I couldn't even order him a cup of tea because of the Ramadan fast.

'I will give her your name,' said Ayubi. 'But it will not be her first name because it is too strange.'

The good news seemed to have broken down the courtly formality with which Ayubi always spoke to me and he suddenly confessed that he was thinking of leaving the mujaheddin and had asked Ismael to release him so that he could go into business.

'I love my commander and he is a good friend and a good man but six lakh a year [600,000 afghani – about $120] is not enough to support two wives and eight children,' he explained. 'I went to Tora

Ismael and greeted him and said, "You have all these cars confiscated from the Taliban, please give me one." But he said, "Don't even think about it for if I give you a car then I must give to all." Yet many mujaheddin have just taken them.

'I am no longer a young man but after all these years I have nothing. My family were not poor and some years ago my father, a mullah but a learned man, saved money to buy me a motorbike, a very nice one. But when Ismael heard he called me and said that motorcycle will feed two thousand of my men and he took it from me. That was the only thing I ever had.'

With his fine clothes and silver ring, I had imagined him to be a wealthy man but I realised that I did not even know how he had become a mujaheddin. He told me that he had become a 'rebel' as he put it at the age of sixteen in the mid-1970s when he was studying for a law degree at Kabul University and joined Rabbani's party Jamiat Islami to fight against Daoud.

'We caused trouble for the government, we published leaflets and wrote slogans and organised strikes and were very excited and very young and wanted to bring down the regime. Then in 1978 the Communists came and we wanted to fight. We had our own group of guerrillas in a village called Mullasia about twenty kilometres west of Herat. Our commander was friends with Ismael Khan so when he went to the hills we joined him. That was almost twenty-three years ago.'

'I know compared to many mujaheddin I have a comfortable life. My family has a little money which they give me and I do get paid something by Ismael whereas many fighters have not received anything for years. But Ismael is a very tight person. We say water doesn't stop in his hand.

'If I hadn't been a mujahid, I would have had a better life. Because we were ideological people, believers, we had to fight. But now I am tired. We have fought so much and for what? I am not sure that at the end of all this anyone but a few warlords has a better life. The tribes are weakened. Our children are illiterate. Our cities are in

Boarding the first Ariana flight from Herat. The airline's slogan is:
Be a Second Marco Polo, Fly ARIANA.

rubble. Even now the Taliban is gone people are scrapping for power like vultures after meat.'

It seemed wrong that such a noble figure should be disappointed and I was touched when he invited us to dinner at his family home that evening, though as usual no time was mentioned. After Ayubi had taken his leave, the interpreter said, 'He doesn't want you to go to dinner. The language he used means he is ashamed. There will be no dinner.'

That evening Ayubi did not show up. When he appeared again the next morning he mentioned nothing about the dinner, only that he had slaughtered a goat and cooked it then distributed the meat to poor people to celebrate his new daughter.

There was a rumour that Ariana Airlines were to run a flight to Kabul the next day on their only remaining plane and while we were talking a man came with tickets. On the back there were photographs of the giant Bamiyan Buddhas that had been scribbled out with black felt-tip

by the Taliban after they blew them up. I told Ayubi that we were planning to leave and he seemed sad. From his pocket he took an inkpen
and pad of pink paper then wrote me a letter in turquoise-inked script
of curves and dots like tiny long-tailed birds flying across the page.

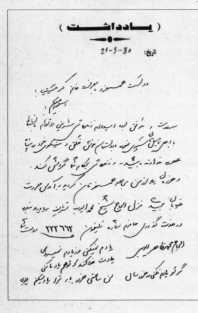

*My dear intuitive co-traveller
   Miss Christina
I hope you will be healthy
   and successful
And for you and your family
   to always enjoy the
   sweetest taste in your
   mouth
And to be sheltered by the
   Almighty's grace along
   with your friends
And any time you remember
   me write to residence of
   Al-Haj Sheikh Mohammad
   Ayub Sharif near Ice
   Factory, Mashad
I am always ready for your
   service
Your friend Zahir Ayubi
I'll never forget you and you
   will forget me
Though I will ask God to
   remind you
If you don't think of me in a
   thousand years
I'll think of you a thousand
   times in an hour*

When the Persian was translated, there were tears in my eyes. I would never forget Ayubi's big gentle smile and sad expression.

'Come with me,' he said.

I followed him to a taxi and we drove east of the city on a rutted road, past the walled tomb of Khwaja Abdullah Ansari, an eleventh-century Sufi poet and philosopher, the city's most famous shrine. Inside the garden of calligraphed white and black headstones, work was underway on the roof of the latticed pavilion guarding the saint, which had been destroyed by an American food drop. We did not stop but continued past a dusty grove of trees and along a track up towards the hills. The driver looked uncomfortable and said something to Ayubi which I didn't catch and then suddenly before us I could see thousands of tiny flags fluttering in the wind stretching along the bluff as far as the eye could seen. I realised what we were looking at. This was the mass grave of the thousands of Heratis killed in those three days of furious bombing by the Soviets in 1979. Ten thousand according to some, twenty-four thousand Ismael had told me.

There was nothing to say.

MARRI'S DIARY
Kabul, December 16

Eid Mubarak! Last night rockets and guns were going off all over town to announce Eid-ul Fitr, the end of Ramazan, and for once it was a sound to celebrate. Today father brought in a box of Eid biscuits and sweets and some many-coloured bangles. No new clothes this year but we dressed up in our best to go visiting friends and neighbours. Latifa and I put on make-up, lipstick and eye shadow and painted our nails in bright red, and it was so strange not to have to hide. There were lots of people on the streets and everyone happy, the children with toys.

The new government is to be sworn in on Saturday. How we pray this will bring peace. Father says it is a cabinet of Old Enemies and maybe they will all shoot each other. He says he will not believe in peace until the old cannon that used to fire to announce Eid and at noon every day is back on the hill above Babur's tomb. He told me it was so famous that a Swiss watch company used its picture for their calendars. The cannon was destroyed by Hekmatyar's men who took the hill and no one knows where the old man is who used to fire it – it was always the same family who lived on the hill and looked after the cannon.

I so hope that Karzai quickly opens the schools again and I can go back to teaching. I long to be useful and we have so little money, it is many weeks since we afforded meat. I *know we are luckier than most people but I long to have nice things again and to go to bed with a full belly instead of always this emptiness.*

But sometimes I fear, how can I teach children whose eyes have seen so many terrible things? I have read foreign books like Shakespeare with all his kings and treachery but anything we read in books will seem tame compared to what has happened here. Father says we are a country which started off with murder and looting so what can we expect.

7

Unpainting the Peacocks

O, but everyone was a bird
And the song was wordless;
The singing will never be done.
Everyone Sang, SIEGFRIED SASSOON

IT WAS TOO ABRUPT arriving in Kabul by plane, even on Ariana's labouring Antonov, which had to be jumpstarted at Herat airport. The city felt drained of colour, everywhere small flat-roofed houses made of sundried mud clinging like swallows' nests to the mountains, the trees long ago stripped for firewood, and the December sky was pigeon-grey and heavy as if waiting for snow. Had one reached there exhausted after a long journey over mountains by mule and foot or a bone-shattering ride along unmade roads, I suppose the city would have come as a relief and its washed-out Cubist landscape might appear attractive. But skittering to a halt on the taxi-way of Kabul airport (the main runway was full of craters from bombing) amid the wreckage of helicopters and war-planes, it was like arriving at the denouement of a tragedy without having witnessed the preceding acts.

Too many people had moved in from the countryside during the last twenty-three years of war, swelling Kabul's population from half a million to two or even three million, no one knew, and bringing bleakness with their broken families and baked-brick houses. It was hard to find any trace of the charmed city so beloved of the Moghul Emperor Babur who had counted sixteen kinds of wild tulips on its hillsides and asked to be buried there in a tomb describing Kabul as 'the light garden of the god-forgiven angel king'.

The hotel was bleak too. The Kabul Hotel, where I had stayed back in 1989 in a room on the same corridor where the US ambassador Adolph Dubs[1] had been murdered ten years earlier, had a large hole in the side from a rocket attack and looked darker and gloomier than I remembered. I still shivered at the recollection of the sinister one-armed telephone operator who doubled as the hotel's taxi-driver, his one hand cased in a black leather glove switching back and forth between the wheel and the gear-stick. Instead I found myself at the Mustafa, whose owner Wais (pronounced 'wise'), had moved back to Kabul after twenty-one years of exile in America, and presuming that with the Taliban in power there would be no tourists or foreigners in the capital for years, had decided to convert his family's old hotel into a moneychangers' and gem-dealers' bazaar. After repairing the holes made by mujaheddin rockets, he knocked out all the walls between rooms, replaced them with glass, and put bars on the doors. He was just finishing when the attack on the World Trade Center occurred, prompting the American bombing of Afghanistan. Within two months the Taliban were gone and journalists and aidworkers from all over the world were pouring into the city so he had quickly painted over the glass partitions in white, put back the beds and the hotel sign, and reopened it to cash in on media dollars.

Even Wais would admit it was not a luxury establishment. At 6000 feet above sea level, Kabul is a high city with harsh winters and inside the glass cubicles it was bitter. On the sporadic occasions that the

---

[1] Ambassador Dubs was abducted by members of a Maoist group in February 1979 and held captive in the hotel. He and his four captors were all killed when Afghan troops and Soviet advisors stormed the room.

capital had electricity, the one-bar heaters did little more than partially thaw a foot or hand placed on top. The glass was so thin that you could hear the person next door scratching. I had a snoring Australian one side and a Japanese who got up in the middle of the night for a high-pitched chatter with his office on the other.

However compared to most people in Kabul with their medieval lifestyles collecting water from wells and foraging for firewood, or kerosene if they could afford it, we lived like kings. It was close to Chicken Street, the hippie mecca of the 1960s, and a narrow road of shops hung with old carpets, pelts of snow-leopards and mountain foxes, or displaying trays of pebbles of lapis lazuli from Badakshan which the artists of Herat used to grind to produce deep blue pigment. At the end was the Chelsea Supermarket, where Osama bin Laden and his Arabs used to shop, in which one could buy tins of John West tuna and Cadbury's chocolate, although to get there involved battling through a forest of hands of women in tattered burqas and thin-faced orphans carrying small cans of coal to keep warm and demanding 'dollari, dollari'.

But the Mustafa had one enormous advantage and that was Wais, 'the Fonz of Kabul' as we quickly nicknamed him for his New Jersey accent and fast-talking 'tell me whaddya want, Wais can geddit' manner. A short but powerful-shouldered man of thirty-one with a jutting chin and passion for Al Pacino movies, he was a former body-building champion and knew everyone in town. He was bursting with plans for the hotel, building a restaurant, hot showers, installing a gym, and dreamed of reopening the bar and nightclub it had once featured. From morning to night a stream of men came to his office to take tea with his white-bearded father who always looked as though he was about to go somewhere in his dark overcoat and astrakhan hat but never stirred from his armchair, and was as silent as Wais was talkative.

Wais had been born in a sprawling white house with its own cinema not far from the hotel, and his family, he told me rather nebulously, had been 'in the import-export business' and owned five or six properties. They had left Kabul for the United States in 1979 when the Communists came. 'They killed a whole bunch of my family, my grandfather on my mother's side, some uncles who were Governors and one who was a general,' he said. But in 1991 his father had returned, met President Najibullah and managed to get the family property back including the old hotel. 'Then the mujaheddin came and it was a mess so he left again.' Finally, in the summer of 2001, Wais had decided to sell up the Nissan dealership he ran with his brothers in Ridgefield, New Jersey and 'give Kabul a go' as he put it. The clash of cultures was so great that neither side seemed to know what had hit them.

'Hey Christina, wanna come for a ride?' Wais asked me one day, looking pleased with himself. 'I fixed up the crown prince's car!'

I followed him down to the garage where one of his men was polishing a white 1968 Chevrolet Camaro. The temptation of driving around in probably the only convertible in Afghanistan on its first day out was irresistible. Wais opened the door with a great flourish and I wrapped my scarf round my head, donned my sunglasses and lowered myself down onto the beige leather seat. The car used to belong not to the crown prince but his brother Prince Nadir Shah, the father of Mostapha whom I had met in Rome, and had been part of his classic car collection, along with a Thunderbird that Wais was also trying to locate.

'Cost me six, maybe seven thousand dollars,' said Wais as he turned the key and we set off, spluttering at first but then smooth. The car dealer in him soon came out. 'Six cylinder, listen to that baby purr. Pure magic.' As we drove through the untidy streets, everyone turned to watch. Turbanned men fell off bicycles, children ran after us, shopkeepers and bakers came out onto the street to point. Up above us the sky was brilliant blue and the air was crisp and invigorating. Waving to people as we passed, I felt like the Queen of Kabul.

Driving round Kabul in Afghanistan's only convertible.

'There are no rules here, man,' complained Wais, shaking his head as he swerved to avoid a man with a rifle on his shoulder leading a flock of muddy goats down the main road. It was more a matter of compromise as the yellow taxis, blue rickshaws and black government saloons tried to find spaces between the shepherds and beggars and robed men. I laughed as Wais proceeded to go the wrong way round a traffic island on which a flummoxed traffic policeman in a long white coat and peaked cap was standing brandishing a Stop–Go sign. Seeing the convertible, the traffic cop looked astonished then began to wave excitedly. 'These guys all know us,' said Wais. 'They're all in our pay.'

'Oh man.' He stopped talking and covered his nose and mouth as we crossed the Kabul River, which emerges from between the mountains to the south and west of the city and meanders through the middle. Wishing momentarily that we were not in an open-topped car, I tried not to breathe in the nauseating odour from the almost dry riverbed into which people had evidently dumped their waste. Once the river was shining blue, there had been gardens all along the side and Emperor Babur would sit on a specially built stone terrace to drink wine and admire the view. But the grass had died, the trees been cut down and the banks had become a sprawling bazaar of the old and the rotten. Children with wooden pushcarts were selling brightly coloured sherbets from glass bottles with marbles as stoppers that were cloudy inside and almost certainly contained river effluent. There were men with piles of old clothes, a few stalls of black bananas and one of eggs, and in the midst of it all beggars with arms or legs missing, in some cases both.

It was hard to equate with Nancy Hatch Dupree's breezy description in my 1976 guidebook of Kabul as 'a fast-growing city where tall modern buildings nuzzle against bustling bazaars and wide avenues fill with brilliant flowing turbans, gaily striped chapans, mini-skirted school girls, a multitude of handsome faces and streams of whizzing traffic'. There was nothing modern about the city at all; on the contrary it felt like going back several hundred years except for the yellow taxis and occasional four-wheel drive bearing the militia of one warlord or another. Even the lampposts and roadnames had been looted for the metal. The only women were ghost-like figures in burqas and the girls' schools were still closed.

The Kabul I remembered from twelve years earlier, although still a city at war, had almost a festive air. It was June, the wedding month, flowers and blossoms perfuming the air, the Kabul River swollen with molten snows, and I had sat in the sunshine licking ice-creams in the university café with lively young women in high heels, some with dyed blonde hair, one even wearing a T-shirt proclaiming 'I'm not with this idiot' tightly pulled across her large breasts. At the apartment of a bureaucrat I had met, I had danced at a party where a well-known singer called Wajiha had strummed her guitar in between puffs of her cigarette. The only real signs of war apart from the large number of men – and women – in uniform and the drone of planes, had

Kabul was once a cosmopolitan city.

been the dawn queues at the bakers as people waited for the daily rations of five pieces of *nan* per family and the music and ideological commentary blaring from the loudspeakers hung in trees around the city which bizarrely sometimes included work-out classes and the theme from *Love Story.*

The fashionably-dressed women and the flowers may have disappeared but the handsome faces of the men were as I remembered, providing the only real colour in a city that had become a meeting point of all the races of Afghanistan. There were hawk-nosed Pashtuns in silk turbans or gold-threaded Kandahari caps, shorter coarser-featured Tajiks in karakul caps, darker-skinned Baluchis, sloe-eyed, flat-haired Turkmen and Uzbeks in bearskin hats, stocky Asiatic-looking Hazaras and fair-skinned, light-eyed Nuristanis from the impenetrable northern mountains, believed to be descendants of Alexander. Apart from those trying to sell rotten fruit or old clothes to each other, most seemed to be just waiting, standing or crouched by the roadside, their long pyjama tops over their knees. Almost all had leather belts slung around their waists or across their shoulders bearing knives and ammunition, and gave the impression of great strength, for tough conditions in Afghanistan where the weak die young have created a natural selection process. One group was watching two men playing a kind of speed-backgammon using Coke bottle tops and another surrounded a man showing off the beak and legs of a fighting cock he was trying to sell, but most stood slightly apart from each other and the years of civil war and massacres of different ethnic groups had left their faces furrowed with suspicion.

As we drove over newly-woven carpets laid out in the road to be 'antiqued' for gullible foreigners and into the celebrated Dar-ul Aman avenue, the brilliance of the sky seemed to fade as the winter sun dipped towards the horizon. In *The Road to Oxiana*, Byron described Dar-ul Aman as 'one of the most beautiful avenues in the world, four miles long, dead straight, as broad as the Great West Road and lined with tall white-stemmed poplars'. There was no sign of poplars or the grass-banked streams that had run in front of them. Instead the area looked more devastated than the photographs I had seen of Dresden after the Second World War. For as far as the eye could see there wasn't a single block undamaged, just row after row of ruins. The façades of some buildings still stood including one which resembled a Greek temple with its colonnaded pillars, but all were pockmarked with holes from hundreds of rockets and bullets, and, like a film set, there was nothing behind.

I had heard about the destruction and seen pictures of it, but to be confronted with it for myself instantly turned our afternoon joyride

Dar-ul Aman.

into something more sinister. On my previous visit to Kabul, four months after the last Russian soldier had left, the city had appeared almost untouched as the natural defences of the high mountains, rising like the scaled backs of dinosaurs from the plains all around, meant that during the Soviet occupation the mujaheddin had been unable to do much more than send a few rockets round the airport. In a vast concrete bunker of a compound near the start of Dar-ul Aman avenue, I had interviewed the Soviet ambassador Yuli Vorontsov, the First Deputy Foreign Minister, who was said to be the most powerful man in town. Now, feeling disoriented, I looked around in vain for that building but like the school and the cultural centre, the carpet bazaar and the match factory, it was gone. All this damage had been caused after the mujaheddin had taken the capital in 1992 and started fighting each other, first everyone against the luckless Hazaras, then the forces of Hekmatyar and Massoud continuing their long-running rivalry no matter who or what was in between.

These ruins were the work of weapons supplied by the Americans, British and Saudis.

'This is too spooky man,' said Wais after we had driven about a mile further, in stunned silence. 'I've seen it before but it don't get any better.' It was the first time I had seen him quiet and he was clearly uncomfortable with the attention his car was attracting. There was no other traffic on the wide avenue but lots of dark-looking characters hanging about, some sitting round a fire, apparently living in the ruins. I shivered. Dusk was falling and the cold felt like a dentist's drill on my gums.

'I don't think other young people will come back,' he said as he performed a hurried three-point turn. 'What's here? Just rubbish and ruins. Nothing works. Most guys my age have mortgages and kids and have been working six or seven years and are in good jobs. They ain't gonna give that up to come here where the most you could earn has gotta be $100 a month and no schools for their kids. No way. Back in Ridgefield I was clearing forty or fifty thousand easy after tax, you could pick up a burger or a pizza on the way home or take in a movie and when you turned on the shower out came hot water like "pow!", fast and powerful. Coming home is good but it ain't that good.'

'Look out for picturesque walled castles, cultivated fields and poplar groves', recommended the indefatigable Mrs Dupree in my guidebook but all I could see was rubble and the familiar painted skull and cross-bones warning of landmines. Both intrigued and repelled by what I had witnessed with Wais, I had hired a taxi and set off back up the avenue of Dar-ul Aman, this time intending to travel its whole length. Dar-ul Aman means City of Peace and the road leads to the place that Amanullah, the king who tried to make his citizens wear Western clothes, had built as his new capital.

About two thirds of the way along, I stopped to take photographs.

In the distance the white Dar-ul Aman Palace loomed, a large square building with a cupola on each corner, like some Gothic house of horror. The sky was grey and soulless, and the high mountains behind the palace dark and forbidding. Once again the wide avenue was deserted, and the only sound was the creaking of a cart on pram wheels carrying a man with no legs who was propelling it along furiously with his arms. A woman in a blue burqa clutching the hand of small boy drifted into view as if from nowhere and, amid all this bleakness, the vision was jarring as if some colour had seeped into a black and white photograph. Stopping in the road in front of me, she astonished me by lifting her burqa to reveal the moon-like face of a woman in her forties, kind if weary. Speaking in English, she invited me to lunch. 'Please it's all ready, just you come with us,' she said, 'it's just across the road.'

'I'm sorry,' I replied. 'I have an appointment.' It seemed a very British thing to say in a city where nothing worked including the telephones.

'Welcome,' she replied. 'We are very happy to see Britishers in our country, especially women. God will go with you.'

The taxi-driver hooted his horn. He had warned me that I would almost certainly be robbed or murdered on this road. I got in the car and we drove off, the woman and the boy still standing in the middle of the road gazing after us. When I looked back again there was no sign of them.

My driver, whose name was Yaqub, the Muslim equivalent of Jacob, was a classic-featured Kabuli with hooked nose and dark deep-sunk eyes, and looking at him it was easy to understand the once widely-held belief that the Afghans were one of the Lost Tribes of Israel. Just as with Afghanistan, land of the Afghans, no one seemed to know where the name Kabul originated. There were plenty of legends, many with Biblical links. Babur believed that it was founded by Cain, the son of Adam, and wrote of visiting his tomb in Kabul. Some credence is lent to this theory by the fact that in Persian, the

Dar-ul Aman avenue with the ruined palace in the background. Kabul Museum is to the right of the palace.

word for Cain is Cabil. Mountstuart Elphinstone, in his *Account of the Kingdom of Caubul* about his travels from 1808–10, the first British description of the country, wrote, 'the origin of the name of Afghanistan is entirely uncertain. They maintain they are descended from Afghaun, grandson of the King of Saul.' Sir Alexander Burnes, the British envoy hacked to pieces at his house in the city he loved in 1841 by protesters against British occupation, wrote that it was popularly believed that two sons of Noah called Cakool and Habul were the founders of the Afghan race. When it came to naming their greatest city the two brothers could not agree and finally each gave a syllable of their name, hence Ca-bul.

Much of old Kabul was built by Babur who captured the city in 1504 and lived in the Bala Hissar fort on a mound south of the Kabul River until 1525, writing poetry, laying out gardens, and disposing of various rivals within his own family including a rebellious step-grandmother, before moving on to Delhi and founding his great Moghul Empire. He described the city as 'an excellent mercantile centre' with 'the most pleasing climate in the world', explaining, 'within a day's ride it is possible to reach a place where the snow never falls. But within two hours one can go where the snows never melt.' In his own inimitable way, he added, 'Kabul's rhubarb is excellent'.

Yet it only became a capital city in 1776 under Timur Shah, second son of Afghanistan's first king Ahmad Shah Durrani and his chosen successor. Timur moved the capital from Kandahar out of spite because he was so angry with the Kandahari tribes who had opposed his accession; he spent his entire reign quelling revolts. Apparently not learning anything from his own experience, he went on to have twenty-three sons and left no designated heir, which meant they all ended up killing, blinding, and locking each other up in the dungeons of the Bala Hissar, and never completed their father's tomb.

Little remains of Kabul from Babur's or even Timur's days, not because of the jihad, as with the destruction of the ancient *musalla* and minarets in Herat, but because of two British punitive expeditions in the nineteenth century.

The first demolition mob, the Army of Retribution, arrived shortly after the murder of Alexander Burnes, in response to the massacre of thousands of retreating British officers from the Army of the Indus along with their wives and children, on the road to Jalalabad in January 1842. The attack had been led by Akbar, the son of Dost Mohammed, the king ousted by the British to install their puppet, Shah Shuja. The massacre was followed in April by the slaying of Shah Shuja outside the walls of his own palace.

One of the warring sons of Timur, Shah Shuja had been king before from 1803–09 when he was described by British envoy Mountstuart Elphinstone, who visited his Court in the winter capital of Peshawar, as being 'surrounded by eunuchs' and wearing so much gold and precious stones that 'we thought at first he had an armour of jewels'.[2] Pearls were strung across him like belts, the Koh-i-Noor flashed from one of the emerald bracelets above his elbows and his crown was 'so complicated and dazzling that it was difficult to understand and impossible to describe.' But for all this magnificent show, the 'Luckless Prince' as his troops called him, was ousted shortly after by his half brother Shah Mehmud, who he himself had toppled in the first place, then spent thirty years in exile in India before he was restored to the throne with the help of the Sikhs[3] and the British. His return on a white charger draped with gold had been met with such indifference and hostility on the part of the Afghan people that the Army of the

---

[2] Elphinstone writes that the British gifts which found most favour with the King were 'a pair of magnificent pistols, an organ and some pairs of silk stockings he had earlier admired'.

[3] Sikh aid did not come cheap. In return Shah Shuja ceded all territories on the banks of the Indus (including Peshawar) to Maharaja Ranjit Singh, gave him the Koh-i-Noor and promised to send him yearly 55 high-bred horses 'of approved colour and pleasant paces', 11 Persian scimitars, 25 good mules, an abundant supply of pomegranates, musk melons, grapes, figs, quinces and pistachios, as well as furs and Persian carpets, altogether to number 101 items.

Indus had had to stay on in Kabul to keep him in power. Realising they would be there for a while, they had built cantonments, brought in their families (though there was also said to be considerable 'fraternisation' with the local women) as well as fine wines, crystal chandeliers and servants, and occupied themselves with amateur dramatics, ice-skating and hunting.

The killing of Shah Shuja meant that British honour was at stake. It also sparked a national outrage at one of the worst massacres in the country's history, and by September the Union Jack was flying over the Afghan capital again as the Army of Retribution fought their way through the Khyber Pass and exacted their revenge, burning down Kabul's famous seventeenth-century covered bazaar. Accounts from travellers describe the Char Chatta or Four Arcades Bazaar as a beautiful place, four painted arcades linked by open plazas in the centre of each was a fountain. It was one of the great crossroads of Central Asia where one could buy silk and paper from China in the north; spices, pearls and exotic wood from India in the east; glass, pottery, silver and wine from Persia and Turkey in the west and slaves brought from both directions. The British forces destroyed all this, and set fire to so much of the city that flames were said to have still filled the sky two days later when the troops left. Having learnt their lesson, this time they did not attempt to stay and the following year, 1843, Dost Mohammed quietly reoccupied the throne, telling the British, 'I am like a wooden spoon, you may throw me hither and thither but I shall not be hurt.' After four years of disaster and the terrible human cost of the First Anglo-Afghan War, the British had left Afghanistan as they had found it.

The Second Anglo-Afghan war was founded on the ongoing rivalries between Victorian England and Tsarist Russia whose army maps had stopped showing any southern boundary to their territories, and was precipitated in 1878 by the refusal of the Afghans to join an alliance against the Russians or accept a British Mission to Kabul to counter an uninvited one from St Petersburg. The capture of the

Second Anglo-Afghan War.

Khyber Pass, Jalalabad and Kandahar by 35,000 British troops forced a change of heart and in July 1879 Sir Louis Cavagnari rode into Kabul on the back of an elephant with an escort of seventy-five Indian soldiers from the Guides Cavalry to become the first British Resident in Kabul since the murder of Burnes. Six weeks later he too was dead, killed when the British Residency inside the Bala Hissar fort was stormed by mutinous Afghan troops, just one day after Cavignari had sent a cable which concluded with the words 'all well'. The mayor of Kabul carried his head in triumph through the city.

When the hastily assembled Avenging Army marched on the Bala Hissar in retaliation a month later, their commander General Sir Frederick Roberts described finding 'the floors covered with blood-stains and amidst the embers of a fire we found a heap of human bones'. He set up a commission of inquiry offering rewards to those who came forward with information, which meant many Afghans used the opportunity to settle old scores, then hanged more than a hundred protest-leaders and tribal chiefs including the mayor, from gallows erected in its courtyard. The following spring the British troops demolished it altogether in what General Roberts called 'a lasting memorial of our ability to avenge our countrymen'.

They then handed the throne over to Dost Mohammed's grandson Abdur Rahman. But the war was far from over. Ayub Khan, the ruler of Herat and Abdur Rahman's cousin, decided he would drive the infidel British from Afghanistan and seize the throne. He marched on Kandahar, then occupied by a small British garrison. At Maiwand, on the plains just west of Kandahar, the British suffered one of their worst-ever defeats in Asia, losing more than 1000 men. Once more General Roberts mobilised his forces for revenge and marched from Kabul, taking sips of champagne to keep up his strength as his 10,000 men inflicted a decisive victory on Ayub Khan's Afghans with just thirty-five British losses.

The last British troops on Afghan soil marched from Kandahar in April 1881, leaving Abdur Rahman in charge of his country though he agreed to accept British control over his foreign policy in return for being able to call on their help against foreign aggressors. He was fascinated by Britain and constantly quizzed British envoys about monogamy, eventually announcing that it must be because of the damp climate that British men could only manage one wife.

'My life as king was not a bed of roses,' he wrote with wonderful understatement in his autobiography, 'here began my first severe fight against my own relations, my own subjects, my own people.' During his twenty-one-year reign he crushed over forty revolts by non-Pashtuns, usually in the most brutal manner involving wholesale executions, and he became known as the Iron Amir. According to Frank Martin, an Englishman who worked as the king's chief engineer, even his bookkeepers were made to sign declarations to say that if they interfered with his papers they would have their hands cut off.

His punishments were so severe that when a married man and married woman who had run off together were brought before him he told the man 'as you are so fond of the woman you should have her as completely as possible', then had the woman thrown alive into a huge cauldron of boiling water and boiled down to soup which the man was forced to drink before being hanged.[4]

It was Abdur Rahman's grandson Amanullah, declared king in 1919 after the murder of his father King Habibullah while hunting in Jalalabad, who came up with the idea of building a new capital. His Grand Tour of Delhi, Tehran and Europe in 1927–8 made him realise the backwardness of his own country; he became determined to modernise it.

French and German architects were commissioned to construct his new capital and told to make it 'monumental'. Ornate European villas were built for the ministers and noblemen who would live there, as well as the vast white Dar-ul Aman Palace set in formal gardens that was planned to house the parliament. German engineers were brought in to build a narrow-gauge railroad to connect Dar-ul Aman and the centre, open trolley cars running the six-mile journey three times a day on the only railway in all of Afghanistan.

Not satisfied with building a new capital, King Amanullah also decided to transform one of Babur's favourite places, the nearby village of Paghman in the foothills of the Hindu Kush, into a hill-station based on Simla. Swiss-style chalets and Italian villas were built among its pine-wooded glades along with bandstands, an ornate theatre, a red mosque, a victory arch modelled on the Arc de Triomphe, and a racecourse for elephants.

Years later, after the Russian occupation, both Paghman and

[4] The object was to punish him not only in this life but also the next for a cannibal cannot go to Paradise.

The gardens of Paghman were modelled on those King Amanullah had seen in Europe.

Dar-ul Aman became battlegrounds between factions during the mujaheddin fighting. Paghman was the base for the forces of Sayyaf, one of the seven mujaheddin leaders, and was flattened apart from the arch, its population of 40,000 fleeing to leave just five families. Dar-ul Aman changed hands several times and though the Dar-ul Aman Palace remained standing, it was a charred skeleton of what it had once been and the blown-out windows and jagged rocket holes in the walls and domes gave it a haunted appearance.

Across the road from the ruined palace stood Kabul Museum which still had the opening hours on the gate even though the whole of the west wing had collapsed, the roof had caved in and the ground all around was covered by expended ammunition shells. The door was padlocked but as I approached three men appeared. One with a white beard and sad gentle face under a rolled cream *pakol* hat introduced himself as Umar-akhan Masoodi, the director, whom I had arranged to see.

'Our museum was one of the great museums of the world,' he said as he took a large iron key from a chain around his waist and opened the padlock. 'We had probably the best collection of Central Asian art and artefacts. But as you will see it is now one of the great tragedies.'

As Mr Masoodi pushed open the door and waved me into the entrance hall it was evident what he meant. On either side of the stairs leading up to the museum was an empty stone plinth and on the wall to the right the smashed remains of what had once been a large wall cabinet. On one of the plinths there were a few pieces of rubble and a small black and white Polaroid sellotaped to the wall showing an impressive Gandharan statue of a warrior. 'This was a statue from the second century, of Kanishka, one of our great Kushan kings,' he said pointing at the photograph, 'and that was a Kushan princess.' He pointed at the other empty plinth and then to the cabinet. 'In this cabinet were two giant stone birds not like anything you ever saw and as tall as you or I. When these things were made Caesar was ruling Rome and the Han emperors ruling China. That's how old they were.'

'What happened?' I asked. 'The Taliban,' he replied, shaking his head with a sigh. 'A high-ranking delegation led by Qadratullah Jamal, the Minister of Culture, came last February, with an authorisation from the Ministry of Vice and Virtue. I wasn't here because I had quit my post as deputy director of the museum when the Taliban took over and I saw what kind of people they were. I couldn't be witness to the breaking of our history so I stayed at home. I didn't care about not having money for food. But Mr Khalilullah here, one of our curators, was present and saw it all.'

A man in a belted black leather jacket took over the narrative. 'There were about sixteen of them with armed guards and they started breaking statues with hammers and axes. They were happy and laughing like children.' Pointing at the Polaroid of the Kushan king, he said, 'The minister himself who is from the Popolzai tribe broke this one. The statue was very big and hard to break so he tied his shawl around it to pull it down to the floor then smashed it with an axe.

After that they came every day for three months, smashing things until there were no more statues. Some of the statues were solid marble so they brought big pick-axes like those used for breaking rocks in the mountains. It was a few weeks after they started coming here that they blew up the Bamiyan Buddhas.'

'What did you say when you saw what they were doing?' I asked.

'We were employees and we just had to watch it all because it was dangerous to protest. The order had come from Mullah Omar himself and was announced on the radio. Nobody could question it. By Allah all we could do was pick up and save the pieces.'

We walked up the steps, past a large stone urn, and down a long corridor with all its windows blown out and most of the roof missing. 'It was not just the Taliban who destroyed the museum,' said Mr Masoodi. 'This area was the centre of fighting between the Northern Alliance and Hekmatyar's men and it became very dangerous to be here. In 1993 a rocket came through the top floor and burnt the entire area. We managed to save a lot and box the things up. Then the warlords started looting. First we fitted padlocks, then steel doors but still they came. Even huge things they took, bigger than a man. We kept hearing about parts of our collection being sold in Islamabad, London, Paris and America, and one of our archaeologists even saw an artefact he had dug up on display in a case in the Metropolitan Museum in New York, but what could we do? By the time the Taliban came we had already lost seventy percent of our collection.'

He told me that he had worked twenty-five years in the museum, all his working life, and I asked which had been his favourite piece. He looked at me like a parent asked to choose between his children. 'We used to have so many things, prehistoric tools of flint found in Badakshan, fifteen-thousand-year-old inscribed stone tablets from Ghazni, one of the world's largest coin collections with first-century Greek silver coins, ivory panels from India, Alexandrian glassware, Buddhist statues, the Hindu Venus, the Bactrian gold . . . all of them were special . . .'

Buddhist sculpture in Kabul Museum, photographed before the years of the Taliban's regime. Kabul Museum once had one of the most impressive collections in Central Asia.

The arrival of the Taliban in Kabul in September 1996 with their insistence that the depiction of live creatures on paintings or in stone promoted idolatry and was un-Islamic, proved catastrophic for the museum.

'It was our most vulnerable time,' said Mr Masoodi.'We had managed to hide some things from the warlords in the basement of the Culture Ministry but of course when the Taliban came with their ideas against faces and animal forms they destroyed them. Here in the museum we tried to fool them by turning things upside down so they would not realise that they were figures but in the end they just destroyed everything. Come, you'll see.'

The tour took less than five minutes. Founded by King Amanullah in 1924, the museum had once boasted a collection of more than a hundred thousand items reflecting the many different cultures and invaders who had passed across Afghan soil over the centuries. The Bactrian gold alone, discovered only in 1979, consisted of around twenty thousand gold artefacts dating from the first century. Of all these many treasures, all that was left to see was one nineteenth-century marble door, a wall frieze from Helmand, and the large

Kandahari urn inscribed with squiggles and swirls. 'They left this because these are Islamic phrases,' explained Mr Masoodi.

I asked him how he had felt when he came back after the Taliban had fled and saw the destruction. 'I cried,' he said simply. 'This museum was so precious and now we've lost everything. Of course all things fashioned by artists are precious and valuable but the oldest things cannot be replaced.

'They wanted us to be a faceless land with no history,' he continued. 'Pakistan was responsible. They thought they had captured Afghanistan through their Taliban puppets and wanted to destroy our history and culture because they are a land with neither. They ordered this and as far as I am concerned what they did is an international crime and should be punished as such.'

I followed him as he walked through a doorway which had obviously only recently been unbricked, took another key from his waist and unlocked a door into a storeroom.

'This is the real museum now,' he said.

On the floor and on shelves, laid out as if in coffins in numerous labelled wooden boxes, were the rescued fragments of various statues. A few pieces were large enough to be identifiable as parts of a hand or a face but the majority were as pulverised as if a bulldozer had run over them. Some of the boxes had black and white photographs or museum guides open at pictures of the figures and scenes that they had once been. Thousands of years of history smashed into bits by a few men with beards and axes intent on cultural genocide.

'These are all the pieces we saved,' said Khalilullah proudly, 'we hid them from the Taliban and now we will try to reconstruct them.'

The page open next to one box of rubble showed a marble chariot drawn by two horses guided by the charioteer Dawn and bearing the Sun God Suriya which had been part of a fifth-century Brahmanic temple. I couldn't imagine how you would start to reconstruct such a thing but there was a look in Khalilullah's eyes that stopped me from saying more.

*The Taliban, led by the Culture Minister, had smashed centuries
of history into smithereens.*

'We have pictures and documents and UNESCO has promised to
help,' he said.

We walked back to the entrance and I felt Mr Masoodi's hand
lightly on my shoulder. Tears were running down my face and I felt
foolish that after all the death and tragedy I had witnessed in this
land I should cry over broken statues and pots.

'Don't be pessimistic about the museum,' he said. 'We can restore it again. You know twenty-three years of war is a long time and it's difficult to cry all that time. Every family in Afghanistan has lost people and yet we're still optimistic. My brother who was strong and handsome was injured in a rocket attack and paralysed. That's just a small example. Maybe we have lost our past but it's the future that matters now.

'You know we still have a few objects we managed to hide. Now they say peace has come but we don't tell anyone where we have hidden the things, even the ministers. If they ask we just say "under the sky". Some of the people who were shooting the rockets before are now running the government.'

Bidding me farewell at the entrance, Mr Masoodi cupped his right hand to his ear.

'Listen,' he said, 'have you noticed?'

I strained my ears but all I could hear was distant rumbling of heavy guns in the mountains. Then I realised what he was listening to. Across the road on top of the charred stump of a tree in the ruins of the palace gardens, a bird was singing.

Mr Masoodi smiled. 'For years there have been no birds in this city. When I was a boy this was a place of many trees, cherry trees, mulberry trees, poplars. The city smelled of trees. But first the Russians cleared them to get rid of cover for the mujaheddin. Then the people cut them down for firewood. I guess there was nowhere for the birds to go.'

He disappeared back into the forlorn ruins of his museum with its missing roof and windows.

Just that morning I had been reading Alexander Burnes' description of Kabul on his first visit in 1832 when he likened it to Paradise. 'There were peaches, plums, apricots, pears, apples, quinces, cherries, walnuts, mulberries, pomegranates and vines all growing in one garden', he wrote. 'There were also nightingales, blackbirds, thrushes and doves and chattering magpies on almost every tree.' He was so captivated by the birdsong of Kabul that an Afghan friend later sent him a Kabul nightingale which he named 'the nightingale of a thousand tales'.

In the taxi on the way back I realised that I had never asked Mr Masoodi about the origins of Kabul. Maybe he was right. In a land where the past had always been everything, people's lives governed and destroyed by the feuds of their forefathers, it was the future that mattered now.

That future depended on my old friend Hamid Karzai. He had been named leader of the interim government which had been chosen by Afghan delegates meeting in a castle in Bonn under pressure from the international community as well as the Teutonic hotel management, who needed it to be wrapped up quickly as they had hired the place out to a conference of dentists. Hamid was to be sworn in the following Saturday and had been flown into Kabul from Kandahar. He was already installed in the Arg, the old Royal turned Presidential Palace, where so many of his predecessors had been brutally murdered, and he had invited me over for supper.

As I arrived at the palace gate, the city was echoing with the rattle of machine guns and barrages of anti-aircraft fire. The mullahs had announced the sighting of the crescent moon, which meant that it was finally the end of Ramadan. The guards at the gate, clearly all former mujaheddin, dressed in camouflage but with open sandals which must have been freezing in the below-zero temperatures, stopped firing into the sky and lowered their Kalashnikovs, to regard me with suspicion.

'What do you want?' their captain demanded.

'I've got an appointment to see Mr Karzai,' I replied.

'You're a journalist. No journalists allowed. Come back tomorrow morning.'

'No, I'm a friend,' I insisted, 'he's expecting me for dinner.'

'We don't know anything about that. You look like a journalist. Go away.' He spat noisily onto the ground and walked off.

Hamid Karzai, President of Afghanistan, in the palace where so many of his predecessors were killed, December 2001.

I was shocked. It was the first time anyone had been rude to me in Afghanistan and I stormed after him.

'I think you will find that Mr Karzai will be extremely angry if I am not shown in. Please radio him immediately.'

'We don't have a radio,' said one of the other mujaheddin. All of them had bloodshot eyes and I guessed what they were chewing and spitting was opium paste.

'Anyway Mr Karzai is not anybody yet and we are President Rabbani's guards.'

Burhanuddin Rabbani, as head of the Northern Alliance had declared himself President of Afghanistan immediately after his forces had liberated Kabul and was not at all happy about the meeting in Bonn that had led to Hamid being chosen as leader. It was Rabbani's liking for power which had sparked off the destruction of Kabul such as that at Dar-ul Aman, because of his refusal to relinquish the presidency at the end of his agreed term in 1992 when all the mujaheddin leaders were supposed to take turns at six months in power. I had had no idea that the two men were now sharing the Presidential Palace.

We were at a standoff with the guards refusing to let me in and laughing at my insistence that I would not move from the gate, when the headlights of a car approached from inside the compound. The driver was one of Hamid's cousins who had met me back at the house in Quetta. It was just in time.

Hamid was horrified when he heard what had happened as I was shown into the barely lit palace an hour late. He, his brother Shah Wali who had flown over from America and was looking miserable, and uncle Aziz, were all gathered round a small electric fire in a long sitting room with brocaded wallpaper and a tapestry on the wall. Clad in a fur-lined emerald green and black-striped *chapan*, one of the Uzbek long coats, with an astrakhan hat on his head, Hamid looked thin and drawn in the large winged leather armchair. For the last two months he had been in the mountains of Uruzgan trying to rally people against the Taliban, then negotiate a surrender, and his beard had turned almost white.

Hamid was perhaps the only tribal chief in Afghanistan without his own militia and within a few days would take charge of a cabinet of squabbling warlords, many of whom had killed each other's men and taken their lands. But he seemed unfazed and full of his customary fierce pride by which he would lay down his life for his country at the first perceived slight.

'When I arrived in Kabul, I was met by the Defence Minister, General Fahim [military leader of the Northern Alliance] and the Interior Minister, Mr Qanuni [another senior member of the Northern Alliance] and they asked me where are your bodyguards. I told them you are my guards from now on. They were shocked!'

I was not surprised. While I admired the principle, in Afghanistan's bloody politics it had to be madness to trust these people who hated a Pashtun being in charge again and clearly wanted his job. I wondered why he did not call in some well-armed Popolzai tribesmen from Kandahar. But Hamid insisted, 'I would not kill an ant to remain in this position.'

It was hard to adjust to seeing him there in the palace in Kabul about to be made head of state in a ceremony that would be celebrated from Downing Street to the White House and shown live on television all over the world, after all those years of frustration in exile in Peshawar and Quetta, and our adventures in Kandahar living on trenchwater and mud-crabs. But instead of being exhilarated, I felt strangely depressed and, as I watched the tell-tale tic in his cheek, it seemed to me that his own feelings did not match his brave words.

We hadn't been talking long when he was called away to deal with a problem with Rabbani. Uncle Aziz, who had been deputy chief of protocol to King Zahir Shah so knew the palace very well, gave me a tour of the quarter in which they were camped with a running commentary, mostly stories of Afghan kings getting one over on the British as well as a few digs at the 'ignorance' of Rabbani who had apparently insisted on taking down what he had called 'that old rug', not realising it was a rare Gobelin tapestry sent as a gift to Amir Abdur Rahman by Queen Victoria.

First he took me to the Peacock Room where he and Shah Wali were sleeping. The room was decorated with silk wallpaper printed with hundreds of peacocks but the heads of every single one had been painted over in white by the Taliban. 'Can you imagine the time that took someone to do?' asked Aziz, 'the madness of it all.'

It was a similar story in the dining room. The line of white discs along the wall had once all contained birds but had all been painted over. Someone had taken a knife to all the oil paintings, gifts from monarchs such as King Victor Emmanuel of Italy, and cut out any figure. This left some bizarre results such as the fishing scene over the fireplace which showed a fishing rod going into a river but no man holding it, next to a field with a cow's body but no head. Even more strange, to cover some of the holes, black ink drawings of trees on white paper had been inserted behind the canvas.

Outside, the stone lions guarding the entrance had all been carefully decapitated. 'This is a country which cannot feed or educate its children, that has no healthcare, where people die by the age of forty, yet our government spent all their time removing heads and faces from things,' said Aziz, laughing.

By the time Hamid returned it was almost curfew so we talked quickly about his plans to 'rid the country of warlordism' and hopes to disarm the population. I tried to imagine him asking Ismael Khan or General Dostum to give up their arms. 'Even the government became a warlord,' he said. 'That must never happen again.'

A few days later foreign forces would arrive, mostly from Britain, to keep him in power just as they had tried to with kings in the nineteenth century. For all Hamid's fierce protestations of independence and being 'nobody's puppet', Italian troops would be patrolling the dark palace grounds with their avenues of bare trees and ruined buildings around which the castrated Najibullah had been dragged over and over again behind a Taliban jeep. As he stood at the door, a headless stone lion either side of him, the untrustworthy Rabbani guards watching on sullenly, he seemed the loneliest man in the world. I wondered if I would ever see him again.

One morning a piece of pink paper appeared under the door of my hotel room inviting me to the re-opening of the National Gallery the following week. I thought I would stop by and see how preparations were going.

The gallery was a strange insubstantial sort of building resembling a Bavarian chalet that had landed in the middle of an untidy Kabul street. It was a day without electricity and it was gloomy inside. On a table near the entrance was a pile of paintings with the faces scratched out. Upstairs a thin-faced man of about forty was swabbing furiously at an oil painting with a sponge, dipping it back and forth in a bucket of water.

'What are you doing?' I asked him.

'I am the artist,' he replied with a half-bow although with his cream suit and neat-trimmed beard he did not look like one at all, 'and I am also a doctor. My name is Dr Mohammed Yusuf Assefi and every one of my paintings is done in oils so when the Taliban wanted to destroy our heritage, our paintings, because they had people and faces, I covered them over with watercolours. Any figure or animal I changed to trees, flowers or mountains. I pretended to be repairing the paintings and instead I painted over them. Look, you see.' In front of my eyes he rubbed at a shadow on a lake and a swan appeared swimming under the autumn trees.

'And here.' He sponged away a pot of flowers by a canalside and a peasant woman appeared carrying a bundle on her back.

It was hard not to laugh. I'd never seen anything like it. 'How many did you do?' I asked.

'I painted over as many as I could, not just mine. I did eighty here in the gallery and forty-two in the Foreign Ministry. I did the ministry ones first, then when they started destroying the museum I knew they'd come here next so I did these too.'

Unlikely as he looked for the part, particularly when I later saw him again driving along very slowly in his battered Volkswagen Beetle, clasping the wheel, I had come across one of Kabul's cultural heroes.

'How did you get the idea?' I asked.

'I used to have eight paintings hanging in the Presidential Palace and of course I was very proud. When the Taliban took over and executed Najib I heard they'd torn up those paintings because they had people and animals in, so then I hit on this idea of repainting the others to save them.'

'That was an incredible risk. How on earth did you get away with it?'

'The Taliban didn't understand what was going on. I just walked into the ministry one day and told them I had been contracted to restore all the paintings. It took about a year to do all of them but I kept moving paintings around so they didn't realise what I was doing and an official in a room with a painting wouldn't suddenly realise a horse had disappeared. Of course it was risky and I could have been beaten and gone to jail but I love my country and wanted to preserve our heritage. And you see it took three or four days to do each one but it only takes a minute to bring the figures back. It's like magic.'

I stood there watching for a while as figures came to life under his sponge in front of me. Once I knew what he had done, the subterfuge was quite apparent, in some cases comically so. The scene of a man on horseback in the countryside had become a rather bad painting of a large tree with an immensely swollen trunk. A boat of a family outing on a lake had become a boat of sacks with no one rowing it.

From outside suddenly came the sound of children's laughter. I realised it was the first time I had heard this since arriving in Kabul, and we both went to the window. Thick flakes of snow were starting to fall and children were dancing about in the street trying to catch them. 'It's *barf-i-awal*, the first snow,' said Dr Assefi. 'Maybe finally the drought is over. Then we can start to live again.'

MARRI'S DIARY
Kabul, January 2002

Snow again today and all the mountains are white. Everyone
is hoping that this may finally be the end of the drought and
Qargha Lake will be full again. Outside children are playing
in the streets making snowballs and riding down the hills on
trays and everyone smiling.

Yesterday I went with Farishta to the city to the Womens
League office by the old Zainab cinema to find out about
jobs for women. There were so many other women there and
everyone praying but no one knows yet.

We hear on the radio that the world has promised our
government a lot of money so surely they will soon reopen
the schools. But there are still so many shortages and the city
is a place of orphans. Even the Arg is without heat and light
and water. We are all poor now.

It was very busy in the city, many people coming back, the
traffic hardly moving. It's odd to see taxis coming into the
city laden with things rather than leaving and trucks
bringing in televisions and electronic things. The Post Office
is open again. Everywhere there is the sound of hammering
as people are repairing their houses.

There are lots of foreigners in the city. My brother says every
day there are television cameras in the bazaar. I wonder if
Jamil's friend, the lady journalist, will come. I heard from a

*friend who saw Tawfiq in Kandahar that he took my letters
to Quetta. He says the Taliban are all in Pakistan.*

*The loud planes still fly over but for now it is calm here in
Kabul with all the foreign troops driving around, flags from
their jeeps. Farishta is very naughty and persuaded me to go
to Chicken Street and says some of the soldiers are very
handsome. Sometimes the burqa is very useful for being able
to watch and no one knows. She told me of one girl who
sings Beatles songs as she passes foreign men and they don't
know if it is for them. We stood for a while and watched the
British soldiers. Boys asked them for cigarettes and they drew
pictures for children.*

8

The Story of Abdullah

*'He is the hero who does not ask the number of his foes
but asks as to where they are'*
ALEXANDER THE GREAT

IN KANDAHAR FOOTBALL STADIUM, a dusty pitch with concrete stands either side, two men, one in baggy cream shalwar
kamiz and large plastic-framed glasses, and one in a shiny blue and
purple tracksuit, were standing in the centre of the field, holding a
hose and watering the same spot over and over, forming a small
pool. The rest of the ground was grey and bone-dry. The man in
shalwar kamiz, who introduced himself as Mohammed Nasir, head
of the Sports Board, shook his head. 'However much we water, we
can't get it clean,' he complained, pointing at the muddy water
through which a dark stain was just visible. 'It's where they used to
erect the gallows to hang people. For the first three weeks the water
ran bright red as all the blood came out of the soil.'

'There's also that patch over there but it's not as bad.' He pointed
towards the goal on his left. 'That's the goalpost where they used to
tie women and stone them.' He returned to his hosing and I went
and sat on one of the stands, my mind filled with baying crowds
cheering on an execution. In the distance I could see the shining

Washing out the blood at Kandahar football stadium.

turquoise dome of the tomb of Ahmad Shah Durrani, Afghanistan's first king, who was himself not averse to executing those who stood in his way.

After a while I became aware of someone watching me. A teenage boy with a dirty face under a silver-embroidered scarlet skullcap had arrived on a bicycle and stopped in front of me, tapping his blue flip-flops on the ground.

'Where are you from?' he asked.

'Inglistan,' I replied. 'And you?'

'Over there.' He pointed in the direction of some tumbledown buildings behind the stadium.

We chatted a little and he told me his name was Nida Mohammed, he was fourteen, and that he did not go to school because he had to earn money carrying goods in the market as his father had 'disappeared' in the jihad.

'Did you ever come to an execution?' I asked.

'I've seen more than a hundred,' he said proudly. 'I used to come because it was entertainment – there was nothing else to do. And it was interesting to see the reaction of the victim, if he would be scared. The best time was during Ramadan because then there would be at least one hanging or amputation a day, sometimes three or four.'

'How did you find out about them?'

'The Taliban announced them on the radio two days before – this man, son of this man, who killed that man, son of that man, will be executed on Tuesday at 2 p.m. They were usually either at noon or 2 p.m. Thousands of people came. I would meet my friends and if we had money we would buy pistachios or oranges. The left-hand side of the stadium would be full but the right empty in case they chose to shoot the man.'

'Who chose?' I hadn't realised there was any choice involved.

'The family of the injured party could choose the manner of death. Sometimes we would bet on what they'd choose. The person could be shot, hanged or sacrificed.'

'Sacrificed?'

'You know, like sheep. Their hands and feet would be tied and they would be laid on a block then their chest slit open with a long knife so all the blood and guts spilled out. Women were tied to goalposts and shot down or if they had committed adultery, they would be stoned. Once I saw some homosexuals have their hands and feet tied and a wall collapsed on top of them. That was interesting.'

He was as matter of fact about it as if he were recounting a television documentary. I asked him to describe a typical execution.

'Just before the time the Taliban officials would drive into the stadium in their Land Cruisers wearing their big black turbans. They would announce that this person, son of that person has committed this crime and the injured party has chosen this form of death. Sometimes they put hoods over their heads. During the shooting or sacrificing people would go very quiet then afterwards there would be all the crying of the relatives. They always made the family come and watch and collect the dead bodies. They used to keep an ambulance at the gate so when people had their hands or feet amputated they would be taken straight to the hospital.'

'Did anyone speak?'

'Afterwards the Taliban would say, "Learn from this. This is what will happen to you if you commit crimes. Remember what you have seen." Then we would all go home. People were quiet then.'

Nida told me he had to go. Before he left I asked him when the Taliban had held their last execution.

'It wasn't here,' he said. 'It was in the centre of town, in Herat Chowk just the day before the Taliban left.'

'Do you know who it was?'

'Of course. It was Abdullah. Everyone knew him. He was a hero. His uncle works in the woodcutters' bazaar.'

He rode off on his bike before I could ask any more. It was too big for him and he wobbled as he looked back to wave. I sat there for a while puzzling about what he meant by 'hero' as Mohammed Nasir carried on hosing the same spot. The water gave a last spurt and cut out so he came over to join me and I asked him if, apart from amputations and executions, the stadium had actually seen any football in the seven years of Taliban rule.

He laughed. 'To start with they banned it altogether. But football is our national game so eventually they allowed us to play matches but only before 4 p.m. The players all had to be completely covered, arms and legs. You can imagine in the summer, what that was like for them, when it is a furnace here, more than 40°C. The Taliban used to come and catch those players who had rolled up their sleeves or whose beards were too short. They would drag them from the pitch and beat them with the butts of their Kalashnikovs.'[1]

'And did people come and watch the games?'

'Yes, football is very popular here. In the past, before television

[1] The Pakistan youth football team that went to play in Kandahar in summer 2000 were dragged off the pitch by religious police and had their heads shaved for not wearing long trousers.

and foreign radio were banned and we became so cut off from the world, we even used to follow foreign teams. My favourites were Brazil and Manchester United. But the Taliban did not allow people to cheer or even clap. If a goal was scored all they could do was shout *Allah-o Akbar*. Now we must rebuild everything. I want a football federation where no beards are allowed. But we had a game last week and everyone was quiet and saying holy words because they were scared that there are still many Taliban here. We will have to teach them to clap and cheer and whistle again.'

On my way out of the stadium, I noticed a plaque on the wall. In English and Pashto was written; 'This Project has been completed with UNHCR and WFP funding on 21 May 1996'. It was the date that caught my eye for that was more than 18 months after that Taliban had captured Kandahar. Did Taliban officials laugh, I wondered, every time they passed by that sign to carry out their barbaric practices in a stadium paid for by well-meaning Western 'infidels' who thought they were encouraging sport.

The place where I was staying was not really a guesthouse, just an empty house abandoned by Taliban and commandeered by one of the Karzai cousins, in which myself and an American TV crew from CBS had landed up. It was in the new part of town near the Red Mosque (no longer red, but cream and turquoise as the Taliban had repainted it), and it was a peaceful area of wide avenues away from the crowds and dirt. There was no electricity, often for days at a time, and sometimes no water, but it had a small army of guards who sat round a fire outside, and every time we paid rent, new things appeared, first carpets, then curtains, a plastic table and chairs, paraffin heaters, potted red and pink geraniums and eventually even a roaring log fire, making it almost homely.

It also had a talented if rather languid cook called Humayun who was such a late-riser that breakfast was long after we had all set off for the day. He was a sensitive soul with long delicate fingers who had somehow decided that his destiny was to be a pastry chef; a job there was little if any call for in Afghanistan where it was hard to find butter or sugar and most people survived on *nan* bread. In the meantime from the limited produce available in Kandahar bazaar, he managed to concoct wonderful spicy dishes of tomato and aubergine, which he ate with us. He was waiting with lunch when I arrived.

'I'm sorry Humayun, I've just been to the stadium and it's put me off eating,' I explained, toying with my food, knowing how moody he got if we didn't eat everything. 'I can't believe the awful things the Taliban used to do.'

Humayun cleared his own plate and helped himself to more. 'Executions were good,' he said, heaping forkfuls of stewed aubergine into his mouth. 'I went a couple of times. I saw the execution of a woman who had shot her husband and the amputation of the hand of a robber. Another time I saw a man hanged who had been stealing lots of sheep.'

'Didn't you find it shocking?'

'These people were criminals and deserved to be hanged. Under the Taliban you could leave a bar of gold outside your house and no one would take it and you could roam the streets at 2 a.m. and be perfectly safe. Now if we didn't have ten guards here even this plastic chair would be taken. Already last week the owner of a gold jewellery shop and his son were shot dead on their way home just for his gold chain and watch. Things were better before.'

Humayun's defence of executions turned out to be a fairly common view in Kandahar. Unlike Herat, Kandahar had always been a conservative place, and a month after the Taliban surrender, their main stronghold and spiritual heartland seemed – perhaps unsurprisingly – still a city of Taliban.

I had arrived in the town well after sunset, coming through the arch that was all that remained of the city walls much later than I had planned because thick snow had blocked the Khojak Pass from Pakistan. The only hotel in town, the grimy Noor Jahan, already had four to a room so I stopped at a *chai-khana* on the main street to enquire about places to stay. Sitting cross-legged on wood and string charpoys under a large canopy, drinking glasses of tea from small blue enamelled pots, were a crowd of men in black turbans with kohl-rimmed eyes who regarded me with hostility, in between puffing at their water pipes.

'Taliban!' whispered my driver Hakim, 'better we go.' It was getting near curfew so he announced that I would have to stay with his family and whisked me off through a maze of alleyways between earthen-walled compounds, the way getting narrower and narrower until eventually we had to abandon the car and walk. The only light was the glow of the swollen yellow moon above and I bumped my head as I followed Hakim through a low archway into a courtyard and then up a few steps to a typical Pashtun house with barrel-vaulted roof.

The house belonged to Hakim's father-in-law Mohammed Daoud, a white-haired former mujaheddin commander with a noble nose who stared fiercely ahead as Hakim apologised for the humble sur-roundings. I was taken to meet the women who were giggling and self-conscious, then embarrassed me by presenting me with a gold-tasselled white handkerchief. I had nothing to offer them except half a jar of Nescafé, which I handed over rather grudgingly, knowing that I would miss the coffee in the mornings. A young girl with a pink headscarf framing her gipsy face produced a tin bowl of warm water for me to wash, trembling so much that most of it spilled out as she led me to the 'bathroom' – a small second courtyard off the first. The ground felt rather soft and, needing to relieve myself after the long drive, I shone my torch around in vain for the usual hole in the ground. Then I noticed a spade and the little brown deposits all around and realised with a sinking feeling what it was I was standing in.

We ate dinner seated on cushions in a windowless room under the stairs. The room was also used for sleeping, judging by the pile of quilts in a corner. The young girl brought in an oil lamp and one of Mohammed Daoud's sons came in bearing trays of *qabli* rice decorated with raisins, almonds and shredded carrot; mutton bones in a porridge of *nan* bread soaked in meat juice, and bowls of gristly meatballs, as well as a large jug of curd drink, all of which he laid out on a sheet on the floor.

We had just started eating when there was a knock on the door, followed by another, then another. The neighbouring men had all come to see the *firangi*, the foreign woman, greeting Mohammed Daoud by pressing him to each side of their chests, as was their tradition, then laying their Kalashnikovs against the wall as they joined in the feast. For a while there was silence apart from eating, and an occasional popping noise as someone gobbed into the blue spittoon, then a young boy came in, deftly pulled the four corners of the cloth together with all the remaining food inside and tied it in a bundle. Tea and a hookah pipe were brought in, and the men leaned back on their cushions, regarding me intently.

Once I told them I had been to Kandahar before, during the jihad, the ice was broken and we discussed the commanders I had travelled with and what had happened to them. When I said I had known Bor Jan, the commander who became a founding member of the Taliban then was killed, one of them produced a photograph from his pocket of Bor Jan against a backdrop of flowers, which he insisted I kept. As was common among Pashtuns, getting information took a long time because each mention of someone new would involve enumerating all their forenames. The talk then moved on to Mohammed Daoud's son who was due to arrive from Quetta. His right hand had been chopped off by the Taliban after he had borrowed money from Haji Lalik, the city's biggest moneydealer, then been accused of stealing it from a moneychanger's shop.

'They put a hood over his face, tied a cable round his wrist then

Bor Jan.

cut it off,' said the old man. 'It was in the stadium in front of everyone. When he took off the hood and saw his hand on the ground he fainted. He was a builder, a brickmaker but what good is a builder with one hand? We have found out who made the accusation and asked for compensation but he has not agreed. Under Pashtunwali we have a code of an eye for an eye. Only a weak person wouldn't take revenge. If my son doesn't then his son will.'

It became clear from the conversation that everyone in the city was suspicious of everyone else. To survive and have a decent life in Kandahar it seemed many of the city's residents had become collaborators just as thousands did in Second World War France and Holland, only in the Kandaharis' case the occupiers were from their own country, their own town even.

Dusty, impoverished Kandahar with its bitter winters and fishgrilling summers was to the Taliban as the Vatican to the Catholic Church. It was where Mullah Omar had lived as a virtual recluse. Even in Kandahar, most people I met said they had never seen him nor knew what he looked like. If he really did cruise the bazaars at night on his motorbike to hear what his people were saying, he had gone unnoticed. But the Amar bil Marouf, his Moral Police, were every-where for Kandahar was the centrepiece of his project to impose Shariat law on Afghanistan and village ways onto urban life.

Although Mullah Omar had fled into the mountains and the head-quarters of the bil Marouf stood in ruins at the end of Kandahar's main road, bombed by the Americans, there were more reminders of the rule of the one-eyed cleric than that of its first king.

The city walls of mud and stone which once stood twenty-seven feet high with a twenty-four-feet wide moat, and six giant gates, had long since disappeared, but it was still possible to discern the rectangular grid system laid out by Ahmad Shah Durrani on land given to him by the Popolzai tribe, and in giving directions people referred to the gates as geographical points as if they still stood. Like Kabul, Kandahar had been an important trading post on the caravan routes linking India with Persia and Turkey and was famous for its four bustling bazaars. In the tiny open-fronted shops one could buy birds in wooden cages, gunpowder or opium inside the skins of sheep, sandals made from car tyres, old Persian scimitars, embroidered hats and shawls, and prayer beads made from a glassy green stone found in the mountains north of the city. The air was thick with the smoke of fires grilling kebabs sprinkled with coriander seeds and the

The Ministry for the Promotion of Virtue and Prevention of Vice, after the American bombing in 2001.

occasional whiff of musk or other ancient perfumes. Probably the only thing that was not on sale in Ahmad Shah's day was Tupperware. Near Char Suq, the square where the four bazaars met, were the extensive foundations of a partially built mosque, Jamia-a-Umari, named after Mullah Omar.

But it was in Shahar-i-Nau, the New Town, that Mullah Omar had really left his mark.

First there was his house, a walled compound inside a vast walled estate including a mosque and farm which I explored with a group of guards who kept asking for their photographs to be taken in unlikely places, such as standing in the cot bed of one of Mullah Omar's children. Just as Mullah Khalil Hassani, his former bodyguard, had described to me back in Quetta, in front of the iron gates to the inner compound was a twenty-foot-high fountain consisting of a fibreglass log out of which sprouted strange plastic palm trees. We climbed the stairs to the roof terrace of his house where a large crater from a cruise missile revealed the six-feet-thick protective cushioning of rubber tyres and steel stopping the missile going through.

*A guard perches on a child's cot inside the house owned by Mullah Omar,
Kandahar 2001.*

Not far away, on the edge of the Sufi Saheb desert southwest of
the city, where Arab sheikhs used to come hunting and caravans of
camels laden with opium still trod gently through tracks in the sand,
rose a shimmering dome of eggshell blue. This was the Eid Gaha
Mosque, meant to be Mullah Omar's great legacy and completely to
eclipse the dome of Afghanistan's first king that had dominated the
city for more than two hundred years. Set in a ten-acre walled compound planted with rows of saplings, thousands of men had been
working on it for four years but the project was far from finished
and the hundred-and-fifty-foot-high dome was still supported on

Mullah Omar's fibre-glass fountain, Kandahar 2001.

wooden scaffolding. Next to it were unfinished blocks of housing meant for students and teachers in what was intended to be a religious seminary. No expense had been spared in its construction, employing numerous gardeners and importing equipment and engineers from abroad, and also relocating the national engineering institute from Kabul to Kandahar.

Just as in Mullah Omar's house, the inside of the dome was painted with garish murals of flowers in pinks, blues, greens and yellows and beneath them, depictions of historic monuments such as the mosque of Herat, the minaret of Jam, and curiously, once again the Hotel Continental in Kabul with its swimming pool. A monument to bad taste, its decoration was the sort of thing one might expect to find in a second-class brothel, rather than a place intended to be the holiest site in the land.

While all this was being built, allegedly with funds provided by Osama bin Laden whose own house in Kandahar was said to have had jewelled door handles and bath taps of gold, the Taliban had done little for the city. Afghanistan remained one of the poorest

The vast Eid Gaha Mosque was meant to be Mullah Omar's great legacy, paid for by bin Laden.

nations on earth, struggling under two sets of UN sanctions imposed in response to the Taliban's appalling human rights record. Many people in the city told me that Kandahar had just five schools (all boys) and five hundred mosques and I could see for myself that the canals were all dried out, the famous orchards withered, and piles of rubbish everywhere. One day Hakim threw a Coke can out of the window onto the street and I reprimanded him, saying, 'Oh Hakim, you'll make your city dirty.'

He laughed, replying, 'The city is already dirty.'

It wasn't just the infrastructure that had been neglected. Something had happened to the spirit of the city. It was partly the years of drought which meant that the lush pomegranates which Persian princesses used to breakfast on and the forty varieties of grape sweet enough to make men cry, were nowhere to be found. But it seemed a town with no soul. I remembered Kandahar even in the midst of the war, as a place with a lot of laughter, loud belly laughs and locals always described themselves as the Texans of Afghanistan. There had been music, searing mournful melodies sung by boys strumming lute-like instruments or tapping tabla drums. Now the only music was muzak from Hindi films, and the Kandaharis looked cowed, scurrying along, heads bent in the shadows of buildings.

In the centre of town, people kept passing close to me and whispering, 'be careful, there are al Qaeda around'. Four tanks kept guard outside the new Governor's office and bunkers being built along the roads into the city. The intermittent roar of American warplanes overhead, carrying out raids in the pink cliffs north of the city, added to the tension. One day posters appeared all over the city, warning, 'Be Careful of Present Government. Don't be Associated with it. Its Fate is Short.'

My young interpreter Ahmed Jan was terrified. Though his family was from Kandahar, he had grown up as a refugee in Quetta, and while I found Kandahar infinitely preferable to Quetta, he was horrified by the place. 'I can't understand these people,' he would complain. 'They are my people but they speak differently, eat differently, even sleep differently. They spit. I don't like it. Not at all.'

Most of our time together was spent by Ahmed Jan telling me I couldn't do this or that because it was dangerous and he was furious at my refusal to hire a jeepload of bodyguards to travel round with us as the American television crews were doing. 'Can't we even have one bodyguard?' he would whine. He loathed being given instructions by a woman and sometimes instead of translating my interviews, told me they were stupid questions that no one would answer. He rudely refused to take tea when we were offered it by commanders, telling me I would catch terrible diseases from using their cups. Every afternoon he would say he wasn't feeling well and insisted we stop at a pharmacy so he could stock up on pills. He was nineteen-years-old yet claimed he needed an after-lunch nap.

Ahmed Jan was an only son who had left the city with his mother and uncle when he was just six, and remembered nothing of Kandahar except the photographic shop. 'My father was killed because of enmity with another tribe, the Alkozai. We're Popolzai and they killed so many members of my family. One of my uncles was a very good-looking boy and he was abducted and found in a garden two or three days later. His body was unrecognisable, not even bones left they said. They did the same thing to my father. It is not good to be handsome in this city. My grandmother and one uncle went to New York and we went to Quetta.'

Once he told me this I could understand why he might not like the place and I kept encouraging him to go back to Quetta or even to America but he spoke fluent English, a rare skill in Afghanistan, and had decided there was money to be made. At least he was not handsome – he had a doughy complexion with lips that were too thick and drooping eyes – so was unlikely to attract the attentions of a lovelorn commander. My hopes of palming Ahmed Jan off on some other journalist were dashed when he moved into the ground floor of my guesthouse from where he would emerge each morning, managing to look ever more doleful about the day's plans. When I told him we were going to look for Abdullah, the last victim of the Taliban, he insisted it was impossible.

'But the boy at the football stadium said everyone knows about him,' I protested.

'Everyone here lies,' he replied. 'They are incapable of telling the truth. Asking them things is as useful as speaking to stones in the yard. I don't know why you waste your time.'

The next afternoon we set off to the woodcutters' bazaar to try and find Abdullah's uncle. The sweet smell of balsam brought back the night more than twelve years before when I had hidden there with the motorcycling mullahs as they waited to launch an attack on the Communist defence post. Even though the street was now crowded with honking rickshaws and jingling pony traps and people going about their business, I could feel the fear tightening my chest remembering how every breath I took had seemed to be amplified in the quiet of the night.

As Ahmed Jan had glumly predicted, we could not find Abdullah's uncle but in a small shack where a man was sawing away at a plank sending woodchips flying, we did discover his brother-in-law Agha Gul. 'Abdullah,' he said, shaking his head sadly. 'They hung the body at 4 a.m. One of my sons Sardar Gul is a driver and he drove through Herat bazaar early that morning and saw his cousin hanging there and came home to tell me. I was asleep and he took me to see the body. When I saw that I vowed I would kill the man who did it. They had taken everything from his pockets. His skin had gone black from so much beating and all his bones were broken like a rag doll. His face was all swollen and he had been hung from the neck.'

'Why did they do it?' I asked.

'You need to speak to his cousin Nazzak,' he replied, 'they were inseparable'.

We followed his directions to find ourselves bumping over a rutted lane amid the crumbling earth walls and dried canals of the Ajarab district just as the sun was swelling crimson in the sky ready to disappear below the horizon. Either side of the road were small brick kilns and bombed-out shells of buildings that in the dusty light and smoke of people cooking on dung-fires looked like the remains of an ancient city. A little way off I could see a tall grape-drying tower with slotted windows just like that which was blown up by Soviet tanks when the mullahs were firing on the airport and I had hidden in the trenches.

'It's too late,' said Ahmed Jan, 'there must be al Qaeda everywhere here. Perhaps it's a trap. We better go back.'

Darkness had fallen quickly and heavily and the pallid glow of the moon gave the ruins a ghostly appearance. The area seemed deserted apart from a man with a donkey cart loaded with freshly cut grass. Then a small boy, who looked English with a white freckled face and red hair, appeared. When we told him we were looking for the house of Abdullah, he told us to leave the car and beckoned us along a track between mud-walled compounds, one of which had a satellite dish perched on top.

The young boy, who we later discovered was Abdullah's son, disappeared behind a pink-flowered curtain across the doorway. A whispered discussion ensued, then I was shown into the women's quarters. A kerosene lamp was brought in and, as my eyes accustomed to the dim light, I could just make out a handsome woman of about forty on the floor surrounded by a group of small children, and in one corner a much younger woman, head wrapped in a black shawl, sobbing softly as she rocked a gaily painted wooden crib inside which a baby girl with rosy cheeks and black olive-pit eyes lay still, wrapped in thick swaddling. She turned her head away and I realised she was pregnant.

Ahmed Jan, mortified at being dragged into the women's quarters, explained why we had come. The older woman nodded, took something out of an envelope and silently handed me a photograph. For a moment I studied it blankly, seeing only a crowd of robed men and a few cars in Herat Chowk, just in front of the bakery where I stopped every morning to buy hot *nan*. Then I realised what the people were all looking at. In the centre was a tall makeshift gallows made of bamboo poles with someone hanging from it. It was a medieval scene so vivid that I could almost hear the poles creaking as the body swung slowly back and forth. The date scrawled on the back in Pashto was 6 December 1422 or the year 2001 in our western calendar. One day before the fall of Kandahar and the end of the Taliban.

Tea was brought and the woman whose name was Bibi Zahra, Abdullah's sister, began to tell his story while in the corner his widow Latifa snuffled quietly, eyes expressionless as she held her daughter Rahmana who was eight and wore a turquoise veil sewn with gold sequins and rocked baby Roxanna, named after the Afghan wife of Alexander the Great. The orange-haired Rahmatullah sat alone,

Abdullah's widow and children.

watchful, the man of the house at just eleven. Latifa had been only fourteen when he was born.

In my travels across Afghanistan I had heard many stories but none mirrored the tragedy of Afghanistan more than that of Abdullah. 'We were just two,' began Bibi Zahra, 'I was the elder and Abdullah younger, born in 1973 just before King Zahir Shah was overthrown. Our father Habibullah was a civil servant here in the Governor's office but when the regime changed he was sacked because our family were from the Barakzai tribe and royalists. He was forced to work as a carpenter, which he wasn't very good at. I remember people coming to the house, complaining about their tables or chairs falling apart, but he always made sure we were well-educated.'

As she spoke, a little boy, younger than my own two and a half year-old son, plucked at her silver bangles and turquoise beads, whimpering for attention, but his older brother yanked him away, throwing him towards the doorway where he sat tracing the flowers on the curtain with his fingers. There was nothing in the room that might constitute a toy and the plaster walls were bare apart from a mirror in a red frame the shape of an upside-down heart.

'We watched the Russian tanks come into Kandahar, Abdullah and I. We were standing on the main street holding hands and wondering what it meant, then our father went away and we knew then it was bad,' continued Bibi Zahra. He had joined the forces of Haji Latif, a white-bearded bandit leader who despite being spoken of derogatively as a 'dog-trainer' was one of the most powerful mujaheddin commanders in the region, and whose son Gul Agha later became Governor of Kandahar after the fall of the Taliban. Like Abdullah's father, Haji Latif was from the Barakzai tribe, the branch of the Durranis from which some of Afghanistan's kings had come such as Dost Mohammed. The two children and their mother stayed in the compound with their widowed aunt and her children including Nazzak, the man we had been told to look for. The area was heavily bombed by Soviet planes, but somehow the family survived and Habibullah occasionally returned for snatched visits, sometimes wounded.

'One day, after the Russians had left, he went away and never came back,' said Bibi Zahra. 'We heard he was kidnapped by Hekmatyar's men and stoned or maybe torched to death. That was about ten years ago.'

Abdullah was determined to avenge his death, even though his father had been angry when he left school to join Gul Agha's forces at the age of fifteen. Like most children of his generation he had learnt to use a Kalashnikov by the time he was eleven and had grown up expecting to fight.

Yet his sister described him as a gentle soul whose greatest joy was to sit under the mulberry tree in the courtyard writing poetry, unlike the other boys who spent their time flying kites and trying to steal birds. 'Everybody loved him,' she said, 'he would stop to help anyone in trouble. Look at this.' From one of two tin trunks in the corner of the room she took out a photograph album. Inside were numerous photographs of a young man with earnest eyes who always seemed to be smiling. One showed him laughing with delight as he bit into a watermelon while picnicking with friends by the local dam. In another he stood surrounded by the white doves outside the blue shrine of Hazrat Ali, cousin of the Prophet Mohammed, in Mazar-i-Sharif, two doves on his head, another in his hand. Afghans believe that one in seven of the doves is a spirit so they feed them hoping to win favour, and it is said that the site is so holy that if a grey pigeon joins the flock it will become white in forty days.

'He would spend one or two months here then the rest of the year fighting,' said Bibi Zahra. 'We would be very worried. When the mujaheddin took power and Gul Agha became Governor the first time, Abdullah was made head of the Afghan Wireless Communication Company, then was transferred to Kabul. He was working there when the Taliban took Kabul and they arrested him because they found faxes in the toolbox in his car to be sent to the Americans. But they couldn't prove they were his so they released him and he joined them so they wouldn't be suspicious. But all the time he was still working for Gul Agha. I was the only one who knew what he was doing and I tried to stop him. I knew it would only end in tragedy.'

It was getting late so we arranged to come back the next afternoon to hear the rest of the story from his cousin Nazzak who lived in a room across the compound. His name was actually Hamidullah but everyone called him Nazzak which meant skinny because he was so thin, his khaki uniform hanging off him and though he was only twenty-two, he had an important job working in the Governor's office in charge of disarming the local population. There was respect in people's voices as they spoke of him.

There was a collection of dusty shoes outside Nazzak's room and inside he was lounging on cushions surrounded by five of his men

Commander Nazzak.

in combat fatigues all glued to a large television, presumably booty from one of the Arab houses, run off a car battery. The programme was a concert by the English teen pop group, Steps, on the satellite music channel MTV. They looked up in bored irritation at the interruption.

Nazzak said something to his men who got up, each spitting noisily into a silver spittoon before swaggering out, their eyes red and unfocused. I asked him to tell me about Abdullah and he took a small red notebook out of his pocket. 'This is one of his poems,' he said, opening the book. 'It's called "A Quiet Scream". He used to

publish them under the pseudonym Khayal which means "The Con-
templative One" and we would distribute them in the town.'

> *I have been screaming but no one can hear me*
> *All the people who can hear me have died*
> *The country I am living in I thought was a garden*
> *But it turned out to be a forest full of snakes*
> *Fate brought me where I can find no one*
> *I lost all my relations, all my friends*
> *The laws are torn up, all I could hear is screaming*
> *Blood is pouring out of my pen*
> *How can I write?*
> *I cannot say anything*
> *Because if I write the truth*
> *I will join the other ghosts*

I watched Nazzak's face as he read it in his soft voice. He looked
so innocent, his beard and moustache out of place in his gamine
face, and he wiped away a tear with a hand adorned by a thick gold
ring and jewelled gold watch.

'Since childhood we were inseparable,' he said. 'I did everything
Abdullah did. Nobody could differentiate between us. When he joined
Gul Agha I did too. And when he joined the Taliban I followed him.
All our family are supporters of His Majesty.'

He showed me a card with Abdullah's photograph on one side and
on the other, a picture of the king and the old red, black and green
royalist flag of Afghanistan with the Herat citadel in the centre. 'Both
of us grew up always with fighting. I was born just six months after the
Taraki Revolution. My father and his father, my uncle, were famous
commanders with Haji Latif. They wanted us to study but when I was
fourteen I left school and became a builder to support the family as my
father and uncle had been killed. I built this room. Then like Abdullah
I became a fighter. I've taken bullets in almost every part of my body.

'When the Taliban first emerged we were very happy because they brought peace to the city. It had been very bad with different groups controlling different parts. Just in one small stretch of the main street there were five different checkpoints. Our women were frightened to go to market. Gul Agha was Governor but could not even move about the city. We thought with the Taliban at least the whole city was under one hand.

'For a while it seemed better. Then we kept seeing Pakistani military. They brought in Chinese and Arabs and we did not know who was running things. Abdullah and I talked a lot and decided we would join the Taliban to see what was going on from the inside.'

The discovery of the faxes to the CIA in Abdullah's car and his subsequent arrest meant that Abdullah had little choice. To prove his allegiance he volunteered for the front line, fighting the Northern Alliance, north of Kabul. 'It was perfect,' said Nazzak. 'Being on the front-line and fighting bravely no one could suspect he might be working against the Taliban.'

Abdullah used his position to start collecting information and building a network of extremely trusted people. 'Over time we amassed an enormous dossier of atrocities by the Taliban, but also crimes by the Northern Alliance.' He showed me some photographs of Abdullah standing by a mass grave in a sandy desert near Mazar-i-Sharif where he said General Dostum's men had massacred hundreds of people.

The following year, 1998, on his cousin's advice, Nazzak also joined the Taliban. 'I went to the Taliban and said I'm a fighter and you need fighters. I had my own car so I joined the patrol team going round the city looking for people doing actions they said were against Islam such as scissoring their beards or having long hair or listening to music as well as looking for those with membership cards showing they were supporters of Zahir Shah. All the time I was carrying my own card in my pocket.'

I asked him why he supported Zahir Shah as by the time he was born the king was living in comfortable exile in Rome. 'I support the king because my relations tell me that there was peace and calm in his time and there were schools for girls and boys.'

Dusk was falling and Nazzak looked at his watch. 'Excuse me, it is time to pray,' he said. He splashed water on his hands and face from a jug in the corner, lay his patou on the ground, then prostrated himself on it as if it were the most natural thing in the world.

After a few minutes he got up and sat down next to me again, carrying on the conversation as if it had never stopped, telling me that his duties as a Taliban included stints in Kandahar jail. 'In my whole life I have never slapped a man but I had to watch my own friends and my uncle being beaten. We used the clutch cables of motorcycles as whips.'

He made notes of who was carrying out the most gruesome tortures and added the information to Abdullah's swelling files in the trunk under his bed. The more he had to do with the Taliban the more resentful he became of the Arabs in Kandahar, who by then numbered 3000–4000, and would roar around the city in Japanese Land Cruisers with black windows, Dubai number plates, and machine guns mounted on the roof. 'The Arabs entered our city and acted as if they were rulers. Sometimes even when we were on patrol they would stop us and check our pockets.'

By 11 September 2001 they had about a hundred trusted people in their network and a hundred and twenty files but no idea what to do with the information. 'We had all sorts of files both on the Taliban and Northern Alliance, usually between two to five pages long on incidents and people. Abdullah used to cry sometimes when he was writing the reports. They weren't just about torture and killings, some were on Pakistanis that Abdullah had seen in Samangan who were pretending to be fighters but were actually digging in the mountains for minerals. We also had a video that Abdullah made, interviewing Rabbani pretending to be a journalist. It was all in a hidden compartment of a big black briefcase that we were going to try to get to Gul Agha or Zahir Shah.'

Gul Agha, who was in exile in Pakistan, had long been discussing military action against the Taliban with King Zahir Shah's office in Rome but without outside help it seemed an almost impossible task, particularly as he had no great desire to work with the Northern Alliance. 'The king had lobbyists in Washington and his grandson Mostapha Zahir had long been travelling around the West warning of what was happening to our country but no one cared,' said Engineer Pashtun, advisor to Gul Agha.

Two planes flying into a building that neither Abdullah nor Nazzak had ever heard of changed everything. The Pentagon, desperately short of Pashto speakers and without a single agent of their own on the ground in Afghanistan at the time of the attack, found a ready-built resistance network in the Kandahar area. Abdullah had been working as assistant to the Governor of the northern province of Samangan but after September 11th, he knew the Americans would be searching for Osama so he told the Governor he was suffering from kidney disease and needed treatment, then returned home.

'Gul Agha still had plenty of arms from the jihad and I knew where there was an arms cache and decided I was going to start killing Arabs for the black name they had given our country,' said Nazzak. 'Just one week after September 11th, I threw a grenade at three Arabs in the Kabul bazaar [in Kandahar] at the place where the buses and taxis leave for Kabul and killed them. There was a huge house and office where Osama bin Laden himself used to come and plan missions and one evening about 6 p.m. I drove past with a friend on a motorbike, stopped just in front and threw three grenades over the wall. We later heard three Arabs were killed and two injured. Another time I shot eight Arabs in a house in the New Town.

'Then Gul Agha announced he was planning an operation and needed volunteers so we went to him in Quetta and he provided us with satellite phones and GPS positioning and laser devices and showed us how to use them so we could give coordinates to the Americans of where the Taliban and Arabs were living. It was about a week before the American bombing started. We were supposed to call in their movements and they gave us a special phone number for the US air force.

'Usually the places I pointed out were then bombed. It was incredible. For example I gave them the coordinates of the house north of the city where Mullah Omar was hiding and they bombed it and wounded him and killed his son. Then when he escaped in a rickshaw and fled to Sanghisar, his old village, I told them.'

Their English was limited so the cousins mostly passed their information to Gul Agha or Engineer Pashtun, a fluent English speaker. He would then speak to the Americans directly or to General Abdul Wali, the king's son-in-law and military strategist in Rome. They were taking an enormous risk. The week the bombing started the Taliban issued an edict that anyone caught with a satellite phone would be hanged. When I later spoke to Engineer Pashtun about the operation he told me, 'People like Abdullah and Nazzak were the real unsung heroes. They were volunteers who were risking their lives. One day we will erect a statue in Kandahar to Abdullah.'

The only member of Abdullah's family apart from Nazzak who knew what he was doing was his sister. 'I knew as soon as he came home with the briefcase and I tried to stop him,' she told me, 'but he said, "The Arabs have blackened the name of Afghanistan in the world and they will never leave unless someone sacrifices himself." I told him to at least get his wife and children out to Pakistan and he planned to do so.'

Abdullah's words were horribly prophetic. Suspecting the Taliban were on their trail, Abdullah and Nazzak stayed up night after night organising to take all their files to Quetta in the large briefcase. The day before they were due to leave, Abdullah was on his motorbike outside an Arab house, talking on his satellite phone, when a man came past on a bicycle. As Abdullah turned to go he was surrounded by Taliban, arrested and taken to the jail.

While he was being tortured and interrogated, four pick-ups of

Taliban soldiers drove at high speed to the family compound and burst in. 'They turned the place upside down and went through everything,' said Bibi Zahra, 'they even opened the Holy Korans looking for things. I knew then that they must have caught my brother.'

Amongst the things they found were the briefcase and Nazzak, who had been waiting for Abdullah so they could leave and did not have time to escape. 'They tore off my turban and used it to tie my hands, then took me to their car and beat me with Kalashnikovs,' he recalled. 'Then they took me to jail and put me in a cell so dark that I could not even see my hands or fingers. I was arrested at 2 p.m. and beaten at 8 p.m. They used to have timetables for beating, always starting at 8 p.m. at night. That first night they beat me with cables and logs across my soles from 8 p.m. to 2.30 a.m. then poured acid on the wounds. They were trying to get information about who we were working with. That's when I knew they also had Abdullah though I never saw him again. I couldn't see him but I could hear his screams.'

For two weeks the pair were beaten day after day. Nazzak got off lightly as many of the torturers were people he had worked with, though he insisted, 'I really believed they would torture me to death.' To him the most painful part was having the soles of his feet beaten with wet logs. 'It is six weeks since they left and I have still not been able to wash my feet,' he said, pulling off his socks to show me his scarred swollen feet. 'As they beat us they would abuse us saying you are not Muslims, you are infidels, you are being supported by infidels and you will die an infidel's death. I could hear the bombings every night and that gave me hope but I couldn't believe the Taliban could be ended so quickly. I thought I would be killed first.

'One evening there was a strange atmosphere in the jail and people started saying the Taliban were going to surrender and might kill us all. The next morning some of my friends came and bribed the prison superintendent Mullah Wali Jan with a car and one lakh rupees

(£900) for my release. I was taken to a friend's house and three or four hours later the Taliban collapsed.

'I said to my friends let's go and free Abdullah, but they said no you must rest, there's lots of confusion in the city, it's better to wait till tomorrow. The next morning I again insisted. By then it was clear the Taliban had surrendered and everyone was rejoicing. I was so happy and couldn't understand why we didn't just go and find him. Eventually in the afternoon my friends agreed. We got in the car. But instead of taking me to jail, they took me to a freshly dug grave. Abdullah had been hanged the day before I was released.'

Abdullah was the last person to be executed by the Taliban.

The last person to be executed by the Taliban, Abdullah's body had hung over Herat Chowk from 4.30 a.m. in the morning to 6 p.m. in the evening. Doctors at the Chinese Hospital to which his friends took the body certified that he had been tortured to death before hanging.

As we talked late into the evening, the depths of horror in Nazzak's eyes made him seem much older than his twenty-two years. I asked him if he hoped that now the fighting had finished, his and Abdullah's children would be able to grow up in peace. He shook his head. He might have been in charge of disarming the local population, but he was already teaching Abdullah's son Rahmatullah to use a Kalashnikov. 'Our family has sacrificed a lot,' he said. 'The son should be like the father and grandfather.'

MARRI'S DIARY
February 2002

The university is reopening, there are entrance exams, my friends Farishta and Najeba went all dressed up in make-up and high heels under their burqas, they were very happy, but I could not go as I am the eldest and my family need me to work. They said it was hard to do the exams after years with no school but it was like a party seeing many friends after a long time. The university was in a bad state, the Taliban had taken all the books from the library and there were some anatomy textbooks displayed in a glass case which they had shot through with bullet-holes!

Karzai has announced that schools will reopen on March 21st, new years day. We will get our jobs back. It will be so good to see the children in the streets maybe even with uniforms and books like it used to be.

They say the king is coming back. I wonder how he will feel after so many years away to see his country all ruined. Where will he live? It must be very dangerous. The Northern Alliance make clear every day they don't want him.

Outside the city in Gardez and Paktia in the south and in Mazar and the north there is still fighting between warlords. Father says it is easier for ten poor men to sleep on one rug than two kings to share one clime.

My brother saw a man selling trees today in the road and people were buying them which is a good sign. Soon it will be spring, there will be cherry blossoms, maybe we will hang up our burqas for good and even start to love again.

9

Face to Face with the Taliban

❧❧❧

'The Game is so large that one sees but a little at a time.'
Mahbub Ali's advice to Kim, in *Kim*, Chp. 10,
RUDYARD KIPLING

THE PHONE-CALL CAME EARLY in the morning. I was back in Quetta and luxuriating in the feel of crisp white sheets on a proper bed, and a heated room. 'The carpet has arrived,' said a voice. 'It's a very valuable one and we can't keep it here long for security reasons.'

For more than five months since the attack on the World Trade Center, I had been in Pakistan and Afghanistan talking to people about the Taliban regime and meeting one after another of their victims. This mysterious phone-call meant I would soon be coming face to face with some of the regime's key members in their hiding places in Pakistan.

Four hours later, after more phone-calls informing my go-between that the carpet had 'changed shop', and a complicated journey round town which involved switching cars so that my friend ended up driving a taxi, bargaining for an Azerbaijani kilim I didn't want, visiting an aid project I wasn't interested in and hurtling round a labyrinth of mud-walled lanes, scattering underfed donkeys and bicycling Afghans, we finally seemed to have lost the two Pakistani agents on motorbikes who had been tailing us in the usual conspicuous way of the ISI.

Down a rubbish-strewn alley, I entered a house through the purdah quarters. To provide me with the cover that I had been interviewing women, I sat for a while impatiently drinking tea, admiring babies and toddlers with runny noses and silver bells round their ankles.

Finally a bearded old man in a swan-white turban summoned me through the curtain into a room where the two Taliban ministers were sitting on floor cushions along with our go-between. For a moment I was confused.

With their beards trimmed short they looked surprisingly young. I knew the Taliban leadership were mostly in their thirties, but somehow I realised that over the months I had built up a picture of them as less youthful and more demonic.

One of the two men, Maulana Abdullah Sahadi, the Deputy Defence Minister, was only twenty-eight and looked vulnerable and slightly scared, greeting me with a wonky Johnny Depp-like smile. It was the first time he had ventured out of his hiding place since escaping Afghanistan after the fall of Kandahar two months earlier.

The other minister, a burly man in his mid-thirties who agreed to meet only on condition of anonymity and was responsible for some of the acts that had most horrified the Western world, looked defiant. It seemed fitting that we should be meeting in Pakistan's western province of Baluchistan, a vast smugglers' land of desert and mountains, much of which is governed by tribal law, where women are kept locked away and federal government officials fear to tread.

'We shaved off our beards, changed our turbans from white Taliban to Kandahari, got in cars and drove on the road across the border,' said Maulana Sahadi, adding, 'before my beard was as long as this.' He gestured down to his chest. His family – three daughters of seven, three and two and a son of five – he had already moved to Quetta when the bombing started.

The Pakistani authorities turned a blind eye and in some cases even helped. While US Special Forces based at Kandahar airbase were going on daily operations scouring the mountains north of the city for al Qaeda and Taliban, it was an open secret that just across the border senior Taliban ministers were sheltering in *madrassas* and houses. Among them were Mullah Nuruddin Turabi, the Justice Minister, Abdul Razzak, the Interior Minister, Qadratullah Jamal, the Culture Minister, and the spokesman for Mullah Omar.

The two men had agreed to meet me because of my past connection with the Mullahs Front (many of whom had later become Taliban) and the trust they had in my friend, a doctor and long-time financial supporter of the jihad, who acted as our go-between.

'You see we don't have two horns,' smiled one of the ministers, as he poured me tea from a brass pot and offered me boiled sweets in place of sugar. 'At the moment anyone can say anything about us and the world will believe it. People have been saying we skinned their husbands alive and ate babies and you people print it.'

We started off talking about how they had joined the Taliban. Maulana Sahadi's story was typical. His family moved from a village near Kandahar to a refugee camp in Quetta when he was just five after his father, a mujahid with Hekmatyar's Hezb-i-Islami, was killed fighting the Russians and the village bombed into ruins. The family was very poor; living in a tent, which let in all the cold in winter, and in summer became unbearably hot as the burning desert sun was reflected off the rocks and mountains. They survived largely on bread begged or bought with the few rupees earnt from his mother and sisters sewing carpets. His family were delighted when he got a place at a *madrassa* in Nowshera in Frontier Province at the age of eight as his food, board and books were all provided. After that he saw his mother only once every other year; it was too far and expensive to travel back in the holidays. At some point he learnt to use a Kalashnikov though he would not say when or where, claiming 'a gun is such a thing one day you use it, the next day you master it'.

In mid-1994 a delegation of elders and *ulema* or religious scholars from Pakistan came to the *madrassa*. 'They told us we must join the Taliban and fight jihad. Our fathers had all been in jihad and we had worshipped them, then seen it go wrong, people becoming warlords and raping and killing but they said this time it would be different, that the others had lost their way and been corrupted by all the Western things they had seen here in Pakistan. This time we would be really fighting for Islam. I joined with a group of friends from the *madrassa* so we were there right at the very beginning in the first attack on Spin Boldak [a town just over the Afghan border on the way to Kandahar] that October. At that time we were only about a hundred people.

'We were killing men and many of our companions were martyred, but that is part of fighting and we were happy because we were doing it for Islam. We were the soldiers of God. We captured Boldak easily then we moved on to Kandahar where the people were pleased to see us and laid down their arms.'

I asked if he had thought at the beginning they were fighting in order to restore Zahir Shah to the throne and he looked astonished. 'We were never fighting for Zahir Shah. What did he do in the jihad? We were fighting for the *ulema* who supported Mullah Omar as Amir.'

For the next few years Sahadi went on to fight in battles all over Afghanistan including Herat, Mazar-i-Sharif, Kunduz and Bamiyan, commanding a force of five hundred then, two thousand five hundred people, then becoming Director of Defence as by 1997 the Taliban had captured ninety percent of the country. 'I would motivate my troops before fighting by telling them if they were martyred they would go to Paradise and could take with them seventy-two of their family members. I also told them they could take a bride in battle.'

He got on well with Mullah Omar, whom he described as 'a very nice good-natured person with good morals. He treated me like a son. Whoever came to him he treated with respect.'

In 1999 he became deputy Defence Minister under Mullah Obaidullah who was the main linkman between the Taliban and the ISI and as such said he had frequent personal contact with Osama bin Laden, though he insisted, 'The Arabs were not controlling things. Anyone who supports Islam was welcome in our country; we had British, Americans, Australians.'

According to Sahadi, bin Laden had still been in Afghanistan when the Taliban fell and the two of them had laughed at the failure of the Americans to catch him. 'I spoke to him on the telephone the day we surrendered Kandahar and he was in Paktia and he was fine. I briefed him and he wished me Godspeed. I suppose he was going to Pakistan. Now we think he is in Saudi or Yemen.

'The last time I actually met him was in November during the bombing in Herat. We met there to talk about finances; he was helping us buy cars. He may have been thinking about going to Iran at that time.

'He seemed well. A couple of years ago he had some health problems linked to his kidneys but he seemed better. The Americans were bombing the military installations around Herat while we had lunch in the Mowafaq Hotel and we were laughing that if only they knew he was just a few miles away. He was taking anti-anxiety pills, some kind of sedatives, but he was not hiding.'

Although Sahadi admitted he personally had to keep changing houses in Kandahar to avoid being bombed and had lost several of his close friends, he said the Taliban never contemplated handing over bin Laden to save themselves. 'He was a guest in our country and we gave him refuge because hospitality is an important part of our code of behaviour. Besides he was supporting us, giving us money, when no one else was.

'The Taliban leadership do not believe the Twin Towers attack was carried out by al Qaeda,' he continued. 'According to my own opinion the attack was wrong. It is not Islamic to kill innocent people like that. We investigated the attack and it was evident it was not done by al Qaeda.'

How did they explain the videos in which bin Laden talked of the attack? 'We do not believe those videos, they were fake,' he replied, 'it's easy to make such films.'

Having listened silently up till then, the other minister interjected. 'What this war really is about is a clash between Islam and infidels. America wants to implement its own *kafir* religion in Afghanistan. We are the real defenders of Islam, not people like Gul Agha and Hamid Karzai. They are puppets of America.'

'We're not broken, we're whole,' insisted Sahadi. 'We weren't defeated, we agreed to hand over rather than fight and spill blood. Our people went back to their tribes or left the country. Now we are just waiting. Already the fighting for power has begun in Gardez, Mazar, and different provinces. The Presidential Palace is being guarded by foreign troops. We are regrouping, we still have arms and many supporters inside, and when the time is right we will be back.'

'Thank God this war happened because now we really know who are with us and who are against us,' added the other minister. 'Hamid Karzai went to the other camp, once he pretended he was with us but now we see he just wanted power. They will all be brought before justice and punished according to Islamic law.'

What kind of punishment would that be, I asked. 'They will be killed, executed, hanged,' he said, before correcting himself, 'they will be punished according to Islamic law.'

Tucked inside my notebook was the photograph I had been given in Kandahar by the family of Abdullah, the medieval scene of his body hanging on a wooden frame over the busy crossroads of Herat bazaar, and I asked how they could possibly justify such acts.

'These so-called atrocities were carried out by Communists who infiltrated us and committed these cruelties under our turbans to deface the name of Taliban,' said Sahadi.

But I had seen for myself the bare shelves of Herat library after Taliban had taken away the books and burnt them, the ripped-out figures in the oil paintings of the Presidential Palace, and the empty plinths in Kabul Museum after the Culture Minister himself had led a group of Taliban to take axes to all the ancient statues and prehistoric pots. And what about the giant Buddhas of Baniyan?

'Photographs and images are against Islam so we had to destroy them and any books with these in,' said the minister. 'The Buddhas were destroyed because they were against our faith and that's what our court decreed. Like the things in the museum it was not our history but the history of unbelievers and should be wiped out.'

Why did they close girls' schools? They gave the same answer as Maulana Sami-ul Haq had defending Haqqania. 'We were not against girls' education. My own daughters go to school here in Pakistan. The condition of Afghanistan was so bad we could not properly educate boys so how could we educate girls?'

I wondered what they thought of me. 'Women should be completely covered. If you were my wife I would lock you away.' There was no humour in his statement.

I asked why the Taliban regime issued so many edicts such as banning kite-flying and seemed determined to deprive its people of any pleasure. 'Kite-flying was banned for peoples' own protection,' he claimed. 'So many children fell off roofs. Chess was banned because it encourages gambling and is not useful. There were so many other things to do. People could read Koranic texts and walk in parks and appreciate nature. And we did not ban football or cricket as long as players were properly clothed and bearded.

'The world now is so interested in Afghanistan but why did they forget us before? All you did is apply sanctions, which deprived our people even more. The West gave us no option but to accept what Osama was offering us as they gave us nothing.'

I wanted to go on asking questions but the men were looking uncomfortable. We had been talking too long already and the old man in the white turban who turned out to be a *pir*, or holy man, said we might well be traced.

'By whom? Surely the ISI are your friends?'

'At the moment we have no contact with them,' said Sahadi. 'ISI is working with the Americans. Pakistan has betrayed itself. How can it call itself an Islamic country?'

I asked him if he had seen the pictures of Camp X-ray in Guantanamo Bay where America was taking its Taliban and al Qaeda prisoners and feared ending up in one of the cages undergoing interrogation, but he insisted he was not worried.

'The Americans have failed, they have not caught bin Laden or Mullah Omar or any senior Taliban or al Qaeda. All they have done is oust our government. We never did anything to them. Mullah Omar is still in Afghanistan and will stay there making contact with those commanders unhappy with the new government. You British of all people know how unwise it is for outsiders to meddle in Afghanistan. You will see Islam will win out and we will break the Americans into pieces as we did with the Russians and bring back the name of the Taliban.'

I left feeling uneasy, thinking of the words of Irish satirist Jonathan Swift, 'we have just enough religion to make us hate but not enough to make us love one another'. Sahadi seemed such a young simple man, a father of four small children in a land where far too many children had lost their fathers, and on the few occasions he had looked straight at me I thought I could detect some doubt in his eyes, as though something had gone wrong that he could not explain. It was the same look that I had seen in the silent red-haired son of Abdullah whose watchful eyes sought reassurance everywhere yet trusted nobody.

General Hamid Gul and I had a history, and it was with some trepidation that I rang the doorbell of his house in Rawalpindi. Once, twelve years earlier, while I was living in Pakistan, I had received another mysterious phone-call. 'The Chief would like to meet you', said a purring almost feminine voice. I was told to be waiting at eight and on the stroke of the hour, two men in grey shalwar kamiz, silk cravats and dark glasses who could only have been intelligence agents knocked on the door of my apartment in Islamabad. In a dark saloon car with tinted windows I was driven to an unmarked building on the wide Khayaban-e-Suhrawardy just near Zero Point. Behind the high walls and barbed wire stood the headquarters of the Inter-Services Intelligence, or the ISI as it was known, an organisation that struck fear into the hearts of most of its countrymen.

I was shown into a long room with a conference table, a large military map of Afghanistan dotted with coloured pins covering most of one wall. From a corner of the room emerged a short man in grey shalwar kamiz with a long black waistcoat and a moustache that looked as though it were pasted down from nose to lip. His eyes smouldered blackly, his complexion like that of a bruised plum, and he had a commanding presence that I would later come to think of as malevolent. I had learnt by then to resist the urge to put out my hand as it is not the custom in Islamic countries to shake hands with women, and he came towards me with a curt nod of welcome. This was General Hamid Gul, Director General of the ISI.

If any one individual could be said to be the true architect of the jihad it was General Gul. Backed by the financial and logistical support of the CIA, he headed the agency at the peak of its power in the crucial years from 1987–1989 when victory against the Soviet Union was sealed and the fight spread to become a pan-Islamic rather than just an Afghan cause.

Even before Afghanistan, the ISI had been widely regarded by its countrymen as a sinister force. Conceived in the 1950s by General Ayub Khan as a means of keeping watch on politicians, its power grew after he took over the country in 1958, effectively becoming the army's political wing. In the 1970s, the Prime Minister, Zulfikar Ali Bhutto, expanded it to spy on Baluch nationalists in the insurgency in Baluchistan, and began using the agency to damage his political enemies. It ran smear campaigns against politicians, prominent figures and journalists and became known as a 'dirty tricks' brigade.

However, it was after General Zia ul-Haq seized power from Bhutto in 1977 that the agency really spread its tentacles, supporting and arming various extremist and radical sectarian groups within Pakistan in a kind of divide and rule strategy and training militants to fight in Kashmir, another cause close to its heart. It was the Afghan war that enabled it to complete the transformation into a 'state within a state'. When the Soviet tanks rolled into Kabul at Christmas 1979, Zia was quick to spot the opportunity. Relations between Pakistan and America had been at an all-time low and aid was suspended following the hanging of Bhutto and the burning down of the US Embassy in Islamabad that November. With the Cold War in full swing, Washington was anxious to check Soviet expansionism, and the fall of the Shah of Iran left Pakistan as its only ally in the region. General Fazle Haq, then Governor of Frontier province and one of Zia's key advisors, wasted no time making contact with the Carter administration. 'I told Zbigniew Brezinski [Carter's National Security Advisor] you screwed up in Vietnam and Korea, you better get it right this time,' he later said.

The hawkish Brezinski was quick to take the bait, but it was under the Reagan administration that the mujaheddin cause was really embraced. In the autumn of 1981 a six-year package of $3.2billion in economic and military aid to Pakistan was agreed. As it was a covert war against the Soviet Union, the massive CIA weapons pipeline that was put in place to arm the mujaheddin was completely managed and supervised on the ground by the ISI, giving the agency enormous power. The weapons came from China, Israel, Poland and factories set up to copy Soviet arms to disguise their provenance. From the moment they arrived in Karachi they were under ISI control to transport, distribute – or sometimes siphon off[1] – as agents saw fit. 'Paki-

---

[1] Most of the weapons were transported to a warehouse near Rawalpindi, in Ojheri, the headquarters of the ISI's Afghan unit. The warehouse was mysteriously blown up in 1988 just before the first CIA audit was due to take place.

stan insisted they decided who get weapons and we agreed to it,' said Chuck Cogan, CIA Director for the Near East from 1980–3. According to one estimate, the ISI was involved in transferring 65,000 tonnes of light weapons to the mujaheddin, mostly handed out through the seven Peshawar-based parties.

The distribution was a lucrative business. The ISI charged $20 per kilogram to move supplies in to Afghanistan, using the long running smuggling networks of the Tribal Areas. The empty trucks returned filled with drugs. The CIA also deposited money into special accounts in Pakistan, shipped sophisticated intelligence gathering equipment to the ISI and gave the agency a free hand in training. General Gul claimed that by 1989 more than 80,000 mujaheddin had passed through ISI training camps. The CIA even agreed to keep its agents out of Afghanistan, a decision it was to bitterly regret later. 'The Americans weren't even allowed in tribal areas', General Gul told me, 'they could not talk to any of the Afghan leaders without my men being present'.

Although weekly meetings were held with representatives of the three main agencies involved – CIA, the Saudi Al-Istakhabara-al-Ama headed by Prince Turki bin Abdul, and Chinese intelligence, ISI was selective in what it passed on. 'My father and ISI always made sure the Americans had no direct contact with the mujaheddin,' General Zia's son Ijaz-ul Haq told me, 'that's why now they don't know anything about Afghanistan.'

Among the things not mentioned was the fact that ISI agents were increasingly planning and directing operations inside Afghanistan and arms were frequently given as a reward for carrying them out.[2] The agency did not like independent commanders, particularly those like Abdul Haq with civilian support inside Afghanistan because that might make them reluctant to carry out ISI plans that often involved

---

[2] For each plane confirmed downed by a Stinger missile, the commander received two more Stingers.

Hamid Gul at his home in Rawalpindi in 2001.

blowing up bridges or dams. The ISI so poisoned Haq's name that CIA agents referred to him as 'Hollywood Haq'. The feeling was mutual. 'Intelligence communities have their own agendas,' Abdul Haq told me bitterly, 'it's better to rely on arms captured from inside.' With such a deliberately divisive system it is hardly surprising that no unified Afghan national organisation or leadership emerged to establish a government in Kabul when the Russians left.

American aid for the Afghan rebels rose from $30m a year in 1980 to $600m by 1986, an amount said to be matched dollar for dollar by the Saudis, and Afghanistan became the world's fifth largest arms importer. All this money enabled the ISI to build up a vast network of between 25,000 and 100,000 freelance agents, from doormen and taxi-drivers in hotels, to journalists on all the country's leading newspapers; to arm and train militants to fight in Kashmir; and to become increasingly influential in domestic politics.

By the time General Gul took the helm in 1987, the agency was already out of control. When the sudden death of President Zia in a mysterious air crash in 1988 left it orphaned and opened the way to restoring democracy, Gul did everything in his power to try to prevent Benazir Bhutto from winning the subsequent elections. Not only did he force the other political parties to cobble together an alliance against her but also his agents organised smear campaigns, airdropping leaflets showing a photograph of her mother Nusrat when she was Pakistan's First Lady, dancing bare-armed with president Gerald Ford in the White House. The caption warned that the country was about to be taken over by 'gangsters in bangles'.

To Gul's chagrin, his campaign was unsuccessful; the combination of international pressure and massive popular support for Bhutto ensured that she became the country's first female Prime Minister. But in the negotiations that went on between the military, the Americans, and Bhutto before she was allowed to take power, he made sure that the ISI would retain control of Afghan policy.

Iftikhar Gilani, who was Law Minister at that time and one of Bhutto's closest advisors, told me, 'From 1988 onwards no civilian government controlled Afghan policy. We didn't even have any say on it. I complained to Benazir that it was embarrassing and that we should be able to formulate policy and she said, "why do you have to argue?" I replied, "either we're a government and we control things or we're not." She said, "don't touch this subject, these are prohibited areas." We were the cabinet of an elected government, and yet the military, or the ISI, was running our most important foreign policy and we weren't even given real briefs of what they were doing. If I were her I would not have accepted government on that condition.'

Bhutto herself admitted to me, 'It's partially true that the ISI and the army had control of Afghan policy but at least when I was Prime Minister there was a check. It was after my overthrow that they invited Osama bin Laden and turned it into a surrogate state.'[3]

So that evening I first met Hamid Gul in early 1989, he was Afghan supremo. Finally to meet this shadowy figure that I had never even seen a photograph of yet had heard so much about was an un-nerving experience. After initial awkwardness, for the next two hours we discussed the situation in Afghanistan. He gave the most eloquent exposition of the war that I had ever heard and I could understand how the general had brought tears to the eyes of politicians when he made a presentation to parliament urging them not to accept the Geneva Accords allowing the Soviet troops to withdraw safely. It was the first time that I realised that supporting the mujaheddin was not just a policy for the ISI, it had become their whole raison d'être.

Partly it was the desire to run someone else's foreign policy after so many years as a satellite of the United States, and partly its own extreme insecurity, hemmed in by the Indian giant and losing more than half its population in the war that resulted in the formation of Bangladesh. Founded as a religious state, Pakistan's leaders had yet to come to agreement on how the country should be run and had failed to develop a modern economy, relying instead on foreign aid and exporting people and living off their remittances.

A friendly government in Kabul would enable Pakistan to secure its north and western borders and put to rest the Pashtunistan issue. Many Afghans felt strongly that the Pashtun areas in Pakistan should be incorporated back into their territory and Afghanistan had been the only country which voted against Pakistan's admission to the United Nations.

But it was also ideological. One of Zia's Islamic generals, Gul was

[3] Interview with author at Benazir Bhutto's home in London, August 2002.

a committed member of the Muslim Brotherhood, determined to see a fundamentalist government in Kabul and then Pakistan. To him the man to do that was Gulbuddin Hekmatyar and he was blatantly using American money and arms to support those leaders that were most anti-west, spuriously arguing that they were the best fighters.

General Gul played a critical role in developing the Afghan jihad as an Islamic cause, meeting with the mullahs and maulanas and encouraging them to whip up passions in the *madrassas*. It was Gul who had first brought in the Arabs to join the fight, instructing Pakistan embassies overseas to issue visas and free plane tickets even if they were wanted men in their own countries. More than 50,000 young Muslims from 38 different countries from Algeria to Sudan flew in. 'It sort of became a fashion among Arab families for one son to get training in Afghanistan,' he explained.

'The West thinks they can use the fundamentalists as cannon fodder – they were all right to win the war but not to run the future Afghanistan,' he added. 'Well we will not allow that.'

Then in March 1989, Jalalabad happened. I knew the battle was his plan. He had told me it was time for the mujaheddin to take cities and he had boasted they could take Jalalabad 'within three days'. When it all started to go terribly wrong, with more civilians killed than in any other week of the war and the mujaheddin's inability to use conventional warfare exposed, he briefed a *New York Times* journalist that it was Benazir Bhutto who had ordered the attack.

She was desperate to get him out and later that year finally obtained the green light from Washington where the Bush administration was starting to see him as a liability. He was shifted to Corps Commander Multan but he carried on controlling Afghan policy until 1992, and remained influential afterwards, going to Sudan to meet with bin Laden while his faithful lieutenants in the ISI continued his work.

It was some months after the Jalalabad debacle but before his transfer that I got another phone-call to say the 'chief' would meet me and two men in the regulation grey shalwar kamiz turned up at my door. This time instead of going to ISI headquarters, the car carried on past Zero Point to Rawalpindi, the capital's dusty and chaotic twin city where the military headquarters is based. Eventually we stopped at a house in the cantonment and I was taken into a room and told to sit down at a table where I presumed General Gul would join me. Instead, two unfamiliar men appeared with a thick manila file, which they placed on the table. 'Why do you want to bring back the king?' one of them asked.

'What are you talking about?' I laughed.

'Why are you working to bring back the king?'

I realised I was being interrogated. I was accused of being part of a British-Soviet plot to bring back King Zahir Shah, who I knew from our conversations was one of Gul's pet hates. It was ludicrous but there on the table was a bulging file of detailed reports on me and my movements with information which could only have come from some people I had considered among my closest friends. It was my first real experience of betrayal.

I was kept all night in that room, being asked the same questions over and over again. Somehow the mere fact that I had been to Kandahar was seen as proof that I was working for the king. Eventually I was driven back to Islamabad with the warning 'if you know what is good for you, you will leave the country'.

I was determined not to be intimidated and even more so when I got home to find my flat had been ransacked and my telephone cut off. Two cars and a red motorcycle were stationed outside my house which was in a cul-de-sac near Jinnah market. I moved to stay with friends Oliver Wates, the Reuters correspondent and his wife Rosie, but it was becoming impossible to work. The Pakistani newspapers ran stories saying that I was working as a spy under headlines such as 'Lamb to the Slaughter' and eventually the Interior Minister called a press conference to say my visa had been cancelled.

Subsequently the government changed, Gul was prematurely

retired, and I was allowed back to Pakistan. By that time Gul had moved out of the shadows and become an active spokesperson for the fundamentalists, or 'fundos' as they were known in Pakistan, and when the Taliban emerged, he was an ardent supporter, often spoken of as their 'godfather'. Directors of the ISI had come and gone but it was Gul's men still running the show on the ground and he had continued to exert enormous influence.

With the Taliban collapsing, all his dreams for Afghanistan in tatters, it seemed the time had come. I obtained his private mobile number so that I wouldn't have to go through a secretary which would give him a chance to change his mind and he chuckled when I said who I was, as if he had been waiting years for my call. He invited me over the next morning.

His house was in Chaklala, a walled estate of large white villas with neat green lawns for retired military in Rawalpindi. Annoyingly my driver could not find the place and we arrived half an hour late, immediately giving him the advantage that he would use of being able to cut the interview short. He welcomed me into a living room, which had a chunk of the Berlin Wall in pride of place on the table. He had always regarded himself as a key player in the fall of Communism.

There were no pleasantries though there was an amused smile playing on his lips. My heart sank as he launched into a long tirade of how the Jews and the Indians were behind September 11th.

'I had been expecting such an attack for a while,' he said. 'The Americans had been indulging in so many evils there had to be some kind of retribution. As a trained intelligence man and military professional who has been in this business for thirty-six years I have no doubt it was Sharon's boys who did it. But the US is now using this opportunity of having world sympathy to go for strategic objectives and that means getting hold of the eastern flank of the Gulf to counter China and to get control of Pakistan's nuclear facilities.'

I asked him about his contacts with Osama bin Laden. 'You know it was the CIA that first introduced me to bin Laden,' he replied. 'They were very fond of him – a man who's a millionaire coming to fight in a dirty war with his bare hands. They told me with pride how he was digging tunnels – the very ones they are now blowing up. Before that, to me he was just one of thousands of foreigners who came to fight in Afghanistan. I first met him in Sudan in 1993 and he struck me as a very simple, sensitive man.

'The Americans think they can use and discard people. They did the same with the ISI. After all we had done for them to defeat the Russians it was George Bush Senior who had me plucked out. He said "clip the wings of the ISI", the same institution they want to share information with them now. That's what they do, they build something up then when they feel it is becoming too independent they destroy it. He thought we had become ideologically motivated. But it had always been an ideological fight. It was only them that hadn't understood that.'

I asked him about the ISI's involvement with the Taliban. 'When the Taliban first appeared on the scene I thought it was some kind of conspiracy against jihad', he replied. 'It really was spontaneous; the response of the Afghan people to the devaluation of jihad. But then I went to Kabul and saw what they were doing, urbanisation, bringing peace, clamping down on heroin and I couldn't believe it. Hekmatyar hadn't worked out as we had hoped and this seemed to be a good alternative.

'What I would like is to see a similar set-up in Pakistan. Conditions here are similar, the governments have repeatedly failed, people feel they have no protection of their life and property; they are fed up with corruption. The Taliban are not corrupt.'

Why had the Taliban collapsed so easily then, I asked. 'It's not over,' he replied. 'The Russians lost in ten years, the Americans will lose in five. They are chocolate cream soldiers. All this "Get Him" type mood will subside.'

I had been putting off the real question and he knew it. 'The interview is finished,' he said abruptly, standing up, 'it's time for prayers.' My heart was thumping but I could not leave. 'Before I go there's one more question I must ask,' I said. 'I want to know why you had me interrogated and deported.' I had wanted to stay calm but my voice rose. 'I was just doing my job. You know that. Why did you do it?'

The general's eyes flashed with anger and for a moment I thought he was going to have me thrown out. 'Do you know Miss Lamb, it's a mystery,' he replied, the mask of politeness dropped. 'I had it all thoroughly checked out. I had my best people investigate. They concluded it must have been rogue elements.'

Rogue elements? Was that his explanation for the small boy who had lost his entire family in a rocket attack screaming to the heavens in Jalalabad as cluster bombs fell all around him? Or for the death of Abdul Haq, who had been captured by the Taliban near Jalalabad and executed, calling the US airforce on his satellite phone as he was surrounded but too late. His family later told me they believed the Taliban authorities had been tipped off by the ISI.

So many people had blood on their hands over Afghanistan, probably nobody came out of it well, from the commanders who had enriched themselves, to the journalists who had tried to make their name then moved on to other 'sexier' wars, to the foreign powers who used the mujaheddin as Cold War proxies than abandoned them. 'The aftermath of victory was a shameful betrayal of the Afghan people by the US' says Bud McFarlane, who was Reagan's National Security Advisor from 1983–5. But on that bright autumn day in Rawalpindi, as I looked back and saw the general standing at his door laughing, I saw a man who had tried to play God with the fates of innocent people in another country because his own country had failed to live up to its promise.

10

A Letter from Kabul

'Look at your eyes. They are small but they see enormous things.'
RUMI

I STARTED LOOKING FOR MARRI on the first day of the Eid
holiday. It was a sparkling blue day almost the colour of the
dome of Queen Gowhar Shad's tomb in Herat, broken up only by
the handful of pearly clouds over the Hindu Kush that would bring
the next day's rain. Everyone in Kabul seemed to be out visiting,
imp-faced boys playing with Eid presents of plastic helicopters or
paper kites, and doll-like girls in embroidered dresses of vivid oranges,
purples and pinks with velvet bows in their hair and daubs of rouge
on their cheeks. Most were olive-skinned with raven hair and eyes
but every so often I would see a fairer one with eyes like limpid green
pools, and it was terrible to think that such exquisite faces would
soon be hidden away behind purdah or inside burqas. People often
likened the burqa to a birdcage but even through the bars of a cage
one could still admire the beauty of the bird inside and listen to its
song.

In my bag I had the grubby envelopes bearing the letters that
Marri had risked her life to smuggle out to me in Pakistan. Written

in rounded childish hand on sheets torn from an exercise book, I had read and re-read her account of the horrors of being an educated Kabuli woman trapped in a burqa and kept recalling her words; 'maybe when you watch the bombs on television you will think of me and know we are real feeling people here, a girl who likes to wear red lipstick and dreams of dancing, not just the men of beards and guns'.

She had written that she lived in New Microrayon, a large housing estate in the east of Kabul near the airport. Although I did not have the exact address – the block and apartment number written on the envelope were wrong in case it had fallen into enemy hands – I thought I would start in that area as she could not live far away. I knew that her real name was Fatema Siddiqui, her father a former diplomat and mother a teacher, that she was about thirty and single, and had a younger sister and two brothers, and I was confident that I would find her.

Kabul is situated in a large valley surrounded with mountains that rise up from the plains here and there, the Kabul River meandering in between. In a taxi I headed east along the river past a stall where a man was sitting on the ground stencilling black capitals spelling out the word 'Police' on a pile of white builders' helmets and a small group of men were holding down a goat and slitting its neck, the dark blood squirting onto the ground.

Eventually in the shadow of the Maranjan Mountain, Microrayon came into view and my confidence of finding Marri began to ebb. Stretching for as far as the eye could see across the bleached soil were row after row of concrete Eastern European-style apartment blocks. Built partly under King Zahir Shah and the rest under the Soviets for middle-class Kabulis such as teachers, government servants and doctors, it was a vast depressing place that housed 140,000 people.

The estate had been on the front-line during the mujaheddin fighting between 1992–4, captured by General Dostum's Uzbek militia, then by Massoud's men and finally revenge-rocketed by

Hekmatyar's forces. Almost every building was riddled with black bullet holes while some floors had collapsed in rocket attacks or were sagging perilously. A survey from Kabul University of one eight-block section each with forty-eight apartments, found that half of the families had fled between 1992 and 1996. 50,000 Kabulis were killed in those years and in some periods a thousand people were leaving each day, part of an exodus of 300,000 from the city, fleeing the relentless killing and destruction.

Apart from the wounds of war, the rank smell and piles of rubbish suggested it was years since the estate had seen any public services. The doors had all been torn off the entrances, perhaps used as firewood, the stairways were dirty and unlit and the glass had been blasted out of all the windows. Black smoke was coming out of some of the apartments from paraffin stoves.

Yet there was a gaiety about the place as people celebrated the first Eid after the fall of the Taliban. Makeshift fairgrounds had been set up on patches of wasteland between blocks. In one, children were riding on a carousel, which on closer inspection turned out to be made of parts of tanks and armoured personnel carriers with seats from machine gun emplacements. In another there was a miniature Ferris wheel of blocks of crudely cut wood roped together. Stalls had been set up selling cheap Chinese-made plastic toys, boxes of bangles in every colour of the rainbow, and improvised ice-lollies of frozen sherbet in polythene bags for children to buy with their Eid pennies.

In the area known as New Microrayon, which seemed indistinguishable from the rest of Microrayon, I asked the driver to stop in front of a block numbered 153, graffiti-painted with the words 'Nike' and 'Titanic', suggesting somebody spoke English. As I stepped out of the taxi, the soil crunched underfoot. I thought the ground was hard from the cold then realised it was embedded with little broken fragments of building, and so many spent ammunition rounds that children had obviously stopped collecting them.

Instead of doors, most apartments had corrugated iron sheets

padlocked into place, and in block 153 these were scribbled with white chalk to say that the inhabitants had received a bag of wheat from the World Food Programme the previous week. It was less than a month since the Taliban had departed and people were suspicious to see a foreign woman at the door with a strange story about a letter. But the traditional Afghan hospitality won out and at every apartment that I knocked asking about Marri, the people insisted that I came in and eat Eid biscuits or sugared almonds washed down with green or black tea from large Chinese flasks.

It would have been rude to decline and I was interested to see how they lived so I took off my boots and went in. Middle-class in Afghan terms would be poor in just about any other country. The apartments might have been modern in the 1960s and 1970s when they were built, but the country had regressed many years since then and they had no windows or heating. Water that had once run from taps was collected from a well; cooking was done on kerosene stoves on the ground. Oil lamps stood on tables and in several apartments there were chickens in wooden cages. I saw no books. But many had old-fashioned black and white televisions and the government had arranged electricity to the city for three hours that morning so the population could watch a lengthy Eid speech by the outgoing President Rabbani followed by a group of men sitting under a tree drumming. In one apartment they had even fashioned a satellite dish of flattened Pepsi cans which they were about to fix to the roof.

To start with my quest seemed to be going well. I was soon told of a Fatema Siddiqui in block 141 who was a teacher. A woman with light green eyes, a gauzy veil of deep pink over her hair, answered the door and for a moment I thought it was my Fatema. But she looked too old and then her children appeared, three girls and a boy. She insisted I came in and showed me into a room with a large quilt raised up on a stool in the middle and spread right across the floor, which she indicated I should put my feet under. It was surprisingly snug; this was a makeshift heating system known as a *sandalee* and there was a box of charcoal burning beneath the stool which warmed the quilt during the day to then be slept under at night, though after a while the charcoal fumes became quite suffocating.

On the wall were framed photographs of a man in uniform and in a glass cabinet a peaked cap and a medal, and as we sat on the floor, chewing toffees from glass dishes, she explained that she was the widow of a general in the Afghan army who had been sacked by the Taliban then one day never came home again. 'I later heard that he had died,' she told me matter-of-factly, 'the Taliban dragged him off the street and beat him and he had a bad heart.' She received no pension, earning a little money from teaching. In the doorway her three daughters hovered shyly, beautiful in their embroidered dresses with silver bangles, staring out from under deep black fringes. Every time they caught me looking at them they would run away until eventually Fatema called in the eldest, Mughan, who told me that she was eleven and had never been to school. 'But I will go now the Taliban have gone,' she said, 'I want to be a doctor.'

I asked to look in the kitchen. I had read a UNICEF study of war widows in Kabul, which found that they survived on a diet of green tea, *nan* bread and a little yoghurt. In Fatema's kitchen there was one onion, some rice, a bucket of water, the remainder of the wheat donation from the previous week and a small plastic bag of sugar, which she told me one of her pupils had brought.

As she showed me out, protesting at my refusal to stay for lunch, a groaning sound came from another room. Fatema lifted a curtain to reveal several piles of bedding on the floor on one of which lay an old woman with milky film over unseeing eyes.

'My mother,' she said. 'My father was killed in a rocket attack just outside. One night when the fighting was so bad there were flames in the sky, my little brother had run outside and my father ran after him.'

Fatema told me that there was another lady who gave secret English classes not far away in block 146 so I decided to try there. This time the door was opened by a slender woman with laughing eyes and tight jeans who was clearly too young to be Marri. Sonita Nawabi was just nineteen and the youngest of a family of six, none of whom were called Fatema or Marri. But she was desperate to practise her English with a foreigner and almost physically dragged me inside. She told me that she was twelve when the Taliban had come and closed down all the schools but had taught herself English from books and she was very excited because she had just been accepted to start working as a presenter for Afghan television.

Her happiness was infectious. 'When a bird is in a cage and you free it, it sings songs of pleasure day and night,' she explained. 'For all these years I couldn't even dare dream. Now I want to see all the world, to see all the people, how they look like. I have lots of ambition but we don't have any opportunity.'

Unfortunately, she did not know any Fatema Siddiquis. I had assumed that on an estate in a country with such a strong community spirit as Afghanistan, everyone would know everyone else but Sonita pointed out, 'There have been constant comings and goings in Kabul,

particularly Microrayon. Thousands of families fled during the mujaheddin fighting and thousands more when the Taliban came. And
you know we women have been locked away for more than five years
and did not know whom we could trust. No one knows the women.
We are like the invisible species. I don't even know who are the
women living upstairs.'

She suggested going to see a man called Mohammed Hamid who
she said had been involved with the resistance. He was a thin worried-
looking individual with pale skin and a small brown beard carrying a
baby tightly wrapped in swaddling, and he seemed very suspicious, asking what I wanted with Marri. Eventually he revealed that he had indeed
known her as she would come to his house to take messages for her
father who was a spy for the anti-Taliban forces but he did not know
where she lived as these were secret missions. He promised that he
would try to find out and told us to come back at 11 a.m. the next day.

He set off looking purposeful but my interpreter Toryali was sceptical. 'He is pretending he knows her,' he said.

'Why would he do that?'

'To appear a more important person.'

Everyone I had met on the estate had told me that the Taliban
had fled so I was surprised when I was shown into another apartment
by a small boy and a man with a long beard and a black turban came
and sat down on the floor, legs crossed. I decided not to tell him
about Marri. He was hard of hearing and leaned close to me as I
explained I was a journalist getting views about the new government.
He told me he was a high court judge for the new regime and
launched into a passionate defence of Islamic punishments such as
amputations for thieves and stonings of women accused of adultery.
Describing himself as a liberal, he explained, 'I will order the use of
small stones so they have more chance to escape.'

His neighbour was a flight engineer for Ariana, the national airline
on which I had flown from Herat, a hair-raising journey over the
snowy Bamiyan mountains during which the pilot invited me into

the cockpit and showed me that all his instruments were broken. 'So how are you navigating?' I asked. 'By vision,' he replied.

The flight engineer told me that he had more than once had Osama bin Laden on his plane. 'He used Ariana like his personal airline. Once we had to go to Sudan to pick up some of his friends and family for a wedding.'

He was angry about the American bombing which had destroyed Kabul airport and blown up the entire Ariana fleet except for the Antonov on which I had flown and one old 737 that they knew could make it to Europe because it had been hijacked to London the previous year. 'The Pakistanis are the real terrorists,' he said. 'They were worse than the Russians because the Russians came here as men, as enemies, whereas the Pakistanis pretended to be our friends but sent all their fundamentalists here. They have the training camps, the finances, why isn't the West bombing them instead of us?'

'Come with me.' He led me downstairs and across a path into a walled yard. Inside was a burnt-out bus. On the side, he traced the remains of the red letters 'AfghanTour'.

'You see a country of mud and ruin but before we had tourists, foreigners travelled all over the country, we had so many wonders, the giant Buddhas, castles, minarets, mountain lakes and they were so happy to see such things. Now the Taliban and the Pakistanis have tried to dry up our waters and destroy this history but they cannot destroy our memory. The father remembers for the son and the son for his son.'

No one seemed to have escaped untouched by war. Everyone I met wanted to know what the outside world thought of Afghanistan, worried that they would all be seen as terrorists, and I regretted not taking along a picture of the Twin Towers. 'Could one building really have so many thousands of people?' I kept being asked. 'How is it possible?'

But after a while I was exhausted by endless glasses of tea and fending off gifts from people who clearly could not afford it, and we had still only checked out a few blocks. I felt like the Pied Piper, a growing crowd of children following me, laughing and chattering so loudly that it was becoming impossible to hear anything, and the hapless Toryali's attempts at dispersing them by whistling seemed to only encourage them. The special Eid morning electricity had finished and my hands and feet were numb. However the concept of being in a hurry was one that Toryali was clearly having difficulty explaining. 'Stay to lunch', 'Stay to dinner', 'Stay the night', came the refrain from everyone we met. I imagined an Afghan woman turning up on a doorstep in my neighbourhood of north London with some tale about a letter and what kind of reception she might get.

The second day of Eid dawned drab and grey. I got up determined that we would find Marri and after picking up Toryali, emphasising the bonus he would get if we found her, we drove back to the apartment of Mohammed Hamid. In the doorway there was a pair of woman's high-heeled white sandals and inside the room seemed to be laid out in celebratory fashion with a crystal platter of nuts, biscuits and brown popcorn, and plates of the dry yellow cake.

I sat down excited, expecting Marri to appear at any moment. In the next room I could hear hushed voices conferring urgently. Eventually Mohammed Hamid appeared, still clutching the baby which never seemed to make any noise and plonked it down on the carpet where it lay stiff in its swaddling. A long conversation in Dari ensued between him and Toryali, which I found impossible to follow, and sat there growing increasingly impatient. Finally Toryali translated.

'Bad news,' he said. 'Everyone has gone away for Eid so he hasn't been able to find her. But he says maybe the family left during the bombing. Lots of people did. Someone told him they had gone to Herat. Or Wardak.'

Herat. I had just come from Herat. But I remembered Marri's last letter saying how scared they were of the bombing. Maybe they had left. Still it seemed to me that we hadn't really tried many people so I refused Mohammed Hamid's invitation for lunch and dragged the reluctant Toryali off to knock on more doors.

I thought we should concentrate on clandestine teachers but soon discovered this did not narrow things down. Every other block seemed to have one. How could there have been so many secret schools? The Taliban had obviously turned a blind eye. One woman even told me that she had the children of a Taliban minister in her class.

Sonita, the budding television presenter, had given a convincing explanation about all the movement in and out of Microrayon which meant people did not even know their neighbours but I wondered if people were lying to me about not knowing Fatema. Perhaps they were scared of giving information to a *firangi*.

'Don't worry Mrs Christina. God is Great. God is Merciful,' Toryali intoned as a kind of mantra, his long face growing glummer. Whenever a group of women passed by, hidden in their pale-blue burqas, I would speak loudly in English in the hope they would hear me and that one of them might be Marri. Once a lone woman in a burqa, wearing high-heeled shoes and somehow managing to look elegant, stopped and swivelled round. Slowly a long-fingered hand emerged from the many folds and she lifted up a palm etched with henna in greeting.

'Marri?' I asked. But she turned and was gone.

I was convinced that Marri was in Kabul. In her first letter she had mentioned working for the Women's League so I decided to visit General Soraya, one of the city's most prominent female activists, a stout middle-aged woman with a strong kind face and uncovered hair. She also lived in Microrayon and we sat in the gloom of the late afternoon talking in her flat until I couldn't make out her features anymore and she fetched an oil lamp. I asked her how she got the title general, imagining that she had fought in some heroic battles and she laughed. 'I used to be secretary to the Secretary General of the Red Cross here in Kabul so everyone called me general.'

General Soraya claimed to have come up with the idea of the secret schools back in 1992. 'It was too dangerous for the children here in Microrayon to go to school because they had to cross the front-line with all the rocketing and also if the mujaheddin saw a beautiful girl they would take her. Kabul was divided between five warlords and they would stop women and seize their jewellery. I had a codename, Perlikon, so the mujaheddin wouldn't know who I was and I kept moving home. I chose an unusual name that no one had – if I'd chosen a common name like Fatema they would have been constantly picking up and beating Fatemas.

'We spread the word about the courses by going to every wedding party and anywhere women were gathered. I told them this is a short-term situation and if you stand with me your children will be able to go to school and graduate. If you or your husband is a doctor or an engineer or a journalist it will be a humiliation for you if your children are uneducated. I also told them if you can teach this is your chance to bring the moon inside your house and a way to get a little money.

'When the Taliban came it was even more dangerous, they burnt our books, arrested our teachers and beat the families of our pupils. So they wouldn't catch us I would teach courses at 5 a.m.'

In her brave words I recognised the same spirit as Marri's letters but she told me that she had never heard of Marri. Seeing my disappointment, she pointed out, 'We have thousands of teachers all over the city and country.' She had been through so much that she had long ago dispensed with the usual Afghan formalities in address and she was bitter that for all her work she had not been named as part of the new government so I was surprised when she pressed my hand, saying, 'If Marri is out there I will find her for you.'

*   *   *

In another letter Marri had mentioned being a graduate of Hishai Durrani School, the big school on the Kabul River next to the mausoleum of Afghanistan's second king Timur Shah, that had never been finished because his sons had been too busy fighting each other.

The city's largest girls' school until the Taliban closed it, the two-storey building had obviously once been an impressive place with arched windows all along but years of war had left it a shell of its former self, the windows devoid of glass and the roof of the west wing in ruins with pigeons flying in and out of a large jagged hole made by a rocket. But inside there was a buzz of activity as the school was about to reopen for refresher courses and mothers with young girls were coming in and out to register.

I was shown into the principal's office where a group of women were gathered, former teachers, their burqas thrown back over their heads, cheeks stained with tears as they greeted each other. 'I feel like we've been let out of jail,' said Marzia, a former science teacher. 'These last years our homes were our jails and however small we tried to make ourselves, the rooms did not grow bigger.'

I explained my quest but the principal shook her head. 'We had records dating back to 1964 when the school opened,' she said, 'but the Taliban took them all. You could try the Ministry of Education but I don't know.'

Marzia offered to take me on a tour. The classrooms were bare, bereft even of benches, desks, or blackboards, and the winter wind whipped through glassless windows. The banisters had been removed from the stairs, probably for firewood, and the floor above was open to the air, an enormous hole in it where a mujaheddin rocket had come through, and there were pigeon droppings all over the upstairs classrooms. In the courtyard outside the ground was strewn with rubbish and thin plastic bags and there was an unbearable odour coming from the block of cubicles in which holes in the ground served as toilets.

'Our leaders have eaten many cows and sheep in their lives and still they are hungry,' complained Marzia. 'Yet we have no heating, no glass in the windows, no water, no books, let alone luxuries like a ball. Many children will not come to school because they cannot afford shoes or winter clothes let alone notebooks and pencils.'

The library was almost empty, most of the books having been burned by the Taliban. An old man was opening a box of textbooks, which he had just picked up from the ministry. They were thin books printed on cheap paper and instead of the colourful ducks and bunny rabbits that children in Britain use to learn counting, the primary school textbook opened with the following illustrated lesson: One Kalashnikov, Two Grenades, Three Rifles, Four Armour-piercing bullets, Five 9mm bullets . . .

In the Learning-to-Read book, a picture of a carrot with a caption that read 'I like vegetables, vegetables are good for you', was followed by a page to 'Colour in a Kalashnikov'. Underneath it said, 'the bullets of the mujaheddin will fall like rain on the enemy'. A book of sums for older children asked; 'if there are 40 mujaheddin and 20 kalashni-kovs, how many mujaheddin will have a gun?'.

As the days went by, I became more entangled with the lives of people of New Microrayon. Sonita had decided I was going to take her back to England and find her a job in the BBC. General Soraya thought I was going to tell the world why she should be Afghanistan's Minister for Women, perhaps even Prime Minister. The Ariana flight engineer wanted me to take a letter to the head of American Airlines to ask for new planes to replace those destroyed in the American bombing. The high court judge wanted me to explain the British legal system and why we stopped hanging people. I had even been asked to play Cupid by Manija, a lovelorn Tajik kitemaker in block 136 who had fallen in love with a Pashtun girl, the cousin of a friend of his, after he had acci-dentally seen without her veil and been immediately smitten. 'Such eyes like mountain streams, lips like petals of a summer rose,' he sighed. The feeling had been mutual and he would hang around outside her apartment waiting for her mother to go to market so they could see each other secretly. 'If her mother finds out she will beat her and have me killed,' he said. 'Loving is not in our culture.'

I was following unlikelier and unlikelier leads. One morning Mohammed Hamid came to my hotel saying he had found someone taught by Marri. We drove to Gullai Park, a pleasant suburb of small villas only to find that the girl we were looking for had gone to stay with family outside town, about an hour's drive away. Toryali, who by then had learnt the futility of argument, looked at me, then in a resigned voice instructed the driver to head that way.

There are four roads out of Kabul, like four points of a compass, and we drove east past what had once been factories, including a tannery the driver said had been set up by an Englishman, a wool mill and a large estate of housing for the military, all in ruins. The road passed through an enormous mujaheddin graveyard, piles of stones marked with fluttering scraps of white, green or black fabric tied to sticks, then snaked high into deserted mountains. Down below on wide plains near the river I could see the vast Pul-i-Charki prison where the KHAD secret police of the Afghan Communists threw intellectuals and political prisoners, as many as fifteen thousand at one time, and where thousands of people sought refuge when Hekmatyar's forces first besieged the city in August 1992.

I hadn't realised how oppressive Kabul felt in its mountain fastness and it was good to be out of the city breathing the crisp air. Not far out of the city we were stopped at a checkpoint manned by menacing figures, sitting around an anti-aircraft gun from the barrel of which hung a bunch of ostrich feathers and some pink plastic flowers. There were lots of stories of murders and robberies on the road and some journalists had been killed and I drew my shawl further over my head and face as they swaggered up to the taxi.

'This is bad,' muttered Toryali.

One of the men rapped on my window. His hand was ingrained with dirt and his little finger bore a large silver ring with a red stone. I wound down the window, trying to look calm.

'Cigarettes?' he asked.

'Sorry,' I shook my head, inwardly cursing my idiocy in not buying some, always useful currency on the roads. I searched my rucksack. All I could find was a roll of wine gums.

'Sweets,' he said, smiling as he took the packet and waved us on.

What Mohammed Hamid had neglected to tell us was that the girl was staying in Udikhel, known as the Thieves' Village. He had said she was in the country in a place known for its yoghurt. But as we drove in, the driver said, 'This village is famous all over Afghanistan for thieves. If they see you are a foreigner they will bring a donkey out in the road so the car hits it and we will have to stop and then they will demand money for the donkey, saying it was a very new special beautiful donkey, and rob us of everything. It is their special trick.'

The sun had disappeared behind the mountains leaving the village in shadow and as we hurtled through alleyways of mud-walled compounds, I looked out for donkeys. Outside one wall, Mohammed Hamid signalled the driver to pull up. The door opened a crack and some words were exchanged.

'They are inviting us in for yoghurt,' said Mohammed Hamid.

'We can't,' I replied firmly, 'just ask the girl about Marri.'

Not having planned to go outside the city, I had all my money on me, a thick wad of dollars in a belt around my waist, and was anxious to get out of this place before it was completely dark. Mohammed Hamid disappeared into the compound and came back dragging a young girl with the unfocused black eyes of a frightened deer and pushed her into the back seat.

'We are taking her back to Kabul,' he said. 'She does not know Marri but can take us to a lady who does.'

I could feel the girl quivering next to me.

'We can't just abduct her from her holiday,' I protested, 'what about all her things?'

'We are taking her,' said Mohammed Hamid. 'It is the will of Allah.'

I was not surprised when we got back to Kabul and found that the lady the girl knew had emigrated to Canada with no forwarding address. I began to wonder if Marri even existed. Could the letters have been some kind of elaborate hoax? Yet I trusted Jamil who had arranged them and we had met people who said they had known her; a man who had once taught at the same English school with her but had lost contact and a teenage boy who had been her pupil a few years ago and kept repeating 'How are you? Fine?' in English but only had a very old address. We went there anyway and it turned out to be one of the most damaged blocks with the floors concertina-ed together on one side of the stairwell and a group of prostitutes at a second-floor window. Dressed in laced basques and floaty scarves, faces powdered white and adorned with spidery eyelashes and pouting crimson lips, they called down to us as they stood there slowly brushing out fluffy brown hair.

It was time to leave Kabul. I could think of no other leads. I had broadcast a message on Radio Afghanistan and put up posters in more than two hundred blocks. Like so many people, Marri's family must have fled the city during the bombing. They could be anywhere.

In Kandahar a few weeks later, I met Jamil who had arranged the letters for me and he put me in touch with Tawfiq, the student who had actually smuggled them out of Kabul and into Pakistan. To my delight Tawfiq told me he had Marri's correct address and promised to meet me in Kabul and take me there.

Back in Kabul in January, snow was falling thickly, carpeting the mountains and turning the streets to muddy slush. There were far more cars on the road and many more people, giving the city an air of some purposefulness, almost bustling for the first time since I had known it. At the Hotel Mustafa, the ogre-like guard on the door had been joined by some others. Wais greeted me looking woeful with a bruised swollen face and his arm in a sling. 'Got beaten up,' he said in response to my unasked question. 'When you go *mano a mano* with the police you lose.'

'The *police* did this?'

'Hey, when you're a big player, you get big enemies.'

As with everything in Afghanistan it was hard to get to the truth of what had happened. The most common version was that Wais had decided to up the rent of the shopkeepers underneath the hotel and when they did not pay it had their windows smashed. They then called in the heavy mob from the Interior Ministry who swarmed into the hotel, beat up Wais in full view of all the journalists and took him off to a cell where they beat him up some more.

Whatever the truth of the story, the battle had left an uneasy atmosphere in the hotel with dark mutterings of retaliation against its guests, even rumours that Wais's enemies might try to burn it down, so I was relieved when Tawfiq appeared. It was hard to believe I was finally about to meet Marri.

Tawfiq directed the driver to New Microrayon 3 Block 187, a different sector from where my search had concentrated, though a block I had passed many times. We climbed the steps to the second floor, apartment 15, which was on the right-hand side of the landing, and Tawfiq knocked, his knuckles echoing on the iron door. I could hardly contain my excitement. In my rucksack were a pen and a hand-made diary for Marri, as well as some English magazines, and a jar of coffee and some sweets for the family. I thought I could hear noises inside but no one came. He knocked again.

Eventually two boys ran down from the floor above.

'Who are you looking for?' asked one. 'That family left.'

'We're looking for Marri or Fatema Siddiqui. She was an English teacher. She lived here with her mother, father and brothers and sister.'

'Yes, that's them. They left during the bombing,' repeated the boy, clicking his tongue against his teeth. 'They were working for the resistance and one night the Taliban came and raided the flat.'

They had left no forwarding address, no one knew where they had gone, who Marri's friends were, or anything, but everyone assumed they had gone to Peshawar like most refugees.

My search was at an end. There were more than two million refugees in and around Peshawar – I couldn't imagine how one would even to start to find someone there, particularly a woman.

In some ways not feeling compelled to go to Microrayon every day enabled me to enjoy the city better and I wandered around, seeing it come to life more with each passing day. One morning a man even walked past the hotel dwarfed by a huge bunch of colourful balloons for sale. Whenever I could face the mauling by beggars, I walked the Chicken Street gauntlet, refusing the boys selling silver armlets that

I knew from experience would turn black within a month, and the wizened Uzbek man with a long wispy white beard whose eyes barely opened but were of deepest sapphire blue and who was determined to sell me the pelt of a snow leopard.

'Madam, you buy tiger, I make you beautiful tiger coat,' he said every day.

'It's not a tiger,' I replied, 'it's a snow leopard and they are very rare. You shouldn't have killed it.'

'No, Madam, not snow leopard. This Afghan tiger. Also rare.'

'It's not a tiger! It's got spots. Tigers have stripes.'

'Here in Afghanistan everything different,' he would say, shaking his head sadly.

The morning of my last day in Kabul there was great excitement in the hotel. The General Post Office had reopened. Finally Afghanistan was reconnected to the outside world. It was approaching Valentine's Day in England back in my other life, so I decided to go along to Pashtunistan Square to try and send a card. I first stopped at the Inter-Continental Hotel where, to my surprise, Mr Shah's bookstore was still functioning although many of the books had their pictures and covers scribbled over with black felt-tip. I had met the owner, Shah Mirzad, back in 1989 and remembered his passion for books and the history of his country. Pulling out a pile of dusty postcards from under the counter, he smiled, 'We couldn't see these before "because of the people". The Taliban were always in here, taking my books to burn, seizing my postcards. Even this.' He showed me a picture of the shrine in Mazar-i-Sharif that had been banned because there were some doves in the foreground. I chose one with a photograph of children standing waving on a Russian tank; above were the words *Greetings from Afghanistan.*

Inside the GPO there was a crowd of people, mostly just milling. One old man in dirty clothes and unruly turban was clutching a cassette, his grinning mouth revealing just one yellowed tooth. 'I cannot write but I have made a tape of my voice to send to my son

in India,' he said proudly. I helped him buy an airmail envelope then watched as he told the post office clerk the address: 'Ghulam Khan, Bombay, son of Ghulam Khan, Ghazni'.

'How long is it since you've seen your son?' I asked.

'Not since before the Russians left,' he replied.

'And when did you last hear from him?'

'At the beginning of the mujaheddin government. But we have left our village so he would not know where to send a message.'

The mujaheddin government had taken office in 1992. He hadn't heard from his son in nine years.

'He will be very happy to hear my voice,' said the man, his hand shaking as he handed over a pile of afghanis. I feared he would have no food all week and I tried to pay the postage for a parcel that would almost certainly never arrive but he refused.

'What is *nan*?' he said proudly. 'We have gone without before.'

Outside the post office, sitting on stools with airmail envelopes, sheets of paper, pens and glue spread on folding tables in front of them, were the letter-writers. Less than a fifth of the population could read or write so sending a letter often required the services of one of these men. There was a set menu of letters available: job application, begging letter, letter to children or parents informing of death or injury, and love letter, all for five thousand afghanis a time, about fifteen pence including paper and envelope.

The letter-writers were busy and I waited in turn for a man with a large oval face and heavy glasses held together by tape. The bitter cold was making my face and teeth ache and numbing my feet even in their boots and thermal socks but he had no gloves and his feet were in rubber sandals. He told me his name was Pir Mohammed and he was a petroleum engineer but had been sacked by the Taliban in 1996 for being what they considered an intellectual. 'I have nine children to support and couldn't get work but I can read and write and was always doing letters for neighbours so one day I came down here and set up. I would come every morning at 8 a.m. when the post office opened. Some days I would write five letters, sometimes none. Then last year the postal service stopped.'

I asked him what kind of letters he was usually asked to write. 'Sad letters telling of how people died. They were like a catalogue of disaster of our country, I felt like the keeper of all memories. Sometimes I got tired of it all.

'But today it's very different. We're very busy as you can see and mostly I'm writing happy letters, people writing to relatives in Iran and Pakistan to tell them to come back everything is fine. Also some to the BBC and Voice of America and Red Cross to try and find missing people.'

I asked him if he could write a Valentine's for me in Dari and he smiled. 'That's another thing that's changed,' he said. 'People are wanting love letters again.'

'What sort of things do you write?'

'Today I am writing "the snow is all around but I feel warm when I think of you".'

When I got back to the Mustafa, Tawfiq was sitting at one of the tables looking impatient.

'Where have you been?' he demanded. 'I've found Marri!'

We set off immediately, heading northwest past Kabul Gate, a pinkish stone archway and the only one of the seven old city gates still standing. No one knows who built the famous old city walls which once stood twenty feet high and twelve feet thick running along the crests of the mountains with regularly spaced sentry towers but they were thought to date back to the rule of the White Huns in the fifth century. According to Frank Martin, the Englishman who worked as engineer-in-chief to monarchs in the early part of last century, the walls were built 'as a protection against the raids of the wild tribes inhabiting the country southwest of Kabul who frequently fell upon the city in great numbers, putting the people to the sword and carrying off all the loot they could get, including women and cattle, both of which are looked upon in much the same light in Afghanistan'.

On the way Tawfiq explained that Marri's family had indeed fled Microrayon but had not left Kabul, instead moving to the other side of the city to an area called Khair Khana, and he had found them that morning. The roads were like polished glass in the freezing weather and with all the traffic it was about forty-five minutes' drive, mostly on a wide straight road clogged with skidding buses, bicycles and yellow taxis. Through the middle of it all, a group of Kutchi nomads in bright summer colours were leading a train of camels, the animals picking up their hooves distastefully as they slid about. Much of the way was lined with shacks selling satellite dishes made from flattened oilcans and skinned sheep hanging from hooks, their white eyeballs peering sightlessly.

Just before the road snaked up into the mountains beyond which lay the Shomali Plains where the Taliban had burnt down entire villages and raped the women, we turned off right into a residential area. There in a side street of small bungalows we knocked at a green door.

'What if she's out?' I asked Tawfiq. 'I'm leaving tomorrow.'

'She won't be out,' he smiled. 'Where would she go? Anyway if she's out, we just wait.'

He knocked again and a young man of about nineteen came to the door and showed us along an alley by the side of the house. Through one window I could see a large group of boys and girls sitting on the floor around a young woman teacher.

I took off my dusty shoes and entered the house, noticing the line of blue burqas hanging from hooks by the door. The boy showed us into a room with lime-green walls and a red carpet and gestured us to sit on the pink cushions as he knelt down and poured thickly sugared tea from the large white vacuum flask on the floor. There were net curtains across the windows and a gaudy painting of a mountain scene on one wall above a plastic plant. I clasped my hands around the tea-glass to keep warm as the door burst open and a young woman appeared with shining eyes and an irrepressible smile, thick red lipstick and a plum-coloured scarf draped over her hair. It was Marri.

'You found me. I wondered if you would come,' she said in English, taking my hands and kissing me on both cheeks. We sat back down, Marri still holding my hand and beaming happily as I gave her my gifts which she fell upon; the jar of coffee seemed to please her more than the embroidered notebook. 'Since the Taliban left I cannot stop smiling,' she explained. 'The snows have come back to the city and today there was a bird singing in the tree. And now you have come. We say this is *zairay*, it means good news and we must give sweets to the bringer, Mr Tawfiq Massood.'

I noticed that for all her open nature, she never looked at him as she spoke.

'It has been hard to find you,' I told her. 'I first came to Kabul more than two months ago, just after the fall of the Taliban, but I didn't have your correct address. I wandered all over New Microrayon. I wasn't even sure whether I was looking for Fatema or Marri.'

'I'm so sorry,' she said. 'My name is Fatema but everyone calls me Marri. I could not risk putting the right address on the letters in case they found them. And in those days we thought they would still be here forever. Then we moved here because the noise of the planes and the bombing was so bad in Microrayon and my mother became very anxious, and we heard that the Taliban knew of our work.'

'Don't worry. I met all sorts of interesting people I would never otherwise have met.'

'Yes, we say that those who wait hardest for the serpents to go,

find the jewels. So please welcome to my city. But I wish you could have seen Kabul when I was young. It was so beautiful then, there were gardens and flowers and everything was good, the air was good, the schools were good, the teachers. It was safe. People flew in and out and wore fine clothes. My mother even went for studies in Delhi. Imagine now.'

'It was a huge risk writing those letters,' I said. 'Why did you do it?'

'We thought we were the forgotten people,' she replied. 'I was frightened the Taliban would find my letters and I would be put in prison. But it gave us hope that someone somewhere wanted to know ... You know the Taliban were very cruel people. They beat my friends, my brother, they even hit my mother in the bazaar. They weren't Afghans, they were Pakistanis, Arabs and Chechens.'

I asked her about the class we had seen going on in the front room of the house.

'My sister Latifa is teaching now. This house is much nicer than our apartment but the rent is high and we must find many pupils to earn money.'

For all her wide smile, there was a sadness in her eyes and she toyed with the end of her scarf as I asked about her own plans.

'Chairman Karzai has promised to reopen the schools and give us our salaries and jobs back,' she said. 'I wish I could return to teaching in a proper school and be a good teacher. I would like to have proper books to teach from, and the children to have warm clothes and shoes so they can concentrate. I would like to travel but there is no money. So I would like women from other countries to come here and see what has happened to our country. Not just the ruins, but the people, the children. You know my family has been lucky, we have of course lost some of our education and freedom and my parents lost their jobs so we no longer have a nice house and garden like when I was a child, but we have our lives. Many don't.'

She went and fetched a box from which she passed me some black and white pictures of her and Latifa as little girls in pinafore dresses with long cascading hair done up in bows, standing shyly in a garden full of flowers. I could make out roses and a large sunflower.

I took out of my wallet a photograph of my husband and son on a beach in Portugal to show her in return.

'Can I keep it?' she asked. 'They are so beautiful. How lucky you are. And this is the sea? I have read about it and my mother and father have seen it. I would love to see the sea.'

'Would you like to get married and have children?'

'Oh yes! There are lots of weddings now, people feel free, there can be dancing and music, the bride can wear make-up and beautiful dresses. Before what was the point? I didn't even want to think about it.'

I asked if she had someone in mind and she laughed. 'No, my parents will choose. That is our system. My family knows about my future better than me. So it's better.'

She took my hand again. 'Christina, you know it's difficult. I have known war almost all my life. So it's hard to believe in peace. And we never imagined the Taliban would go so easily. Now it seems like a bad dream. But we could just as easily wake up again and find the streets once more filled with the men in black and white turbans.'

Her sister came in to join us and her brother brought in a plate of cakes and biscuits. 'It is not much,' said Marri apologetically. 'It is what we have.' Her father, she said, had gone to talk to people to see if he could get his job back at the Foreign Ministry but I was surprised she did not go and fetch her mother. I wondered if her parents had any idea she had been secretly writing letters to a foreigner.

'It is our tradition to give presents and I am so sorry I have nothing to give you,' she said as we swapped addresses and she kissed me goodbye, 'just this.' She gave me something wrapped in a cloth. Inside the taxi I opened it to find an old exercise book covered over with pages of writing.

It was her diary.

The next morning Tawfiq sat at a table in the hotel translating Marri's diary. It was the most valuable thing she could have given me, a part of her, and much as I wanted to keep it, I knew I had to send it back.

While he was working, I went for a final walk along the road from the hotel. On the right I passed the Interior Ministry Hall where I had watched the new government of Hamid Karzai be inaugurated, all the old enemies like General Dostum, Sayyaf, Rabbani and Ismael Khan glaring at each other as their gunmen brooded outside, and I wondered how long it would last. The foreign embassies were starting to reopen and I crossed over to the left to see the Indonesian embassy. There was a driveway leading to a private estate next to it with lots of activity, jeeps going in and out and trucks bringing in mattresses, wardrobes and chairs.

Suddenly a familiar voice called 'Christina!' Some way down the drive a stubby bearded figure in metal-rimmed glasses was waving furiously.

'Hamid!' It was Hamid Gilani, my old friend from the jihad who I had last had dinner with at the Italian restaurant in Islamabad a couple of years before.

I ran to him and we hugged each other, tears falling to be in Kabul together, not caring whom we shocked at such open physical contact.

'This is my house!' he said, pointing at the large building behind. 'I haven't lived here for almost thirty years. Come and see.'

The Gilanis had been rich and this was the biggest private estate in Kabul. 'It was wonderful growing up here,' said Hamid as he showed me round the destroyed garden with its cracked earth, dead trees and broken-down walls. 'We had a pool, tennis courts, vineyards, ten acres of land and here we would have music and barbecues in the summer. My father built houses here for all his sons.'

He led me to a house with bricked-up windows and armed guards at the door.

'Look what they did. KHAD took over our estate. They turned my brother's house into a prison and carried out their tortures here. The Taliban did the same. It's still full of prisoners that we don't know what to do with.'

'And this.' He showed me the banquet hall in the main house, which was full of grass and manure on the floor. 'My parents used to host wonderful dinners here with candles and musicians.' The Taliban had turned it into stables.

He shook his head. 'What is left of this country that one should fight to be ruler of it?'

'How old were you when you left?' I asked.

'I was just sixteen and left in 1973 to go and study in Cairo and London and by the time I had graduated the Communists had taken over so I couldn't come back. The rest of my family fled in 1978 when the Communists were arresting and murdering all the intellectuals. They abandoned everything, just took the clothes they were wearing and fled to Iran but then the Shah was deposed. Fortunately we had a house in Knightsbridge just behind Harrods so we sold it to have money to eat.

'I was a careless youth with no problems living a wonderful life by any international standards in a beautiful part of London but when the Communists took over my country, I knew I had to fight so went to Pakistan. I had learnt to use a gun at the age of twelve for hunting. My father refused three times to let me join him in the jihad but I came because I thought we owed it to our people. We were born into privilege, myself, my father, my grandfather, and the people who had given us that life had been denied all their rights.'

He smiled at me as we walked down to the gateway. 'But to be honest if I had known it would take so long maybe I would have had second thoughts.'

I smiled back, remembering Elphinstone's words in his *Account of the Kingdom of Caubul* which I had re-read the previous night. 'If a man could be transported from England to the Afghan country he would find it difficult to comprehend how a nation could subsist in such disorder and would pity those compelled to pass their days in such a scene,' he wrote. 'Yet he would scarce fail to admire their martial and lofty spirit, their hospitality and their bold and simple manners.'

Almost two hundred years had passed since he had written those words yet, standing there with Hamid, I thought little seemed to have changed.

It was time for me to go and catch my plane to Abu Dhabi and then on to London. In less than twenty-four hours I would be back in warmth and comfort with my family and though I longed to hold my son again and feel his soft cheeks against mine, all this would seem so very far away and I knew I would be sad.

'Look!' said Hamid as we waited for his driver.

I followed his gaze. Standing all alone on the deserted pavement across the road, the man I had seen earlier in the week with the big bundle of brightly coloured balloons was releasing them, one after another. As we stood watching them floating up into the cottonwool sky, wondering why the man was doing it, Hamid smiled at me. 'We're here now and that's good,' he said, 'but we lost so many people. One and a half million. That's too big a number. Every one of them had their story and we must never forget.'

BIBLIOGRAPHY

Ahmed, Akbar S., *Understanding Islam*, Routledge (London & New York) 1988.

Allen, Charles, *Soldier Sahibs: The Men who made the North-west Frontier*, John Murray (London) 2000.

Babur, *The Baburnama: Memoirs of Babur, Prince and Emperor*, translated by Wheeler M. Thackston, Oxford University Press (Oxford) 1996.

Bodansky, Yossef, *Bin Laden: The Man Who Declared War on America*, Random House (New York) 1999.

Burnes, Lt Col Alexander, *Cabool: A Personal Narrative*, John Murray (London) 1843.

Byron, Robert, *The Road to Oxiana*, Penguin (London) 1937.

Caroe, Sir Olaf, *The Pathans*, Macmillan (London) 1958.

Chatwin, Bruce, 'A Lament for Afghanistan', *What Am I Doing Here*, Penguin (London) 1990.

Diver, Maud, *The Hero of Herat*, Constable & Co (London) 1912.

Dupree, Louis, *Afghanistan*, Princeton University Press (New Jersey) 1973.

Dupree, Nancy Hatch, *Afghanistan: A Historical Guide*, Afghan Tourist Organisation (Kabul) 1977.

Dupree, Nancy Hatch, *Kabul: A Historical Guide*, Afghan Tourist Organisation (Kabul) 1972.

Elphinstone, Mountstuart, *Account of the Kingdom of Caubul and its Dependencies, Vol. I*, Longman and John Murray (London) 1819.

Ewans, Martin, *Afghanistan*, Curzon Press (Richmond) 2001.

Gascoigne, Bamber, *The Great Moghuls*, Jonathan Cape (London) 1987.

Griffin, Michael, *Reaping the Whirlwind: The Taliban Movement in Afghanistan*, Pluto Press (London) 2001.

Hiro Dilip, *War Without End*, Routledge (London and New York) 2002.

Hopkirk, Peter, *The Great Game*, Oxford University Press (Oxford) 1991

Kaplan, Robert, *Soldiers of God*, Vintage (New York) 2001.

Lamb, Christina, *Waiting For Allah*, Penguin (London) 1990.

Levi, Peter, *The Light Garden of the Angel King*, Collins (London) 1972.

Martin, Frank, *Under the Absolute Amir of Afghanistan*, Bhavana Books (New Delhi) 2000.

Newby, Eric, *A Short Walk in the Hindu Kush*, Picador (London), 1958.

Rashid, Ahmed, *Taliban*, I. B. Tauris (London) 2000.

Rubin, Barnett, *The Fragmentation of Afghanistan*, Yale (New York) 1995.

Schofield, Victoria, *Every Rock, Every Hill*, Century (London) 1984.

Shah, Sirdar Iqbal Ali, *Afghanistan of the Afghans*, Octagon Press (London) 1982.

Stark, Freya, *The Minaret of Djam: An Excursion into Afghanistan*, John Murray (London) 1970.

Talbot Rice, David, *Islamic Art*, Thames and Hudson (London) 1975.

Yousaf, Mohammad and Mark Adkin, *The Bear Trap, Afghanistan's Untold Story*, Leo Cooper (London), 1992.

INDEX

Page numbers in *italic* refer to illustrations